TAMESIDE IN TRANSITION

A History and Archaeology of Tameside

TAMESIDE IN TRANSITION

The Archaeology of the Industrial Revolution in Two North-West Lordships, 1642–1870

MICHAEL NEVELL AND JOHN WALKER

1999

TAMESIDE METROPOLITAN BOROUGH COUNCIL

A History and Archaeology of Tameside

Tameside in Transition: The Archaeology of the Industrial Revolution in Two North-West Lordships, 1642–1870

ISBN 1 871324 24 6

First published in 1999 by
Tameside Metropolitan Borough Council
The Town Hall, Ashton-under-Lyne, Tameside
with
The University of Manchester Archaeological Unit

Typeset by Carnegie Publishing, Carnegie House,
Chatsworth Road, Lancaster LA1 4SL
Printed and bound in the UK by The Cromwell Press, Wilts

Contents

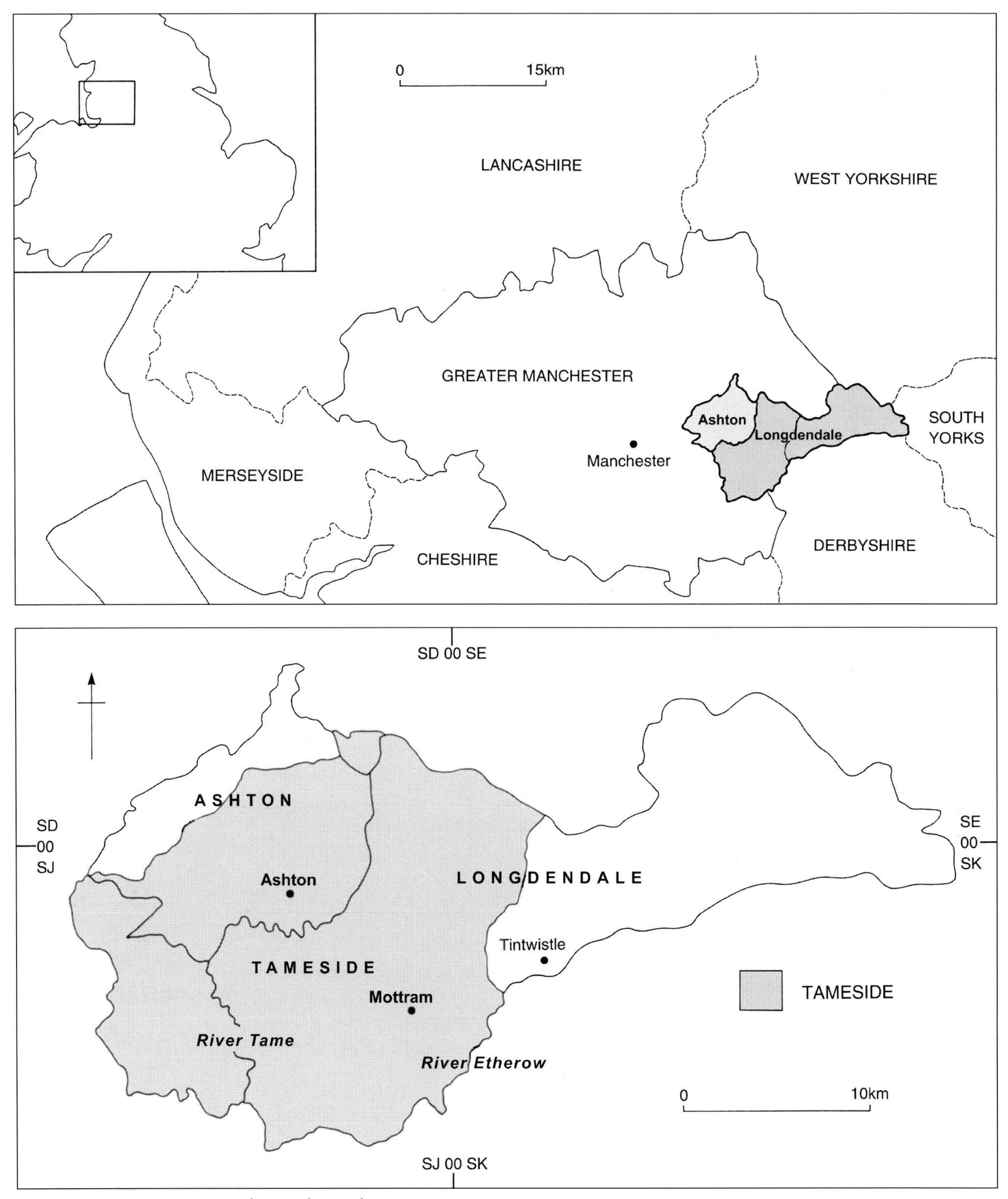

Figure 1.1 Location map outlining the study area.

Foreword

The Metropolitan Borough of Tameside, which stretches from the Lancashire plain to the high moors of the Pennines, was created in 1974 and brought together the nine towns of Ashton, Audenshaw, Denton, Droylsden, Dukinfield, Hyde, Longdendale, Mossley and Stalybridge. Until 1990 there had been no attempt to write a full-scale history of the area. This borough has a rich and interesting past and I felt that this should be documented so that we, and future generations, could increase our knowledge and understanding of our heritage.

The books in the series 'A History and Archaeology of Tameside' have covered the chronological periods up to 1066 (Vol. 1), 1066 to 1700 (Vol. 2) and 1700 to 1930 (Vol. 3). A further three volumes deal with the major personalities who helped shape the borough's history (Vol. 4), the significant buildings of the area (Vol. 5) and the lands and lordships of the pre-industrial society (Vol. 6). A further volume looked at the myths and legends of the area. This final volume in the series identifies the archaeological and historical processes at work between the mid-seventeenth century and the late nineteenth century which transformed the area from a largely agrarian society to one dominated by factory working.

Taken together the complete set of volumes forms a comprehensive reference source on all aspects of Tameside's history. It is an area proud of its past, and one which is now on the brink of a new and exciting period with improved transport links, major opportunities for economic regeneration and industrial development, as well as enhanced leisure and cultural facilities.

It is the intention to continue with a programme of archaeological fieldwork and community based projects which will lead to further pock book publications. Such work will supplement this published series which provides an essential source for education, research and tourism.

Councillor S. Roy Oldham
C.Eng. M.I. Mech.E.
Leader of the Council

Preface

This book, and its earlier companion volume Lands and Lordships, marks a radical departure in the study of the history and archaeology of Tameside. Previous volumes have been written from a traditional perspective with the aim of creating a work of reference immediately available to anyone interested in the area. Once those volumes were completed the whole body of work was reviewed in order to identify the period in which the local history was particularly important in terms of wider issues. The conversion of Tameside from a relatively quiet rural area to a highly industrialised landscape clearly emerged as the most important event in the area's history. At the same time there were growing calls for archaeologists to make a new contribution to the study of the Industrial Revolution.

Combining this interest in the transformation of Tameside with the calls for archaeologists to make a contribution to the study of the period resulted in a three year research project. With the support of the Metropolitan Borough Council the project was expanded beyond the limits of modern Tameside to include those parts of the Lordships of Ashton and Longdendale that now lie within modern Derbyshire. Including those areas, detached from the Borough in 1974, meant that the work could be directly related to the two ancient historic entities that form most of modern Tameside.

This truly collaborative volume, and its companion, are neither works of reference nor traditional analyses of the development of industrial processes. They are volumes, based on intensive local studies and surveys, which seek to approach the years between 1348 and 1870 as if it they were a formal archaeological period. We took this approach as it seemed the only way in which archaeology could provide the type of insights into the period that were being sought by national heritage bodies. Such an approach means looking at the archaeology of the area as a whole and selecting methods and evidence relevant to a particular analysis. The result has been that some things such as the detailed history of industrial processes or the development of monumental inscriptions have received relatively little attention. To compensate for these shortcomings we hope that the volumes present some insights which are sufficiently interesting that, as Harrison said in 1577 'the learned and godly will bear withal, and reform with charity, where we do tread amiss' (Nevell & Walker 1998, 96).

Michael Nevell BA, MPhil, DPhil, MIFA
John Walker BAHons, FSA

CHAPTER I

The Archaeology of Industrialisation

1.1 Introduction

This the eighth volume is in a series of studies produced jointly by Tameside Metropolitan Borough Council and the University of Manchester Archaeological Unit into the archaeology, history and development of the Tameside area. The modern borough of Tameside, an area of 116 square kilometres, lies 18km east of Manchester on the south-western flanks of the Pennines and encompasses the middle reaches of the Tame and Etherow valleys (Fig. 1.1). It is an area of physical contrasts, with wide lowland clay plains dominating the western half of the borough and steep sided river valleys in the eastern half of the area. The Borough, created in 1974, includes two ancient lordships, Ashton and Longdendale, which are the core of the present study.

The first three volumes of the series covered the period prior to 1066 (Nevell 1992), the centuries from 1066 to 1700 (Nevell 1991) and 1700 to 1930 (Nevell 1993). These were followed by a volume (Nevell 1994) dealing with the formative personalities of the area and another (Burke & Nevell 1996) dealing with the Borough's historic buildings and structures. These five volumes were intended to establish an archaeological and historical framework for the area and to serve as reference sources. Volume six, *Lands and Lordships in Tameside* (Nevell & Walker 1998), was a departure from that aim as it was the first publication to arise from a three-year archaeological research project into why and how the area was transformed from an apparently quiet rural area into one of the most active zones at the forefront of the worldwide Industrial Revolution. This volume is a companion to volume six, and follows on directly from where that research finished. Volume seven, *The Folklore of Tameside* (Walker & Nevell 1998) was a popular exploration of the ancient stories of the area which considered the tales of the different social groups identified in the *Lands and Lordships* volume.

Related to, and to some degree shaped by, the Tameside studies are other volumes by the Archaeology Unit dealing with the archaeology of the industrial period in neighbouring areas. *The Cotton Mills of Greater Manchester* (Williams with Farnie 1992) was an in-depth study of the remains of the primary industry throughout the Greater Manchester region of which Tameside forms the eastern boundary. *A History of Stockport* (Arrowsmith 1997) provides a detailed historiographic account of industrial development in the area immediately to the south whilst Nevell's *The Archaeology of Trafford* (Nevell 1997) provides an archaeological account of developments to the south west of Tameside down to 1900. Two issues of *The Heritage Atlas* (McNeil & Stevenson 1996; McNeil & George 1997) contain some articles that deal with general issues arising from the archaeology of the Industrial Revolution in the area.

Whilst there are many modern studies of the industrial development of the cities and towns of England, there are comparatively few which deal, in chronological depth, with the rural fringes where the contrast between pre-industrial and industrial society were often most dramatic. One aim behind publishing this book and its companion volume is to encourage more study of those formerly rural areas, which were the cradle of the Industrial Revolution in this region. Another aim is to attempt to describe from an archaeological viewpoint the way in which two long lived landscape units, the lordships of Ashton and Longdendale, were changed by industrialisation.

1.2 The Research Project

The Industrial Revolution represents one of the great changes in human society, and can be ranked in importance alongside the development of language, the establishment of farming, and the growth of empires. There is a large and growing body of literature about the Revolution, and the transition to an Industrial Society, written from the historians' and economists' view point, but little from an archaeological perspective (Clark 1999, 281–2).

The study area lies on the eastern side of the Mersey Basin, a bowl of land formed by the river catchment of the Mersey. It consists of modern Tameside, formerly part of both Lancashire and Cheshire. The eastern two thirds of this area lie between 76.2m and 496.2m above sea level upon the shales and sandstones of the Millstone Grit or Coal Measures. This eastern zone contains both the Longdendale valley, that provided an historic access route through the Pennines, and many steep sided gorges with narrow floodplains formed by the river Tame and its tributaries. The western third of the area also contains steep sided valleys but is generally much more low lying and used to contain lowland bogs. Throughout the study area the soil quality is generally poor, rainfall high and the valleys subject to rapid flooding (Nevell & Walker 1998, 17–32).

The companion study established that following a severe decline around the 1340s the local population increased steadily against a background of changes in the local climate. These changes in local climate probably encouraged a decline in already relatively limited arable production and a shift towards pastoralism. The historical data suggests that despite this there was no overall or significant shortage of food needed to feed the expanding population between 1348 and 1642 (Nevell & Walker 1998, 17–32; see *The Impact of the Climate*).

By the eighteenth century, the area was part of the centre of an extensive international industrial complex primarily based upon cotton (Aikin 1795). Aikin's contemporary description of the Tameside area in late eighteenth-century, at a time when industrialisation was in full swing, is marked by contrasts; the township of Mottram, for instance, is described as having twelve large manufactories, but also a greater number of small mixed farms, the tenants of which eked out an existence through cottage industry combined with farming (Aikin 1795, 458, 472).

This volume presents a relatively simple account of the process of industrialisation in Tameside and the lordships of Ashton and Longdendale. Today visitors tend to view Tameside as one of the urban areas, like Stockport, Bolton and Wigan that surround Manchester but it is important to remember that Tameside was different to those other areas. Unlike the majority of Greater Manchester Boroughs the area was not dominated by an old and large urban centre. It is true that Ashton has a long history but for many years it was a very small town whilst Mottram, the centre of Longdendale lordship, remained a village. The industrial growth in this area was therefore both more dramatic and less constrained than in other parts of the Manchester region.

The companion volume

For the archaeologist studying this area, with its early and rapid shift from rural backwater to industrial centre, offers models of transition and parallels applicable to other eras of rapid change in the region, such as the shift from hunter-gathering to farming, or the impact of Romanisation on the native late prehistoric population and culture (Nevell & Walker 1999, 11–12). The first part of this research project, published as *Lands and Lordships in Tameside* was an assessment of the archaeology of the area during the proto-industrial period, 1348 to 1642, which was related to wider historical concepts and theories (Nevell and Walker 1998). That work attempted to establish that the archaeological remains within the study area, in particular in the lordships of Ashton and Longdendale, are distinct from many other areas of England and that they underwent various changes with the transition to a proto-industrial society. We suggested that these physical remains can be ordered, or better understood, by relating them to different contemporary classes or groups of landholders; lords, freeholders and tenants.

Although the first part of the study might appear to have been about contending social classes it was as much about competing adaptive systems. The groups that we defined (lordships and manors, freeholds, and tenancies) could all be seen as quite distinctive methods of trying to achieve a sustainable relationship within a changing world. The adaptive strategies of each group were influenced by social rules and those rules, in combination with each group's land holdings, gave them different options for adjusting to change. Manors relied on various methods of exploiting the population; freeholds concentrated on agricultural efficiency or growth; and tenancies upon finding a mechanism, such as crafts, that was not easily exploited by others.

This emphasis on social groups and their relationship to each other seemed closely linked to modern Closure Theory. This school of thought was suggested by Weber and has been developed by Parkin and Murphy (1988). The use of Closure Theory to explain developments during the later medieval period has also been reviewed and elaborated by Rigby (1995).

Closure Theory concentrates upon how individuals within society attempt to bolster their position by acting as a group. To strengthen their position such groups make use of exclusion and usurpation. Exclusion involves the exercise of power downwards to control or restrict others whilst usurpation involves lower groups wresting new rights from more powerful groups. This theory attempts to focus not only on competition between different classes but also on competition within particular classes. It draws attention to three main modes of power, economic, coercive (such as political, legal and military force), and ideological, that are used within and between groups to enhance or maintain their position. Rigby's work (1995) demonstrates how that approach is useful in classifying and categorising the various developments in the medieval economy and society of England.

1.3 The Current Volume

This volume follows on in style, approach, and chronological period from its companion, *Lands and Lordships* (Nevell & Walker 1998) by looking in detail at developments in material culture in the study area, particularly the lordships of Ashton and Longdendale, between 1642 and 1870.

Whilst it was relatively easy to see that the development of different kinds of social groups might shape the simple archaeology of the early period when this volume, the second part of the study, was started it seemed unlikely that the same effects caused by the same groups would be seen in the more complex archaeology of the eighteenth and nineteenth centuries. The first part of this volume is, therefore, mainly about the different types of archaeological site that were introduced or developed in the area during these later centuries.

The core of the volume presents an analysis of the archaeology of the three social groupings, the lords, freeholders and tenants, related to their known historical development within the two lordships. At the end of each chapter an attempt is made at assessing the overall strategy of each grouping during the Industrial Revolution. The final chapter presents an overview of the results of this two volume study and seeks to present a contribution from an archaeological viewpoint to our understanding of the period as a whole.

1.4 Current Economic and Archaeological Theory and the Industrial Revolution

In this study and its companion volume the authors have approached the transition to an industrial society, from a holistic view point. This is not primarily a book about industrial processes and inventions but a broader attempt to analyse the various changes in material culture and society which, taken together, form the Industrial Period.

The scale of the changes produced by industrialisation has resulted in a wide range of economic analyses and explanations ranging from grand theory and macro-economic studies of statistical measures, down to detailed studies of regions and individual industries (see *Population Growth and Economic Change*). In recent years social historians and historical geographers have begun to study the idea of an Industrial Revolution, by asking not only, was there such a revolution, but also whether local social, economic and historical studies might not be as useful as inter-regional and international economic indices in studying the phenomenon.

The contributions to the debate made by archaeologists have tended to lean towards studies of the mechanics, or physical character, of individual industries or structures, with a consequent lack of synthesis. This trend amongst archaeologists is understandable given the volume of available historical data and the depth of the theories of economic historians. As English Heritage have observed this trend may have meant that the contribution of archaeologists to the debate on the validity and origins of the Industrial Revolution as a concept has not been as great as it could have been (English Heritage 1997, 45).

It is not the place of this volume to discuss in detail the various schools of thought about the Industrial Revolution, but a brief review of some of the recent literature will serve to illustrate the vigorous nature of the national debate. Current economic theory about the event can be divided into various strands all of which address, to some extent, the key question of what do we mean by an Industrial Revolution, and how can we identify its time and place?

The idea that there was one period which saw a take-off in industrialisation has been debated since the 1820s when French commentators coined the term the Industrial Revolution to described what they saw as the economic transformation of England (Mathias 1989, 1–2). In recent years economic historians have attempted to refine the empirical database (Crafts 1976 & 1989; Feinstein 1978; Harley 1982; Wrigley & Schofield 1981) in order to address the view that major sectoral, regional and institutional changes, represented by an overall discontinuity in the economic database, mark the take-off period for the Industrial Revolution as the years *c.* 1780 to *c.* 1800.

The lead sector hypothesis was proposed by W. W. Rostow in the mid-twentieth century who argued that the main momentum for economic growth in eighteenth-century England came from a few manufacturing sectors (cotton and iron) which were the 'motors of growth' for industrial take-off (Rostow 1960). This theory has been superceded by later studies which showed that within Britain there was a widely diffused pattern of growth with many sources of momentum (Mathias 1989, 19–22).

'The long view', or proto-industrialisation theory, was revived by Franklin Mendels in 1972, who argued that much of the industrial expansion in Britain before 1800 came from handicraft industries using enhanced artisan technology (domestic textiles, small metal wares and even coal mining; Mendel 1972); it is a concept which has been explored by economic historians ever since (Marthias 1989, 10–13).

Finally, amongst the latest of the many theoretical strands studied by economic historians is the concept of marginality, the view that industrialisation and growth first takes off in the marginal zones of Europe. Professor Sidney Pollard has demonstrated the impact upon growth of two main types of marginality; political and economic during the industrial transition (Pollard 1997, 10–17). Firstly, with the idea of political marginality the debate appears to be about the pull between the centre which seeks to open up, subject, and colonise the fringe, and the fringe which might come to dominate the system of which it was a notional periphery. Secondly, economic marginality, which is more about the natural features of a region rather than its political makeup. In pre-industrial, non-urbanised societies, economic marginality was the result of having poor agricultural land. Many of the marginal lands of Europe with their mountains, forests, fen or marshland were to take the lead in developing the industrial base. The companion volume (Nevell & Walker 1998) to this book clearly established that in terms of environment, agricultural productivity the study area was one such marginal zone in the period from 1348 to 1642. It was also an area that rapidly came to the forefront of industrial development.

In recent years archaeology has moved towards providing its own insights into the processes and effects behind the transition from an agrarian to an industrial society. As noted in the previous volume a number of studies have addressed the issue of the transition to a proto-industrial society in the period 1348 to 1642 (Gaimster & Stamper 1997; Johnson 1996; Crossley 1990) and whilst some went on to look at aspects of the period 1642 to 1870, all took the view that the transition to an industrial society took considerable time.

Post-Medieval Archaeology in Britain by David Crossley (1990) brings together the results of large numbers of individual archaeological studies conducted on remains dating from 1500 to 1800 and shows that much of the basic archaeological framework for these centuries is now in place. The volume also illustrates that local variations were often significant and that various types of archaeological remains seldom figure in the historical record, meaning that the lives of the majority of the population living in sixteenth- through to early eighteenth-century England were barely touched upon by the written word (Crossley 1990, 2).

An Archaeology of Capitalism by Matthew Johnson (1996) is the most explicitly theoretical of the volumes and appears to echo a wider trend in archaeology in explaining how the rise of the concept of the individual, seen by some as crucial to industrialisation, can be demonstrated by changes in a wide range of physical remains.

Since the publication of *Lands and Lordships* various articles and books have appeared that look at the archaeology of the Industrial Revolution from a wider viewpoint. *Industrial Archaeology, Principles and Practices* by Marilyn Palmer and Peter Neaverson (1998) attempts to widen the horizons of the industrial archaeologist by relating industries to their associated housing and transport networks, and by placing aspects of the material culture of industrial production in its social context. The authors introduce ideas about the social controls which are both explicit and implicit in the architecture and spatial organisation of industrial buildings, and the way in which social relations were both constructed and expressed in the housing built to accommodate those involved in industrial production.

In addition to these complete volumes there has been a wide range of articles and smaller studies on the archaeology of England in the more recent centuries. The volume *The Familiar Past?* edited by S. Tarlow and S. West (1999) brings together recent contributions by some of the archaeologists involved in studying the period in Britain. Many of these individual studies deal with particular aspects of the material culture in great depth and in a way that, because of our earlier work and the large amount of available data, is not followed in this volume. In their contributions to this work Brooks, Buckham, Mytum and Tarlow explore in different ways aspects of the relationship between the material culture of the period and its social structure. Giles, Gould, Leech, Lucas, Johnson and Williamson demonstrate the relationship between structures (their layout and planning) and contemporary social issues, whilst Pennell does the same for diet. In the same volume Keith Matthews, of Chester Archaeology, discusses how a classical archaeological approach to the study of the period is both in its infancy and still questioned.

In her summary of present progress Tarlow (Tarlow and West 1999) draws attention to areas where archaeologists are trying to make a contribution. Great attention is being paid to how individuals in the past established and demonstrated their identity in various material ways such as building plans or funerary monuments. This interest in issues of identity is moving archaeologists towards a more subtle notion of social structure beyond seeing the recent historic past as consisting merely of large contending classes. Tarlow also emphasises that an archaeological approach demands or requires by the nature of the discipline the use of long timescales and broad concepts of a type that are not usually found in historical studies. Orser (1999) in his recent article about the progress of historic archaeology in Britain and America called for a new form of archaeology centred upon four main concepts; a global view, an emphasis upon past social relations, the study of social relationships across space and through time, and a willingness to comment upon today by drawing from the recent past. This current study, because of the insight gained in the companion volume, follows Orser's call by emphasing social relations and their development through time.

Kate Clark (1999) in her summary of developments in Industrial Archaeology has also, since the last volume in this study, called for archaeology to consider how best it can contribute to a study of the period.

1.5 The Archaeological Database

Archaeological insight can be quite distinct from that of other disciplines because it deals specifically with the physical remains of the past. The aim of archaeology is to explain the patterns and nature of the physical evidence in all its various forms, from building types to field patterns, from pottery to artefacts.

The previous volume confirmed that the archaeology of the Tameside area, and the western Pennine fringe, from the period 1348 to 1642, was distinct being dominated by the remains of isolated farms and the homes of the owners of manors. In the first part of that study we examined a map of the late sixteenth-century Staley

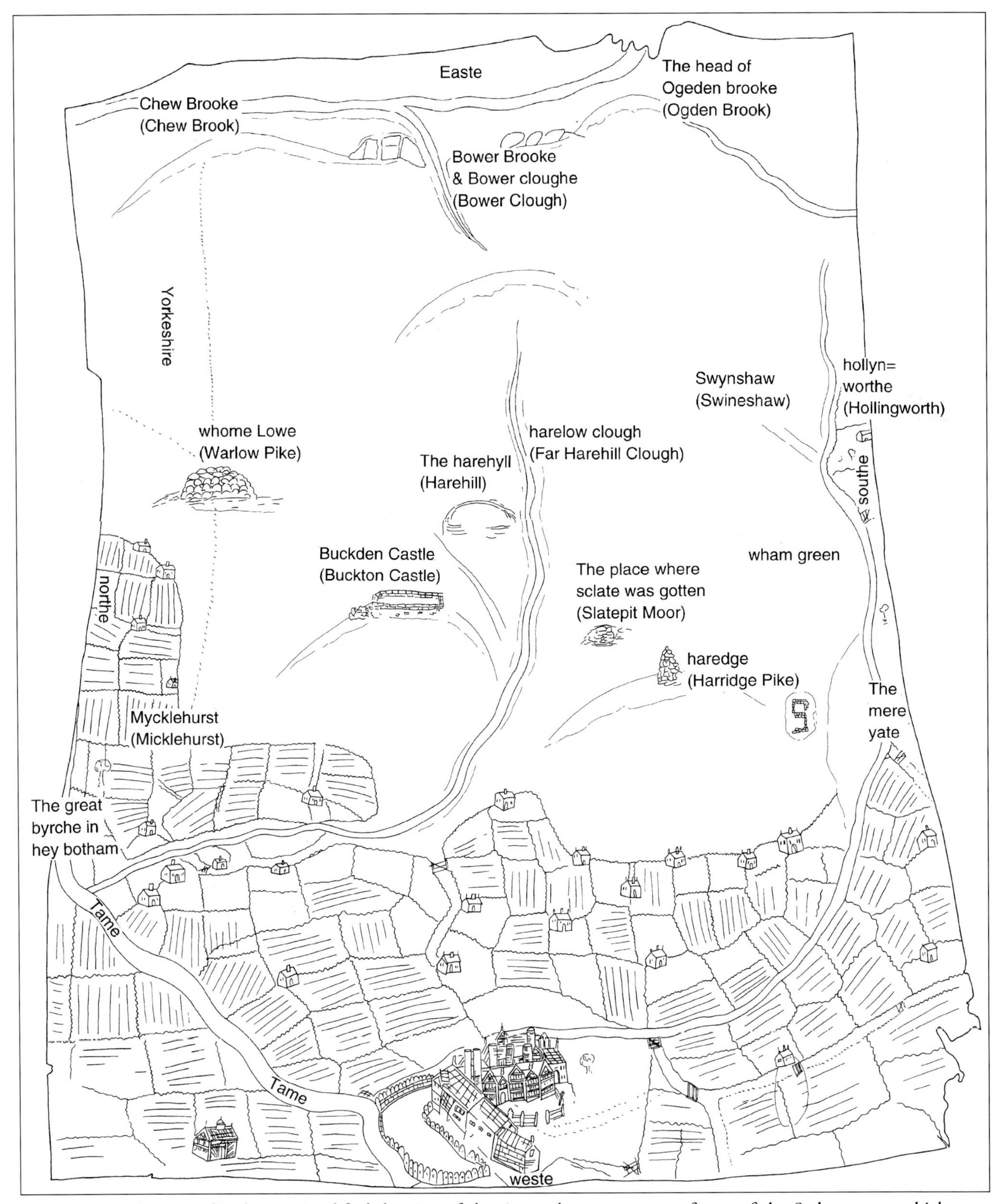

Figure 1.2 Early map of Staley. A simplified drawing of the sixteenth-century map of part of the Staley estates which was drawn for the Booth family, lords of Ashton and Dunham Massey. It shows a pre-industrial landscape consisting of a major hall and isolated farms lying amongst enclosed fields, some of which contain ridge and furrow, beyond which lies the open moors. This evidence is supported by the archaeological data from the area and confirms the distinctive nature of the archaeology of the region prior to industrialisation. (*After LRO DDX 350/21. Reproduced with the permission of the County Archivist, Lancashire Record Office*)

estate (Fig. 1.2) and saw how the sites recorded corresponded with the known archaeological evidence for this area in the sixteenth and early seventeenth centuries. The map shows a pre-industrial landscape consisting of a major hall and isolated farms, lying amongst enclosed fields, some of which contained ridge and furrow. Beyond the limits of the fields lay the open moors or commons containing the remains of Buckton Castle, a cairn, a turf pit and a slate quarry. Allowing access between the two zones was a series of lanes and moor gates. Staley Hall, the manorial centre, appears as a large multi-gabled, multi-storeyed structure, apparently capable of housing many people, joined on one side by a field surrounded by a vertical plank fence typical of a park pale. Other structures were all simple tenant houses with different arrangements of windows and chimneys, each surrounded by fields.

The archaeology of the period from 1642 to 1870 from within the Ashton and Longdendale lordships is as distinct as that for the three centuries before 1642. It was dominated by two new archaeological site types, the textile site, of which 274 were established in

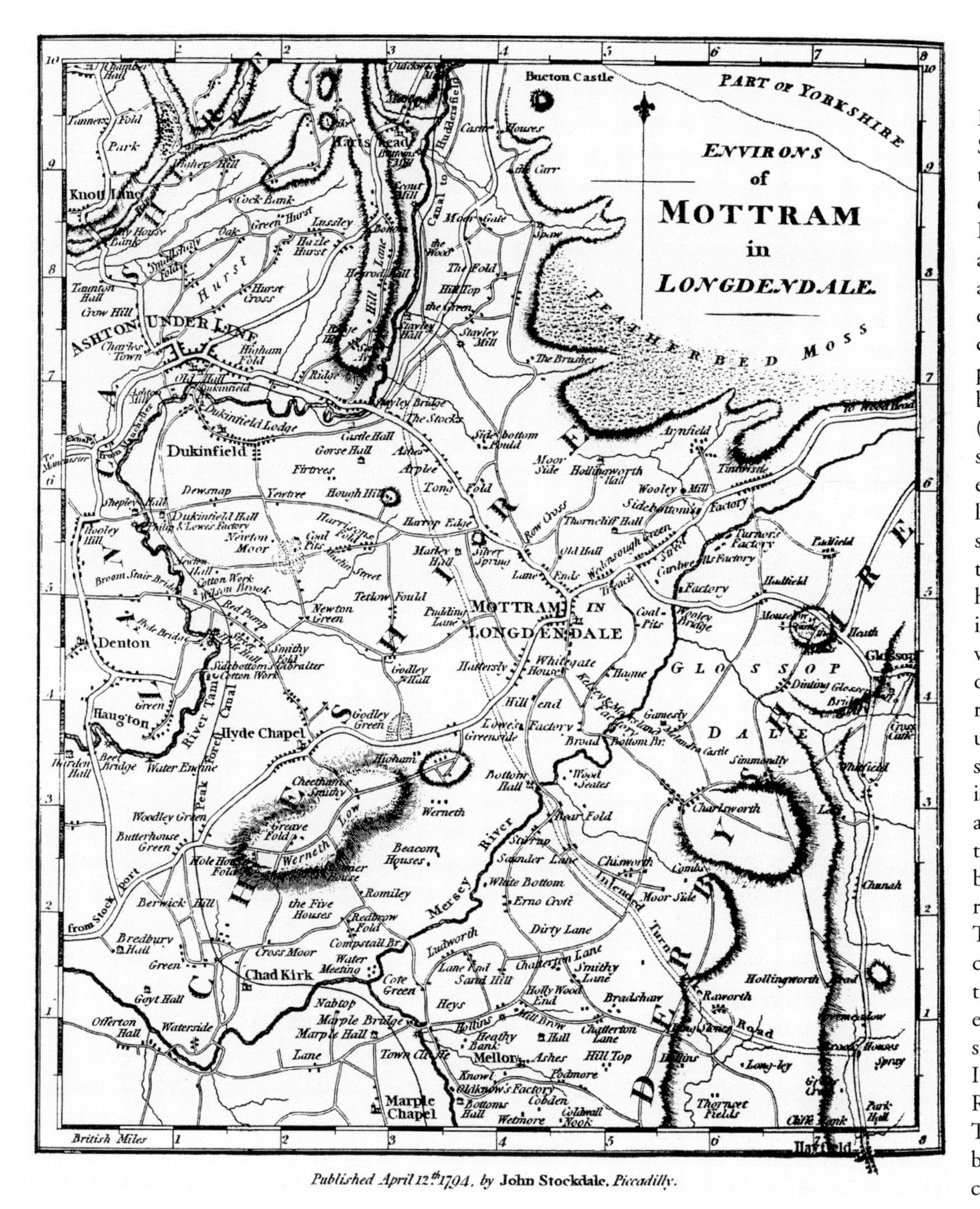

Figure 1.3 John Stockdale's map of the middle reaches of the Tame and Etherow valleys around Mottram and the Longdendale lordships drawn in 1794 and published in 1795 by John Aikin (Aikin 1795). It shows the late eighteenth-century landscape of the study area, showing the area during the high period of industrialisation with the landscape dominated by rapidly growing urban settlements surrounded by isolated farmsteads and rural based textile sites, linked by new turnpike roads and canals. This pattern corresponds with the archaeological evidence which shows that the Industrial Revolution in the Tameside area began in the countryside.

Population Growth and Economic Change, 1642–1870

Most geographers and economic historians agree that there existed a reciprocal relationship between population growth and economic change during the industrial period and particularly in the eighteenth century. Yet whilst such a positive feedback loop can be detected the question arises as to which was the prime mover in industrial change, population or economic expansion?. It has been suggested by a number of economic historians and demographers that the main population check on proto-industrial societies in Europe was the self-equilibrating system, as first suggested by the eighteenth-century historian and social commentator Thomas Robert Malthus. In this system the rate of population growth is checked when it gets out of step with food production by several mechanisms; as the rate of growth rises this pushed up food prices, which reduced the level of real wages, which if severe enough increased mortality levels, ultimately reducing the rate of population growth (Woods 1989, 127–31). The key difference between proto-industrial societies and fully industrial societies appears to have ben a change in the self-regulating system. At the end of the eighteenth century the link between food prices and the rate of population growth was broken allowing population expansion without economic penalty, and has been seen by some scholars as one of the defining characteristics of the Industrial Revolution. This was made possible by the increasing productivity of home-based farming and the import of American and British colonial foodstuffs which allowed the growth of large urban populations. The checking of population growth from the later nineteenth century onwards was related to factors other than changes in food prices and real wages (Wood 1989, 152–3).

The impact of this system can be seen in the way population growth developed within the study area during the period 1642–1870. In the Tameside area the population, after recovering from a collapse in the fourteenth and fifteenth centuries (Nevell & Walker 1998, 29–30), had reached a plateau by the late seventeenth century, with the growth of the early seventeenth century being off set by the excess number of deaths over births in the Ashton and Mottram parish registers visible in the second half of the seventeenth century (Nevell 1991, 103–4). However, aggregate analysis of the Ashton-under-Lyne parish registers for the eighteenth century indicates that from around 1720 births began to significantly outstrip deaths, and from 1731 baptisms were consistently above burials, except for 1794 when they met, the average fertility rate being between 4 and 4.5 births per couple (Moore 1971, 11–13). This increase is reflected in the rise in the population of the Ashton Lordship, which grew from around 550 in the mid-seventeenth century to 2859 in 1775 (Aikin 1795, 228; Nevell 1991, 103). Accurate figures for the Longdendale Lordship are not available for the first three quarters of the eighteenth century, although Booth has used the registers of Hyde Chapel to show that the population of the Hyde area remained stable until the last quarter of the eighteenth century (Booth 1987, 26).

The crucial period appears to have been the last quarter of the eighteenth century, during which years there are indications of rapid population expansion coincident with the arrival of the factory system in Tameside. The Hyde registers show a 50% increase in population in the last two decades of the eighteenth century, whilst the Ashton parish registers show a similar acceleration in numbers (Booth 1987, 26; Moore 1971, 14–5). This is best illustrated by the growth of Ashton town itself, which leapt from the figure of 2,859 recorded by Aikin for 1775 to around 6,500 in the first census of 1801 (Aikin 1795, 228; Butterworth 1842, 94). Accurate figures for Ashton are not available for 1801 because the town was assessed in the census with the Knott Lanes Division, the figure of 6,500 being Edwin Buterworth's estimate.

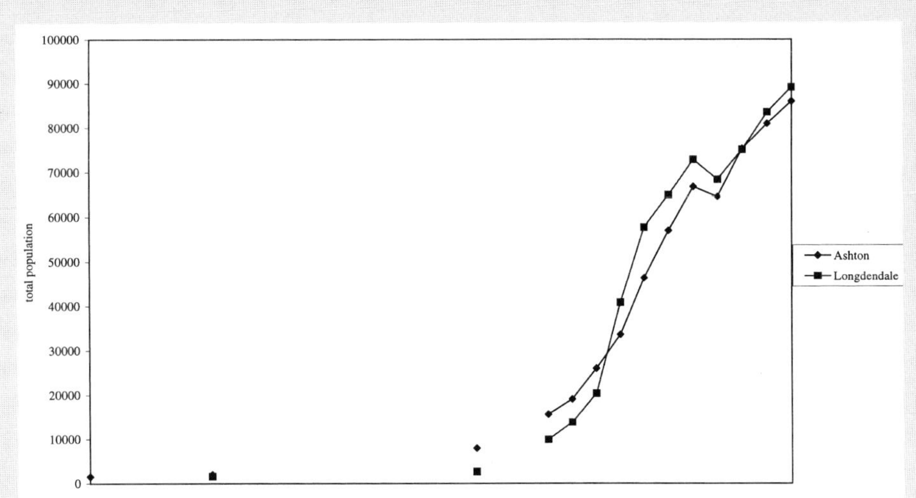

The population of the Ashton Lordship and Longdendale Lordship from 1618 to 1901.

Both Ashton and Hyde were the earliest cradles of the factory system in Tameside, and its introduction during these decades would appear to be linked with rapid acceleration in the growth of the population. The evidence is equivocal as too whether the

Assessment Division	1801	1811	1821	1831	1841	1851	1861	1871	1881	1891	1901	1911	1921	1931
Ashton Town	{7855	{9574	9222	{16883	22678	see Ashton-under-Lyne MB								
Knott Lanes div			3827		5521	6044	7312	divided between Hurst, Limehurst and Mossley LBs						
Ashton-under-Lyne MB	created 1847					29790	34886	31984	36399	40486	43890	45172	51409	51573
Audenshaw div/UDC	2275	2772	3781	4891	5374	5427	6327	7024	7308	7958	7216	7977	7876	8460
Denton tns/LB	1362	1594	2012	2792	3440	3147	3335	5117	7660	8666	see Denton UDC			
Denton UDC	created 1894										14934	16877	17620	17383
Droylsden tns/LB/UDC	1552	2201	2855	2996	4933	6280	8798	8973	8679	9482	11087	13259	13878	13277
Dukinfield tns/LB/MB	1737	3053	5096	14681	22394	26418	15024	14085	16942	17385	18929	19422	19509	19309
Godley tns	270	451	514	636	1399	1353	1185	1222	see Hyde MB					
Hartshead div	5502	6706	9137	11823	12731	18885	19245	divided between Hurst, Limehurst and Mossley LBs						
Hattersley tns/CP	455	473	563	477	610	497	400	276	263	286	287	256	268	280
Haughton tns/LB	1139	1526	2084	2914	3319	3042	3371	4276	5051	5327	see Denton UDC			
Hollingworth tns/LB/UDC	910	1089	1393	1760	2012	2347	2155	2280	2658	2895	2447	2580	2466	2299
Hurst LB/UDC	created 1861							2916	6384	6772	7145	7858	8074	see AuL
Hyde tns/LB	1063	1806	3355	7144	10170	11569	13722	14223	see Hyde MB					
Hyde MB	created 1881								28630	30670	32766	33437	33424	32066
Matley tns/CP	285	311	324	262	251	252	231	207	205	174	196	289	273	348
Mossley LB/MB	created 1864							10578	13850	14162	13452	13205	12703	12041
Mottram-i-L tns/LB/UDC	948	1446	1944	2144	3247	3199	3406	2590	2913	3270	3128	3049	2883	2636
Newton tns/LB	1005	1445	2159	5997	7501	7481	6440	6295	see Hyde MB					
Stalybridge MB	created 1857						18130	15323	16384	26783	27673	26513	25216	24823
Stayley tns	1055	1104	1609	2440	3905	4579	6187	5788	3651	see Stalybridge MB				
Werneth tns	1152	1304	1804	3462	3904	3635	3464	3402	see Hyde MB					

The population of Tameside by township (tns), civil parish (CP), local board (LB), urban district council (UDC) and municipal borough (MB), 1801–1931. Sources: Farrer & Brownbill 1908, 342–4 and Harris 1979, 214–37, with emendations from the census returns of 1871, 1891, 1901, 1911, 1921 and 1931 (HMSO).

factory system was the cause of this population acceleration. In Hyde the population was stable prior to the introduction of the first cotton factory around 1780, whereas in Ashton the population had increased more than five fold before the founding of the first cotton factory in the 1770s. Thus, the present evidence suggests that population growth was a contributory factory in the development of the early Industrial Revolution in Tameside, but that the introduction of the factory system itself boosted the local population by concentrating large numbers of people from the region as a whole in newly created urban areas.

This complex interrelationship between population growth and the expansion of the factory-based cotton industry in Tameside was to continue throughout the life of this industry. During the period 1801–1861 the cotton industry in Tameside rapidly expanded, reaching a peak in terms of the numbers employed and the number of sites in production, although not in terms of the volume of cotton goods produced (Nevell 1993, 11). This period saw the highest rate of population expansion in the township's of the Tameside area listed in the accompanying table, the population of the study area rising from 28,565 in 1801 to 153,618 in 1861, an increase of 437% compared to the national population growth in the United Kingdom during this period of 105% (Cootes 1982, 179). Population growth in Tameside was thus more than four times the national average, although this development was not uniform, some townships such as the rural districts of Hattersley and Matley recorded no significant rise in population, whilst others, such as Hyde recorded a population growth in this period of 1,191%

The cotton famine of 1861–5 caused the arresting, and in some cases the decline, of the population in certain townships within Tameside. Those townships which witnessed population decline between 1861 and 1871 were Ashton, Dukinfield, the Hartshead division of Ashton parish, Mottram, Newton, Stalybridge and Werneth. Among the industrial towns of the study area Stalybridge, which was heavily dependent on cotton, was affected particularly badly with a population decrease of 15.5%, compares to 8.3% in Ashton and 6.25% in Dukinfield. The greatest decreases, however, were in Mottram, by 24% and neighbouring Hattersley, by 31%; this was probably in part the result of the virtual collapse of the cotton industry in Broadbottom which had previously been the major employer locally.

When population growth resumed in the decades after 1871, in most areas the rate of annual increase was considerably lower than for the preceding 60 years, the population of the component districts of the Borough rising only 19.2% in the 40 years from 1861 to 1901, to 183,150. This was a third of the national average of 60% during the same period (Nevell 1993, 13).

The Impact of the Climate, 1642–1870

In the companion volume to this work, *Lands and Lordships* (Nevell & Walker 1998), we explored the link between climatic deterioration and the abandonment of cereal cultivation at altitudes above 100m AOD during the period 1348 to 1642 within the study area. Palaeo-historical climatology is a relatively new field of research, especially for the period 1642–1870. Ancient climatic trends can be collected from a number of sources, including primary written, tree-ring data and the information from ice-cores taken at the North and South Poles. The primary sources for Britain in this period are contemporary written records. The data for North West England is summarised in two articles by Gordon Manley (Manley 1974) And are summarised in the accompanying graph.

This regional information can be added to at the local level through dendrochronology and dendrology (tree-ring dating and tree research). In many cases this evidence reveals climate variance within the annual rings of trees. Though all temperate zone trees may be utilised for this purpose, oak (Quercus spp.) is used primarily because dated master curves exist for Britain from 6500 BP to present. Each of those 8,500 or so rings will contain climatic data for each individual year. Extreme caution in needed when studying tree-rings, as the growth-sites (niches) influence the growth of oak trees, and this will contribute to annual ring growth with climatic influences. Climate interpretation from tree-rings only covers the growing period, five to six months in a given year, from late March through to mid October. Thus dendroclimatology must not be regarded as a detailed source, although growth trends can indicate years of greater stress and by implication variations in the local climate.

Combining the documented data with year by year analysis of tree-rings, produces a far more accurate method of climate interpretation, than from tree-rings alone. Manley's work indicates a number of extreme years of temperature and rainfall within the period 1642–1870. For example, the lowest average temperatures recorded (in centigrade) for January are: **1684** = –3.0 (with actual troughs at <–30), **1695** = –1 (>–10), **1716** = –2.0 (>–20), **1740** = –2.8 (>–25), with **1795** colder than the famous 1684 = – 3.1 (>–35), **1814** = –2.9 (very close to **1684** at >–30) with no more big freezes until **1963** = –2.1 (>–20). The year **1826** stands out as the Great Drought, when between March and June only 10 inches of rain fell in the Manchester area, with one inch of rain in both June and July. This had disastrous results for crops during the spring to mid-summer growing period. Within the Manchester and Tameside areas the evidence from the tree-rings shows some correspondence with these episodes, especially with the cold summers of the 1590s, 1620s, 1695, 1725, 1782, 1799 and 1816, with the tree-rings showing as very narrow bands.

The climatic data for the Tameside area and the North West as a whole it indicates that between 1642 and 1870 there were few extreme years of weather, although a small progressive rise in the average yearly summer temperature is recorded in the written evidence. Even so, the climate in the period 1642–1870 was far more stable than that during the years 1348–1642, and therefore climatic change had far less impact on the settlements of the area. *Ivan Hradil*

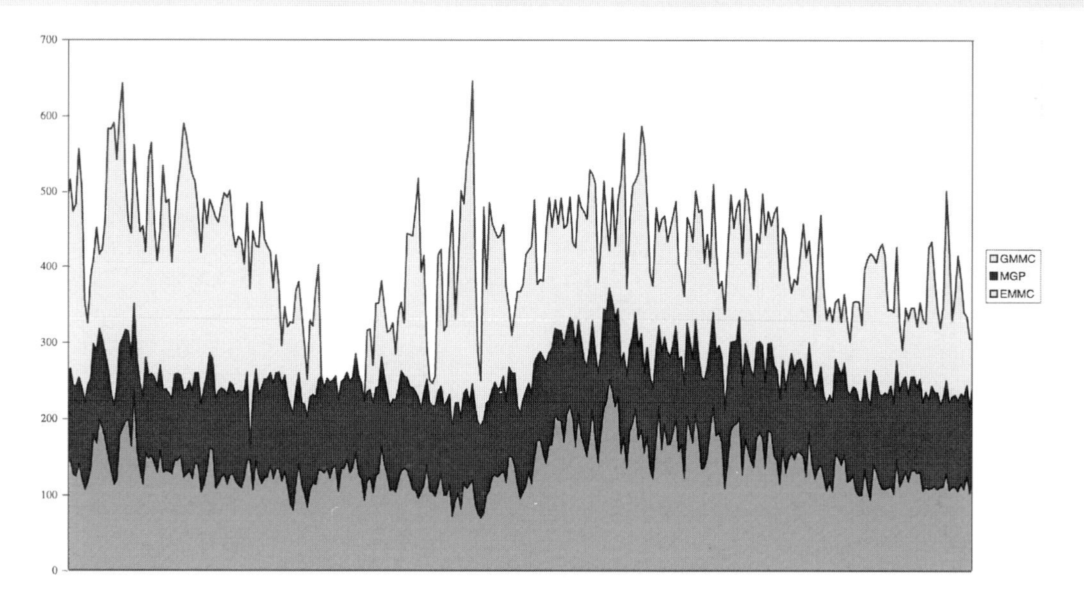

A graph showing the influence of temperature on tree-ring growth during the years 1659 to 1973.
Key: GMMC = Greater Manchester Master Curve (dendro); MGP = Mean Growth Period Temperature (Annual); EMMC = East Midland Master Curve (dendro).

Tameside between 1763 and 1907, and the terraced house of which thousands of examples still survive from the period 1790 to 1870. To these can be added the 273 farmsteads known from this period. An examination of John Stockdale's map of 1795 (Fig. 1.3) shows the correlation between this and the archaeology of the area. Unlike the Staley document this map of the environs of Mottram in Longdendale was not an estate document but an attempt to record some of the more important geographical points of the area in the tradition of the newly improved surveying techniques of the period. Amongst these were many of the other 'new' archaeological sites. These included water-powered mills, cotton works and other manufactories located in the valleys and along the rivers; newly constructed turnpike roads and canals which serviced areas of coal pits and new urban centres such as Denton, Dukinfield, Gee Cross, Pump Street (later Hyde) and Staley Bridge; as well as bridges and non-conformist chapels.

These two maps show a radical change in archaeological sites between the early seventeenth century and the 1790s. Since the archaeology and history of the Tameside area has been intensively studied over the last nine years it is now possible to produce a reasonably complete list of existing and lost structures and sites built between 1642 and 1870. A considerable number of structures have been surveyed and analysed and a campaign of dendrochronological dating has taken place. In the great majority of cases we know who controlled or encouraged the building of each new type of site. In addition to this data there have been a number of archaeological excavations that have produced artefacts from the period, these include, Ashton Old Hall, Dukinfield Hall, Denton Hall, Mottram village and the Black Bull Inn, the Haughton Green glassworks and later colliery, and the field boundaries and tracks of Werneth Low. Individual reports on this work are available from the archaeology unit.

The first problem faced by an archaeologist, confronted by this mass of data and the evidence of a fundamental change in the material culture, is try to characterise or group this new information and new sites in some sort of meaningful way. Archaeology depends strongly upon two similar concepts, typology and seriation, to bring order into any collection of archaeological material from any period (Renfrew and Bahn 1996, 114–18). Typology assumes that objects or sites develop in a coherent fashion whilst seriation is based upon the assumption that similar assemblages of similar types of sites or material objects belong together in some fashion. Put simply, things develop progressively and similar things are created by similar forces.

The most difficult issue in this search for order is how to identify or characterise individual sites. Should we call a seventeenth-century Mottram farm in which a tenant practised both agriculture and weaving a farm

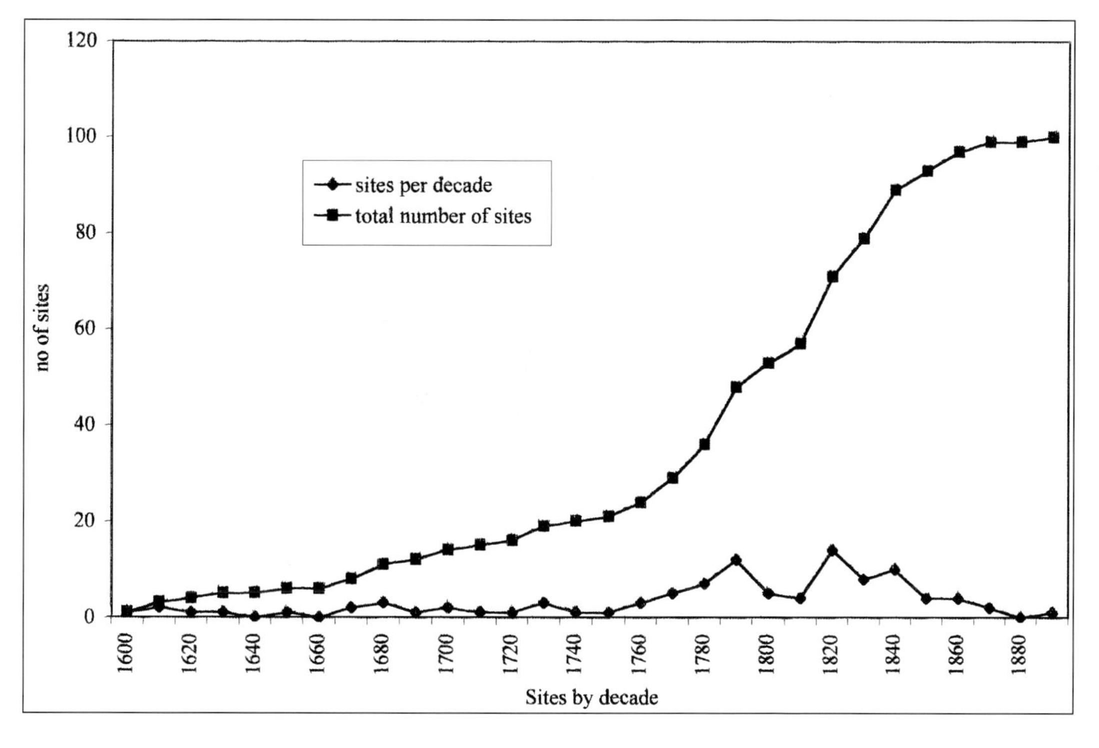

Figure 1.4 The introduction of new types of archaeological site: a cumulative graph.

Figure 1.5 Summerbottom Cottages, Broadbottom. These are the earliest surviving workers' housing built by a mill-owner in Tameside. They were erected in 1790 by John Swindells who was based at the nearby Hodge Mill, later the Hodge printworks. The first phase was a row of six three-storey stone cottages. However the third storey was a single room used as a loomshop which had access to the other third-storey loomshops.

or a workshop or both? In order to categorise much of the archaeological material and to provide a common frame of reference we have used the archaeological site descriptions and monument category classifications contained within English Heritage's and the Royal Commission's *Thesaurus of Archaeological Monument Types* (RCHME 1996).

Using the Thesaurus together with the findings made during the research for the earlier eight volumes, which included targeted archaeological fieldwork, it is possible to draw a graph of when different types of site were first constructed within the study area. As the great majority of sites survived for long periods it is more helpful to draw a cumulative graph showing how the total range of sites expanded through time. Figure 1.4 shows the pattern of introduction of new types of site in the area and how the range of sites expanded.

The slope of the graph is S-shaped with a long period in which new types of sites were gradually developed followed by phases of more rapid change. Such S-shaped (sigmoidal or logistic) growth curves are found in many cases of population growth. We can divide such graphs into four main phases:

1. The adaptive phase in which change is slow;
2. The expansionary phase a period of rapid growth positive feedback;
3. The consolidatory phase in which growth is less rapid and in negative feedback becomes more common;
4. Maturity.

The study of growth curves is dominated by ecological theory (Allaby 1996; Colinvaux 1993; Smith & Smith 1998) and if we accepted some of these insights we might conclude that the graph of new archaeological type sites from the Tameside area is typical of a population where investment in developing new sites (population members) is high and that ultimately the total range is restricted by some form of complex constraint.

This graph and its role in defining the overall form of the Industrial Revolution is considered more fully in the final chapter of this volume. At this stage the more important issue arising out of the conclusions reached in the earlier companion volume is whether or not we can relate different types of new sites to one of the three social groups we have identified.

Using the Thesaurus we have identified 100 new types of archaeological site established in the Ashton and Longdendale lordships between 1600 and 1900, in addition to the sites already in existence by 1600. These new sites fall, according to the schema within the Thesaurus, into one of 15 major monument types; agricultural and subsistence monuments; civil monuments; commemorative monuments; commercial sites; defensive sites; domestic sites; education sites; monuments associated with gardens, parks and open spaces; those connected with health and welfare; industrial monuments; institutional monuments; recreational sites; religious, ritual and funerary sites; transport sites; and those monuments associated with water supply and drainage.

These new sites range from ice houses, such as the fine eighteenth-century example in the grounds of Broadbottom Hall; hatting plank shops, such as that on Joel Lane in Gee Cross built in the late eighteenth century; pumping engine houses, such as at Rocher Vale near Park Bridge from around 1800; and transport networks such as the Manchester to Ashton Canal, built in the 1790s, or the Manchester to Sheffield railway, built in the 1840s. However, the three most common of these new archaeological sites were: the terraced workers' house, the earliest surviving buildings are probably the row of six cottages in Broadbottom known as Summerbottom (Fig. 1.5) built in 1790; the textile site, of which 274 sites are known, the earliest surviving purpose built mill being Gerrards Wood Mill in Hyde (Fig. 1.6), erected in the early 1790s; and the farmstead, of which 273 sites are known one of the more notable being the eighteenth-century Brown Road Farmhouse, a fine example of the new form of symmetrical, double depth, central staircase, plan, farmhouse introduced in this period.

In writing this volume the very extant of the archaeological and historical data has meant that we have had to be selective. Whilst this book touches on many aspects of the archaeology of the period we have tended to focus upon the most numerous substantial archaeological sites rather than upon artefacts or single industrial events such as canal construction. This approach has meant that many topics of interest to archaeologists studying this period, such as gravestones, churches and even tokens, have received short shrift, which is a source of regret.

From our knowledge of the rights and interests of the social groups of the period 1348–1642 we suggested that ownership or control of such major monument types lay within different social groups. If these groups continued to shape the archaeological remains we should expect them to remain as the controlling influence in the main period of industrialisation, 1642–1870. In the following chapters we explore the role of these major groups in detail and how they may have shaped the extent and nature of the archaeological remains of this period within the study area. In this exploration use is made not only of the results published in the previous volumes but of recent fieldwork and historical sources. Our use of historical sources is very much in keeping with the approach adopted by archaeologists studying other historic periods. The sources are used to address or explore archaeological issues rather than either historical artefacts or as a source for a formal history. Using such an approach can lead to distortion but the reader will find a wider consideration of the historical sources and the history of the area in the companion volumes of this series.

The most difficult issue, at a theoretical level, was to be sure that we could reasonably assign ownership of sites to individuals. In a typical local manor such as Hattersley to judge from the Court Leet records a tenant was responsible for building his own house and in the early part of the period could use certain materials obtained from the common land. It might seem, therefore, that the house was the tenant's property but in fact it seems that if they lost the tenancy they lost the house and it became the property of the landowner. However, there is evidence that most tenants thought of themselves as quite secure in their tenancies. In practice the relationship between tenant and owner was a relationship deeply anchored in custom and few tenants lost control of the houses they built. In every case where we have allocated control over the development of different types of sites we have tried to balance

Figure 1.6 Gerrard's Wood Mill, Hyde. This textile spinning mill was one of the 100 new archaeological type sites introduced into the Tameside area during the period 1642–1870. The spinning mill is the archetypal site of the Industrial Revolution in North West England, although in the Tameside area it is only the second most common type site in the period 1642–1870 (274 sites are known) the first being the terraced house. This particular example was built by Samuel Ashton by 1794, and is the earliest surviving purpose built cotton spinning mill in Greater Manchester. The Ashton family were seventeenth-century tenant farmers who diversified into domestic based textile production in the early eighteenth century, acquiring sufficient by wealth to build a series of textile mills from the 1790s onwards, and ultimately becoming the wealthiest landowners in nineteenth-century Hyde.

the evidence of tradition and legal documents and only allocated 'control' of a site to a group where we could be reasonably satisfied that they had a combined influence on the building of the site and its form that was greater than that of any other group.

To enliven this volume, and to allow the arguments to be followed and questioned we have included not only illustrations of individual sites but a number of 'cartouches' or self-contained articles. These cartouches are intended to explain in more depth particular findings relevant to the book as a whole. Also throughout the rest of this book are various quotations from John Aikin's *Description of the Country Thirty to Forty Miles round Manchester,* published in 1795. That book, which offers a unique insight into developments within the area during a critical period, resulted from an extensive survey of a region which included Cheshire, Lancashire, West Yorkshire, Derbyshire and Staffordshire.

CHAPTER 2

The Landholders

There are in Cheshire many very considerable estates possessed by gentlemen who have residences within the county; and, indeed, it has been observed that no county in England has preserved more of the race of its ancient gentry.

John Aikin 1795, page 43

2.1 Introduction

As discussed previously the archaeology of the area from the period 1348–1642 is distinct (Nevell & Walker 1998) and best understood through studying its links to three contemporary social groupings (lord, freeholder and tenant). In this chapter an attempt is made to chart the activities of the lords, with their manorial power, during the high period of industrialisation, between 1642 and 1870, and to see whether they are again shaping sections of the archaeological record.

It was argued in the companion volume, *Lands and Lordships*, that the chief way the lords increased their income during the period 1348 to 1642 was by exploiting their rights to particular natural resources and their control of certain economic elements such as towns. One of the key issues of this period is, therefore, how far they pursued this traditional, medieval, strategy and did this approach leave traces in the archaeological record?

2.2 The History of the Lordships of Ashton and Longdendale, 1642–1870

The core of the present study consists of the ancient lordships of Ashton-under-Lyne and Longdendale. During the period 1642 to 1870, when industrialisation was at its height, these lordships still remained as significant social institutions, dominating the rural economy of Tameside.

Ashton-under-Lyne Lordship

The ancient lordship of Ashton-under-Lyne remained in the hands of the Booth family until it passed through marriage to the Greys in 1758. This was despite the role of the Booth family during the Civil Wars of the mid-seventeenth century and the political revolution of 1689. Initially the family supported Parliament during the 1640s but during the 1650s became increasingly disillusioned with the Republic. This alienation culminated in the younger Sir George Booth leading the Cheshire rebellion in 1659, for which he was imprisoned in the Tower of London. The family benefited from the Restoration of Charles II in 1660, Sir George being elevated to the peerage as the first Baron Delamer in 1661 and the family's estates, confiscated in 1659, were returned. He and his son Henry, who succeeded to the estates in 1684, opposed the accession of the Catholic King James II during the early 1680s and both were imprisoned in the Tower during 1683 for complicity with the Rye House Plot to murder King Charles II and his brother James, Duke of York. They were released without charge but in 1685 when James succeeded to the throne Henry was again imprisoned in the Tower before and after the Monmouth Rebellion. Although tried for high treason he was acquitted. In 1688 William of Orange landed and Henry Booth was the first nobleman to declare openly for him and took around 400 men to Hungerford where he joined William of Orange and his army. After James II's abdication in 1689 Henry was made Chancellor, Under Treasurer to the

Exchequer, and Lord Lieutenant of Cheshire. When he resigned these posts in 1690 the was made Earl of Warrington (Littler 1993, 19–21).

The political activities of the family during the seventeenth century had a lasting effect on the Booth estates. Although these estates were not in debt when George Booth inherited them from his grandfather in 1652 by 1661 he had amassed personal debts of nearly £30,000. Despite the selling of 300 tenements during the next 20 years, when Henry inherited in 1684 the debts had still not been cleared. Henry's political activities over the next ten years meant that at his death his debts had risen to over £50,000. The scale of the debts meant that whilst the family estates had an annual income of £2,100 during the late 1690s annual expenditure, including interest on the debts, amounted to £2,947 (Jones 1982). It was left to George Booth (1675–1758) to rescue the family's finances through marriage to an heiress coupled with careful husbandry (Littler 1993, 24–7). When the family lands passed by marriage to the Grey family in 1758, on the death of the Second Earl of Warrington, the estate's finances had been rectified and the earl died a wealthy man (Littler 1993, 31; Nevell 1991, 80–1; Dore 1966, 78–96).

Throughout the period 1642 to 1870 the chief residence of the Booth and Grey families was Dunham Hall (Fig. 2.1) near Altrincham in northern Cheshire, but the lands owned by the Booth and later the Grey family in northern Cheshire and Southern Lancashire were very extensive and in 1701 totalled over 20,000 acres (Fig. 2.2). Nearly 50% of this land lay in Tameside and included the manor of Ashton, the manor of

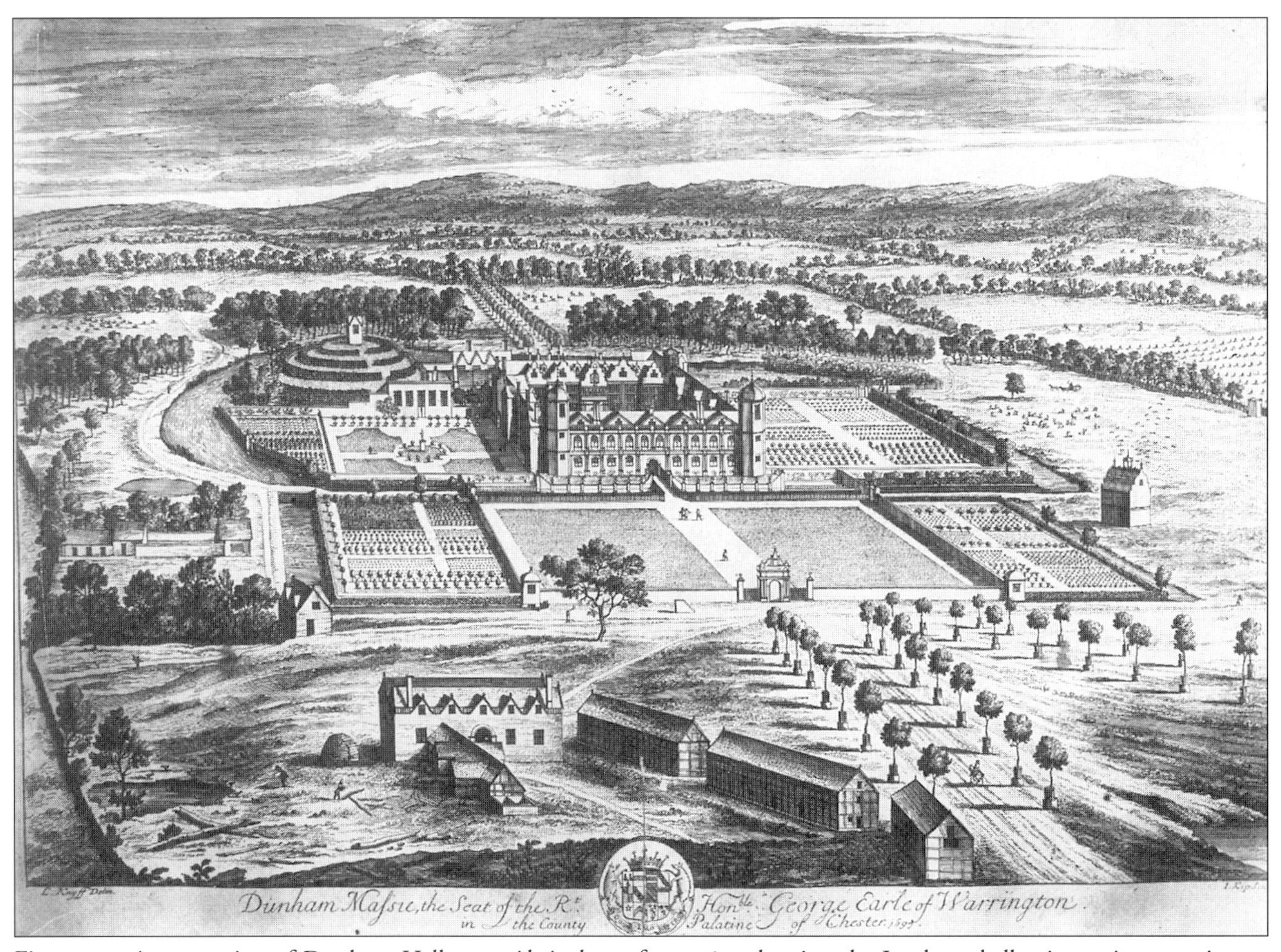

Figure 2.1 An engraving of Dunham Hall, near Altrincham, from 1697 showing the Jacobean hall prior to its extensive rebuilding in the early eighteenth century (the plan), with the site of the medieval castle (the mound) in the background. This was the ancestral home of the Earls of Stamford, who were absentee landlords of the lordship of Ashton and the manors of Staley and Hattersley. This hall complex was more than twice the size of Staley Hall and Ashton Hall, and reflects the position of the family as one of the largest landholders in Cheshire and Lancashire during the period from 1642 to 1870.

Hattersley (inherited in 1577), half of the manor of Matley (inherited in 1457), the manor of Staley (inherited in 1457) and significant tracts of land in Droylsden, and Mottram.

Agriculture

As absentee landlords the Booth and Grey families managed their Tameside estate through a single steward. Ashton Hall appears to have been used as the steward's residence, whilst Staley Hall was maintained as a secondary residence. One consequence of the family's debts acquired during the second half of the seventeenth century was the restructuring of the estate's finances in the period 1694–1715. For the tenant farmers this restructuring included the dropping of all the remaining manorial duties in kind (i.e. the requirements to give the lord so many days for carting coal and turf, reaping and ploughing, and spinning textiles) and their commutation to cash payments sometime between 1704 and 1709 (Littler 1993, 99). In the same period most of the earl's land in Warrington was sold, reducing tenant income from that part of the estate by 82%. However, the earl by the conversion of manorial duties into rents increased the cash income from Ashton-under-Lyne, Dunham and Warrington.

The period saw a considerable increase in arable production in many parts of the families estates particularly in Dunham and on the southern Cheshire estates. However, the family's estates in Hattersley and Staley do not seem to have seen such an intensification, probably because as Pennine fringe areas they were dominated by rough grassland and moss, which accounted for 71.2% of these lands in 1701. The same is also probably true for Ashton where rough grassland and moss accounted for 87.7% of the estate (Littler 58–60). Evidence for the adoption of many of the new farming innovations of the eighteenth century, and a consequent intensification of the farming regime, can be seen at Dunham Hall, with its fine range of stables, hay barns and threshing barns, and at Dunham village with its many new farm buildings such as the Village Farmhouse which dates from 1752 (Nevell 1997, 79). Little of these improvements were seen at the Tameside estate although rebuilding work is recorded at the farms of Lower Fold in 1710, Oakdene (in Mossley) in 1755 and Four Winds in 1775 (Burke & Nevell 1996, 30–49) that might have been financed by the Stamford estate.

The annual requirement for tenants to plant trees on their tenancies imposed in the period 1704–1709 did have an impact on the Ashton, Hattersley and Staley estates (Littler 1993, 90–1). Certainly one consequence of the restoration of the family's fortunes and drive towards farming intensification was the purchasing of land in Ashton; in particular the Cinderland Hall estate which was bought in 1756 (Burke & Nevell 1996, 20). In 1770 the family's lands in the Tameside area, and in particular the Ashton lordship, were still overwhelmingly agricultural in character.

Until the late eighteenth century the majority of the income from the estate came from agricultural rents, the estate keeping tight control over the leasing of property. For instance when Cinderland Hall farm was leased to Samuel Leech in 1756, for fourteen years, the rent was £50, plus '£5 for each acre plowed more than 10 in any year'. Furthermore, the leasee was obliged to keep the premises in repair, pay all levies and taxes, spend any profits on the premises, keep windows, causeways, ditches, and fences in repair, thatch the buildings, and not to plough the meadows (Cordingley 1986, 4).

The estate continued to invest in agriculture in the nineteenth century with the biggest expenditure being the cost of draining and enclosing Ashton Moss between 1831 and 1846 (Nevell 1993, 86). This was a large lowland mossland covering 240 acres on the north-western fringes of Ashton town which after draining and improvement was rented out as market gardens to exploit the growing demand created by the new urban centres of the lordship.

In 1847 over 170 leading residents of Ashton succeeded in a formidable campaign to obtain municipal status for Ashton and the surrounding area and thus wrest control of the town from the estate. Only one councillor called himself an esquire and the great majority were drawn from the minor trades (Bowman 1960, 643–7).

The towns

Until the nineteenth century both the development and economy of the only town in the Lordship, Ashton, lay under the direct control of the Lord. During the period 1770–1830 the character of the Ashton Lordship saw substantial changes, with rapid urban growth leading to the expansion of the existing urban centre at

Ashton. The population of the town rose from around 2,500 in the 1770s to nearly 15,000 people by 1831. A second urban zone arose on the northern bank of the River Tame at the bridge leading into the manor of Staley (hence its name Stalybridge), which by 1831 also had a population of nearly 15,000 (Butterworth 1842, 147; Nevell 1993, 166). This shift towards urbanisation within the lordship was combined with the emergence of the factory system and the establishment of over fifty textile sites within the lordship.

The Earls of Stamford, the Grey family, had begun to lay out in Ashton between 1787 and 1803 a gridded Georgian town grafted onto the south-western side of the existing settlement (Fig. 2.3). This new planned town contrasted starkly with the Charlestown area of Ashton, which lay immediately north of the old medieval market. That area had grown in a haphazard fashion in the 1770s and 1780s and was dominated by the small cottages of workers whose main income appears to have been derived from domestic weaving and spinning. The new town involved the laying out of a grid of streets, named after members of the Earl's family, to create a plan with long vistas and formal open spaces. The estate was responsible not only for laying out the grid-iron of streets in Ashton, and the sale of leases to builders, but also for stipulating in these leases pavement flagging and widths as well as the dimensions of properties and the necessity of proper drainage (Cordingley 1986, 18; Bowman 1960, 637–9). The aim of this project can be seen in the style of buildings being erected, especially around the Old Square area, in the period 1787 to 1803. These were large, brick, three storey Georgian town houses and fixed shops to replace the old stalls. There was a strict hierarchy of road widths defining social divisions within the new town. As late as 1812 detached domestic houses were still being built in this area, but the character of this zone began to change in the late 1790s when the Ashton and Peak Forest Canals were built along its southern edge, and the first three storey loomshops were built on Wellington Street by 1803. By the time a second phase of planned urban expansion began in

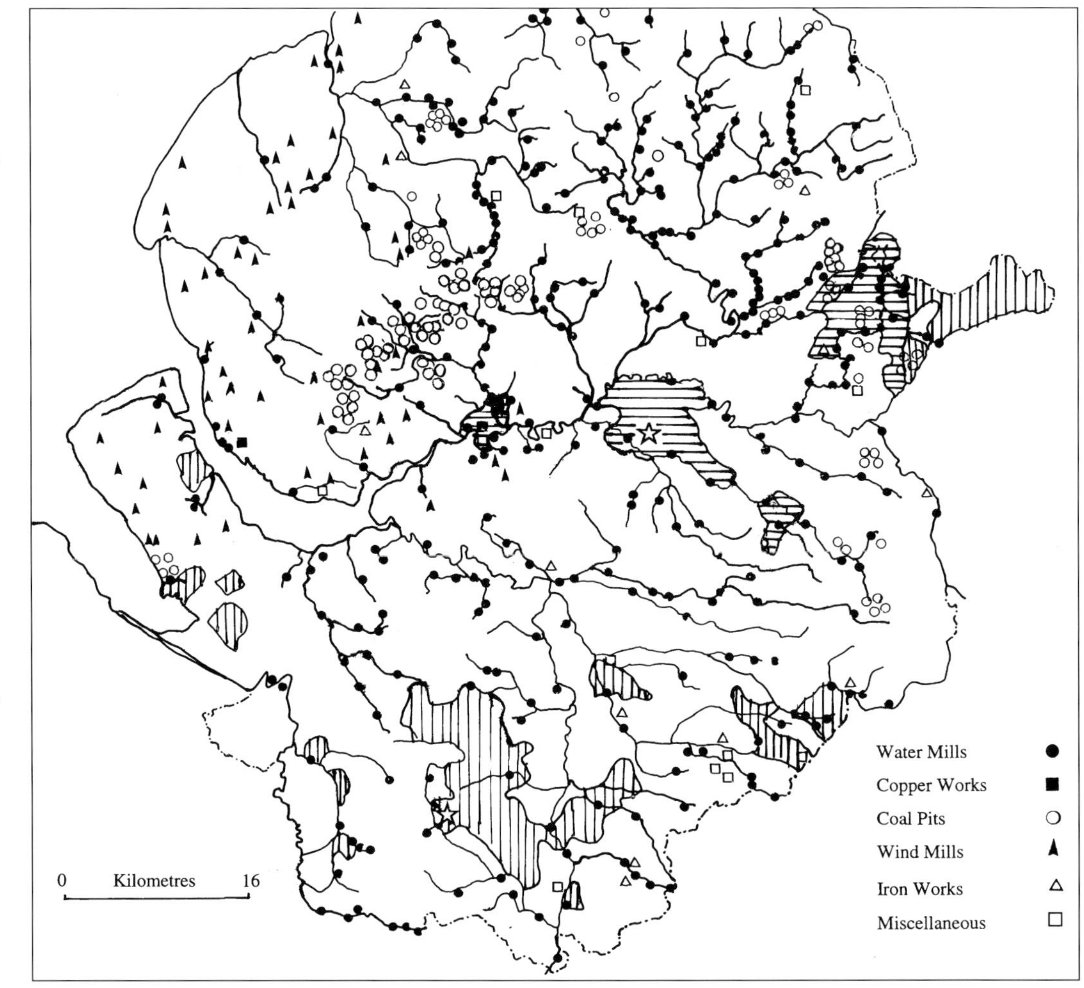

Figure 2.2 The Stamford and Tollemache estates and early industry, 1777–86. These two families were some of the largest landholders in the North West during this period, with over 20,000 acres and 30,000 acres respectively (shaded). Roughly half of each estate lay within the study area and comprised the lordships of Ashton and Longdendale. Note how the distribution of early industrial sites on their estates is concentrated in the lordships of Ashton and Longdendale, away from their eighteenth-century seats (starred).

Figure 2.3 The Old Square, Stamford Street, Ashton-under-Lyne, in 1832. This was the central axis of the Georgian planned town built by the Earls of Stamford from 1787 onwards. Note in the distance St Peter's church, which dominates the vista along the road built in 1821–24 as part of the second stage of urban development initiated by the Stamfords.

the 1820s the proposed new town had more than trebled in size compared to the original scheme, with a new area of middle-class and merchant houses on the south-western edge of the town between the newly designed Henry's Square and a rotunda on the northern banks of the Ashton Canal. This was because the old area of middle-class housing had become swamped by new textile mills and working class housing built between the Ashton Canal and Old Square.

A twenty year gap in the development of Georgian Ashton coincided with the Stamford Estate's construction of a working-class area of housing at another of the estates urban centres; Altrincham (Nevell 1997, 88–91). Here between 1799 and 1835 nearly 400 houses were built on three new roads; Albert Street, Chapel Street, and New Street, on the south-western edge of the medieval market town. The leases for this development specifically excluded the construction of factories.

Immediately to the east of the study area in Glossop and Buxton the local major lords also played a prominent role in developing towns within their land-holdings. In 1780 the Duke of Devonshire developed a new bath complex at Buxton from his profits from the mine at Ecton. The Dukes of Norfolk actively developed Howard Town, now known as Glossop, building a Town Hall in 1837, a market hall in 1844 and the railway station in 1847. To the south in Stockport, Sir George Warren, the lord of the manor, whilst pursuing his claim to an earldom found time to develop the unique urban Castle Mill in 1778. The mill, which lay upon the site of the town's castle was oval in plan and this has led Arrowsmith to suggest the unusual layout might have been a result of Sir George's desire to impress his social contemporaries (Arrowsmith 1997, 102–4).

During the mid-nineteenth century, from 1830 to 1870, the lordship of Ashton saw a further increase in urbanisation, with new mill centres emerging at Hurst to the north of Ashton, Audenshaw, to the west of Ashton town, and at Mossley in the middle reaches of the Tame valley on the eastern side of the lordship.

Industry

In the early period the Lordship played a dominant role both in the organisation of transport routes and in the exploitation of mineral resources. From the 1780s onwards an increasing proportion of the income of the estate came from coal the income rising from £21 per annum in 1758–59 to £827 14*s.* 1*d.* in 1785 (Bowman 1960, 468, 471).

During the nineteenth century the steward of the estate was also responsible for the acquisition and disposal of land to road, canal and rail companies. For instance the steward in 1802, Mr H. Worthington, witnessed a deed transferring all rights of way and 'the reversion and reversions, remainder and remainders, rent issues and profits tenancy, and every part and parcel thereof' to the Manchester, Ashton and Oldham Canal company (Cordingley 1986, 14). The estate had a direct financial interest in these new companies.

The role of the estate in developing new types of industrial buildings and processes that were not associated with their traditional areas of control is less than clear. In March 1816 Lord Stamford wrote to his steward at Ashton that he did not believe it necessary to control the purposes to which the new town buildings were put as long as the rent was secured (Nevell 1997, 91). Although the estate leased land to various new industrial enterprises this seems to have been the limit of their interest with no evidence to suggest detailed involvement.

Social control

Between 1770 and 1830 the traditional forms of manorial government, the court leet and the parish meeting, seemed to have gradually declined and by the 1800s not even the steward seems to have taken a deep interest in individual cases (Cordingley 1986). In 1827, a completely new form of local government, elected and independent of the manorial lord, was established. This was the Ashton Local Board, which had responsibility for its own lighting, cleansing and appointment of petty constables. Although this board only covered the urban centres of Ashton and Stalybridge north of the River Tame it was completely independent of the traditional forms of manorial control, and as such marked the biggest and most fundamental change in local control since the introduction of the manorial system in the early medieval period. For the moment the two systems continued to run side-by-side, with the Ashton Court Leet maintaining its own jurisdiction over the town and countryside.

During this period the population of the lordship rose to nearly 60,000 and local government developed further, with elected local boards established at Audenshaw and Hurst in 1861, and Limehurst and Mossley both in 1864. Ashton town itself became a municipal county borough electing a member of Parliament in 1847 with new, larger boundaries, whilst Stalybridge became one in 1857. Although the Ashton Court leet still functioned in 1870 it had ceased to be the means of local government. Furthermore, the Stamford estate records show that the estate had begun to sell, rather than lease, land within the urban centres of Ashton and Stalybridge.

The Lordship of Longdendale

The Lordship of Longdendale (Fig. 2.4), like that of Ashton, remained intact during throughout this period, although when the last male heir of the Wilbraham family died in 1692 it passed through marriage to the Scottish Tollemache family (Nevell 1994, 93). Unlike the Ashton lordship the Wilbraham family, and their heirs the Tollemaches, did not incur heavy debts due to political activities, even though they were involved in the Civil Wars of the 1640s on the side of Parliament. By the mid-seventeenth century the Wilbrahams owned over 30,000 acres in Cheshire (Fig. 2.2; Hodson 1978, 72), of which around 15,000 acres comprised the manors of Mottram and Tintwistle. The family home was outside of the lordships at Woodhey Hall in the township of Ridley in southern Cheshire, where they had a substantive landholding. Like the Ashton Lordship the Longdendale estates were run by a steward based in Mottram (Nevell 1994, 93) who presided over the manorial court leet. The court met in Mottram and throughout the period 1642–1870 jurors were elected to sit on the court leet from the eight townships of the parish of Mottram-in-Longdendale (Godley, Hattersley, Hollingworth, Matley, Mottram, Newton, Staley, Tintwistle). By the seventeenth century three manors

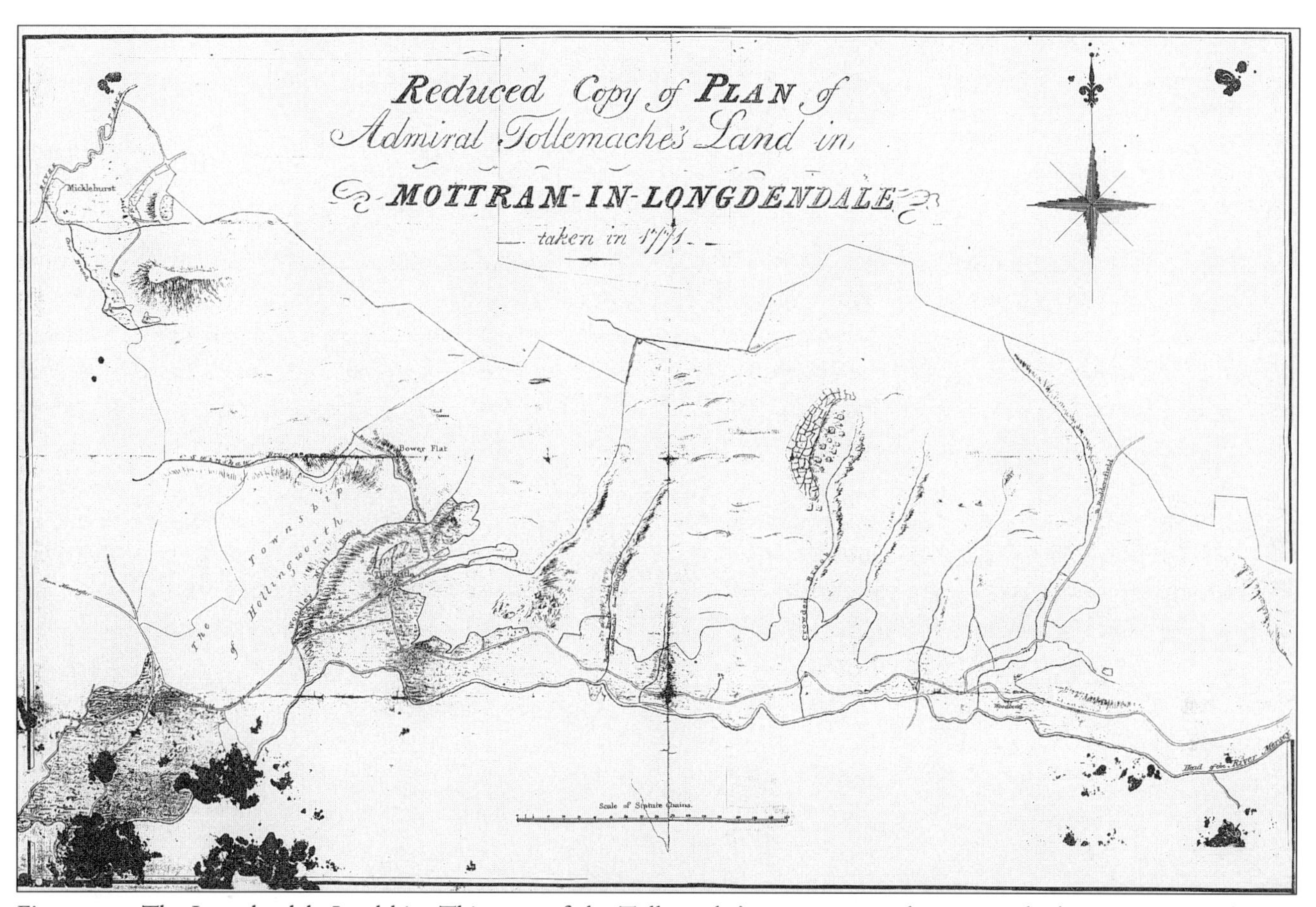

Figure 2.4 The Longdendale Lordship. This map of the Tollemache's estates in north-eastern Cheshire was surveyed in 1777 and shows the lordship at the start of the fastest period of industrial growth in its history. At this date Mottram and Tintwistle are the only large settlements in the area, but within a generation they would be joined by new urban centres at Broadbotton and Hollingworth, and by no fewer than 27 new textile sites. (*Reproduced with the permission of the County Archivist, Cheshire Record Office*)

had been lost to the Lordship of Longdendale; Dukinfield, Hyde and Werneth, all of which held their own manorial courts, which answered to the Duckenfield, Hyde and Stokeport families respectively. The manors of Hattersley and Staley had been inherited by the Booth family in 1577 and 1457 respectively and their court leets were run by a steward unlike the manors of Hollingworth and Newton which still had resident manorial lords. Thus, by the mid-seventeenth century there was a clear distinction within the Lordship of Longdendale between those lands directly owned by the Wilbraham family, namely the manors of Mottram and Tintwistle, those that only acknowledged the Lordship as their overlords (Godley, Hattersley, Hollingworth, Matley, Newton and Staley), and those which were no longer part of it (Dukinfield, Hyde and Werneth).

Seventeenth-century rentals, which only cover lands held directly by the family, survive from the estate for 1600, 1618, and 1640 and these are supplemented by a series of deeds from the 1680s. The evidence from the first three quarters of the eighteenth century is not quite as extensive, with a rental only surviving from 1727, but this is supplement by a series of deeds covering much of the century. Taken together this material shows a steady increase in rents, and the rise of the three life lease, and the same conversion of manorial duties to cash payments as seen on the Ashton estate.

Agriculture

There is no evidence for any intensification of farming on individual holdings at the behest of the estate, and like the Ashton estate there is little evidence of large scale investment in agricultural buildings within Mottram and Tintwistle during the period 1642–1770. Whilst there are a number of new or rebuilt farms, amongst the best examples being Post Office Farm

Transport

Throughout the period 1642–1870 the sponsorship and control of the transport network of Ashton and Longdendale was closely involved with the local lords and local government. Prior to the late eighteenth century the road network was the main means of communication in and through the two lordships and this was maintained by the local townships. With the continual growth in industry and trade throughout the seventeenth and early eighteenth centuries one might expect to encounter clear evidence of road improvement. Much of the wool used in cloth production was probably imported from the Midlands, flax came from Ireland and from at least 1601 cotton was imported from the eastern Mediterranean. In addition coal and stone were from the early seventeenth century being increasingly mined. These are bulky and heavy items that had to be transported, in Ashton and Longdendale, across a high hilly landscape bisected by deep narrow river valleys or lowland bogs. John Cocke, who judging by his will and inventory of 1590 was a considerable trader in cloth and textile raw materials, seems, for instance to have relied upon his team of nine pack-horses (Nevell 1991 89).

Yet until the establishment of the first turnpike through the lordships of Ashton and Longdendale in 1732 (the Manchester to Saltersbrook turnpike) investment in transport system was restricted to bridges at Broadbottom and Ashton. This limited investment might have been due to the fact that road building and repair was a communal task and in this area the low proportion of population to road length could have presented problems. The pack-horse system probably offered the optimum solution within the local context. Although even the hardy ponies of the north are more expensive to keep than any other farm animal their ability to exploit the plentiful grassland wastes of the area meant that in local terms they were relatively cheap. To travel these animals do not require

Figure 1 Woodend Toll Bar Cottage, Mossley. The angle position of the front windows is a typical arrangement and allowed the toll-gate keeper a clear view of the road in each direction. Unusually, at the roadside the building is single-storey, whereas the rear is two-storey, incorporated into the slope on which the building is located. This toll house formed part of the Ashton to Doctor Lane Head turnpike road, which was established in 1765. The building itself is of early nineteenth-century date.

Figure 2 Bridge over the Peak Forest Canal at Portland Basin, Ashton. According to the datestone on the bridge it was erected in 1835. This arched tow path bridge straddles the junction of the Peak Forest and Ashton canals. The shallow gradient of the bridge produces a structure of some elegance.

the wide routeways of waggons but simple narrow paths up to six feet across. Apart from crossing the narrow rivers of the area the only real problem for the horses were the peat beds of the high moors and here a local solution using local materials in the form of gritstone causeways was readily to hand. As a method of transport pack-horsing was capable of supplying fish still fresh from the Lakes to London and with horses capable of carrying 2.5 cwt each coal and stone to major centres.

Overall the transport network of the seventeenth and early eighteenth centuries shows not so much a lack of investment but a carefully evolved system that recognised the potential and limitations of the local environment and capital. The first change to this system was the opening of the first turnpike in Tameside, the Manchester to Saltersbrook Trust established in 1732 and funded by local wealthy land owners such as the 2nd Earl of Warrington (Littler 1993, 31). Several major advantages lay behind this system; the necessary capital could be accumulated, the risk lay with the Turnpike Trusts not local government, carriage travel was possible and the use of wheeled transport required less horses per pound of material moved.

By 1756, with the development of the Manchester to London turnpikes accessible from Tameside, Pickfords were offering regular waggon runs to the capital from Manchester. Twenty years later they went on to offer 'fly-waggon' passenger transport from Manchester to London in 4.5 days.

The next innovation in the Transport network within the two lordships was the introduction of canals, in the late eighteenth and early nineteenth centuries. In the Tameside area these were built with the financial support of the lord lords, especially the earl of Stamford, as a way of increasing the exploitation of the Lancashire coalfield. For instance, the Manchester to Ashton-under-Lyne canal, built in the 1790s, was constructed largely to capitalize on the coal reserves to the east of Manchester (Hadfield & Biddle 1970, 294) and had a branch running to the pits at Fairbottom, which were partially financed by the Earl of Stamford. There was also to have been a second branch, known as the Beat Bank, running to the pits at Denton and Haughton Green. An act was passed in March 1793 at the instigation of the Fletcher family, who were exploiting the coal deposits around Haughton at that time. In 1788 William Hulton of Hulton Park, who had bought the manorial estate of Denton in 1762, leased coal mines in Denton, for fifty years, to 'John Fletcher, Gentleman, of Ashton under Lyne, Collier' at an annual rent of £40 and one sixth of the coal raised (Booker 1855, 34; LRO DDHu 12/32 & 33). Two letters now in the Lancashire Record Office indicate that the Ashton Canal Co. were not keen on the plan, perhaps because two of the chief shareholders in the company were James and

Figure 3 The station building at Broadbottom was constructed in the early 1850s. The station itself opened in December 1842 as part of the Sheffield, Ashton-under-Lyne & Manchester Railway Company's Woodhead line. In 1847 the line passed into the hands of the Manchester, Sheffield & Lincolnshire Railway, which in 1897 was renamed the Great Central Railway.

John Lees, who were also shareholders in the Chamber Colliery Co. based in Werneth in Oldham and thus rivals of the Fletcher family (LRO DDHu 32/3, 32/4). Thus, the plan was abandoned, after poor progress, in 1798, much to the disgust of William Hulton who had hoped to increase the income from the collieries rented on his land. Eventually a tramway was built linking Denton Colliery with the Reddish Coal Wharf on the London and North Western Railway, but this was not opened until 7th September 1853 (TLSL MF/Stockport Advertiser 16/9/1853).

The investment and routes chosen for the railways through the two lordships also betray the interests of the local lords, who by this time included the new nineteenth-century organs of local government, the Local Board. The wealthy local industrial, John Chapman (1810–77) was one of the original and largest shareholders, and later chairman, of the Manchester, Sheffield & Lincolnshire Railway Company and is said to have financially supported the company at times of crisis during the building of the line to Sheffield in the years 1836–45 and the driving of the Woodhead tunnel (Nevell 1994, 72). Elsewhere in Tameside the local boards at Ashton and Stalybridge were anxious to encourage the building of the railway line from Manchester to Leeds via the Standedge tunnel (opened in 1849), through their towns because of the perceived benefits to trade they would bring. The wealthy industrialists remained influential in the promotion of the railway network throughout the rest of the nineteenth century. The Lees of the Park Bridge Ironworks were active promoters and backers of the Oldham, Ashton-under-Lyne & Guide Bridge Railway opened in 1861 with purpose built sidings for the ironworks integrated into the system (Nevell 1993, 129). The owner of the largest cotton spinning firm in the world during the mid-nineteenth century, John Mayall (1803–76) of Mossley, was a chief shareholder in the Midland railway and one of the chief backers of the Micklehurst railway loop, which connected the eastern half of Mossley to the railway network and was opened in 1885 (Nevell 1994, 47–51).

which has a datestone of 1692 and Brown Road Farm which has a fine eighteenth-century farmhouse, there appears to have been no systematic improvement of farm buildings. However, the Tollemaches did add to their Longdendale estates by the purchase of the medieval freehold of Hillend in Mottram, once owned by the Reddich family, in the mid-eighteenth century.

The very good set of rentals for the Longdendale estate in the Cheshire Record Office which cover the period from 1771 to 1919, enable the workings of the estate to be recovered in some detail and present a picture of continuous attempts to improve agricultural productivity. There was plenty to improve. Davies has estimated that in Longdendale during 1805 there was 6,500 acres of rough pasture, and 5,000 acres of waste land. These agents took an active interest in the running of the estate in Mottram. Many of the surveys from 1771 onwards include remarks on the state of the property, and contain valuable details of the acreage and fieldnames on the farms of the township. Comments from the rental of 1824 by the then steward, a Mr Dearnaley, include such observations as buildings in bad repair on Edward Moss' farm, others that needed to be pulled down on Cicely Shaw's farm, and land improved by 'bone manure' on Robert Wagstaffe's farm (CRO DTW 2477/B/10). In that year the income of the estate from the Mottram lands was £4198 14*s.* 7*d.*, which when added to other income from increased rents, £148 0*s.* 1*d.* from coal rents, £26 7*s.* 6*d.* from the sale of timber, and £19 14*s.* 6*d.* for the sale of stone, gave a total income of £4563 3*s.* 9*d.* Total expenditure was £2263 3*s.* 9*d.*, giving a profit to Lord Tollemache of £2,300 (CRO DTW 2343/F/16).

As the Lordship of Longdendale became more urbanised so the Tollemache family began to sell small parts of their estate. The first to go was the Hill End Estate, which was sold to the brothers George and William Sidebottom, members of one of the most successful textile families in Tameside, in 1820 (Nevell 1994, 90). In 1841 nearly half of the estate holding, nearly 300 acres, was put up for sale. Although most went unsold Samuel Marsland bought one lot, Hague Farm (Private Collections, Deeds). Such sales do not compare with the amount of land sold to the Manchester Corporation around 1852 in Tintwistle. In that year around 5,000 acres of the Longdendale valley east of Tintwistle was bought by the City in order to build a series of five reservoirs to supply the population of Manchester with drinking water (Davies 1960, 148). It was not until 1919 that the Tollemache family sold all their remaining estates in Longdendale.

The towns

During the period 1770 to 1830 the Lordship of Longdendale saw similar changes to those seen in the Ashton: rapid population growth; the emergence of new urban centres and the introduction of the factory system. Within the land owned directly by the Tollemache family the population of Mottram grew from around 500 in the 1770s to 2,144 in 1831, whilst that of Tintwistle reached 1,820 people by 1831. Within all of those lands which once had formed part of the Lordship of Longdendale the population grew from 9,901 in 1801 to 40,823 in 1831, spurred on by the growth of new urban centres at Broadbottom, Compstall, Gee Cross, Hollingworth and Hyde, and the continued growth of the existing urban centres of Dukinfield, Mottram and Tintwistle. The Tollemache family were responsible for some of this urban growth through the building of Market Street in lower Mottram during the 1780s and the leasing of land for the building of weavers cottages along this new road during the 1780s and 1790s.

Industry

The rentals from 1771 to 1919 constantly repeat a condition first noted in 1623/4 that the estate reserved the right to search and dig for stone, slate and coal. The 1785 Rental (DTW 2343/A/2/4) of the Tollemache land in Longdendale and Mottram reveals considerable details about the relationship of the estate to industry. Many of the local farms contained public houses and cotton or hatters 'shops' and in these cases the leases were for a standard term of 14 years and charged at the normal agricultural rate. In the case of 'industrial' sites associated with the traditional powers of the estate such as the flag mine (stone quarry), corn mill and turnpike house the leases were again on terms where the total number of years was divisible by seven. With the 'large and valuable' cotton mill of Hardy and Moss and John Swindells' Cotton Mill we have the only lease terms not divisible by seven and marginal notes, in Swindells' case, suggesting attempts were made to raise the land rent above the normal agricultural level.

The evidence from the rentals suggest that the Tollemaches acted in a similar way to the Stamfords by investing in their traditional areas of activity but not in the new industrial processes that lay outside their traditional purview.

Social control

After 1830 local government changes began to supplant the manorial court system in the Lordship. Parts of Dukinfield and Staley manors were included in the new Stalybridge local board established in 1828, and the larger municipal borough established in 1857 (Nevell 1993, 166–7). Other parts of Dukinfield did not have their own local board until 1857, Hyde not until 1863 and Hollingworth and Newton only from 1871 (Nevell 1993, 157, 160). In Godley and Matley the Longdendale manorial court remained the chief form of local government until their incorporation, along with Werneth, within the boundaries of the new municipal borough of Hyde in 1881 (Nevell 1993, 160). Mottram and Tintwistle were amongst the last parts of the Lordship to have their own local boards, which were not established until 1873.

2.3 The Lesser Lords

Besides these two lordships were six smaller manorial holdings in the mid-seventeenth century, both within the historical boundaries of the medieval lordship of Longdendale (the manors held by the Duckenfield,

Figure 2.5 Dukinfield Old Hall in 1795. This was the home of the ancient manorial family of the Duckenfields, who during the seventeenth and eighteenth centuries acquired more land in northern Cheshire, including in 1711 the neighbouring manor of Newton. The success of the family is reflected in the successive rebuildings of the Old Hall, which included the addition of a walled precinct and a gatehouse to the east of the hall, and culminated in the late eighteenth century with the building of a new country house, Dukinfield Lodge, on the northern side of the manor.

Hollingworth, Hyde and Newton families) and elsewhere within the modern Tameside boundary (the manor of Denton which was held by the Holland family, and the township of Droylsden which was part of the manor of Clayton held by the Cheetham family).

Most of these lesser manorial lords had medieval origins within Tameside, apart from the Cheethams who had bought Clayton manor from the Byron family in 1621 (Nevell 1991, 21). Half of these families had either sold their estates or died out by the early eighteenth century. The Cheetham family lands descended after 1664 to Alice Bland and thereafter to the Frere and Hoare families during the nineteenth century, none of whom resided at Clayton Hall (Farrer & Brownbill 1911, 285). The lands of the Holland family of Denton passed by marriage to the Egerton family of Wrinehill in 1683. They in turn passed it on to the Earls of Wilton who held the estate during the nineteenth century. However the hall and its associated lands appear to have been rented since the death of Colonel Richard Holland in 1661 (Nevell 1994, 78). The lands of the Newton family in Newton were sold in 1711 to the neighbouring Duckenfield family, after which date Newton Hall became a farmstead.

Of the three lesser manorial families which survived into the nineteenth century, the Hollingworths had the most complicated history. There were two branches of the family, the senior one residing at Hollingworth Hall as the lords of the manor, the junior branch residing at Mottram Hall, also within Hollingworth, but being freeholders. In the late seventeenth century the senior, manorial, family held *c.* 690 acres in Hollingworth encompassing at least five farms in the township (CRO DDX 87/1/a). Although this branch of the family sold the manor to a Mr Daniel Whittle in 1734, it was bought from this family in 1831 by Robert de Holyngworthe, who claimed to be a descendant of the original lords of the manor (Earwaker 1880, 142–3; Ormerod 1882, III, 870). The estate did not remain long in the family after his death in 1865, being sold by his brother to John Taylor of Booth Hall in Blakeley in 1866 (Nevell 1994, 78–9).

In the mid-seventeenth century the Duckenfield family (Fig. 2.5) owned the whole of the manor of Dukinfield, amounting to 1,690 acres and other lands in Cheshire townships such as Baguley, Brinnington, Cheadle, Edgley, Hyde, Romiley, Stockport and Mobberley (CRO D73/1 & 2; CRO DDX 16/1–5; Stewart-Brown 1935, 193). A survey of Dukinfield from 1692 records 49 tenants in that township alone (TLSL DD 229/1). In 1711 the family bought the manor of Newton from the surviving heiresses of the local Newton family (Ormerod 1882, III, 859) bringing their estate in Tameside to over 2000 acres in extent. According to the will of the third Baronet Sir William Duckenfield Daniell, made in 1756 (CRO D73/2; he died in 1758), the family held lands in Ashley, Aston, Bexton, Brinnington, Dukinfield, Edgeley, Hyde, Knutsford, Mobberley, Newton, Over Tabley, Pickmere, Stockport and Sudlow (CRO D73/2). The title of Baronet, however, became separated from the Dukinfield estates on his death, passing to a descendant of the second Baronet. The last to hold the title was the seventh Baronet, the Reverend Henry Robert Duckenfield who died in 1858 (Ormerod 1882, 818–19).

In 1762 the Duckenfield family estates in Tameside, which had been left to Lady Penelope Duckenfield-Daniel, passed by marriage to the painter John Astley (Ormerod 1882, III, 814). Aikin (1795, 452–7) expounds at length on Astley's development of the estate over the next few years. Astley built a new seat at Dukinfield Lodge to replace the old Dukinfield Hall (Fig. 2.6).

Figure 2.6 Dukinfield Lodge. This was the only new gentry house to be built in eighteenth-century Tameside. It was designed and built in 1770 by John Astley (*c.* 1730–87), portrait painter and lord of the Duckenfield estates. The Gothic style of the building may have been influenced by Horace Walpole with whom Astley was acquainted. This is a view of the loggia or colonnaded walkway on the main façade of the building and was the only structure of its kind in Tameside.

The building was never finished but contained, unlike so many local Halls, the latest facilities such as an octagon room, hot-house and 'a large open bath with a dressing room'. As well as repairing the local roads and building new bridges across the Tame Astley erected the 'Circus' for 'industrious inhabitants' and a large inn. His new water engine on the Tame supplied not only his bath but also the Circus and Ashton. Astley also attempted to develop an iron foundry complete with workers' houses using local ores, ownership of which he let to a Manchester company. Within a few years the foundry failed and was demolished and was be replaced by a cotton mill. The relationship between Astley and the 'industrious' Moravians is uncertain. The Moravian settlement was first established at Dukinfield and they expected their short lease to be extended by the Duckenfield family but after Astley assumed control negotiations failed and the Moravians moved west.

John Astley's son and heir, Francis Duckenfield Astley (1781–1825) took a keen interest in literature and himself writing poetry. He continued his father's investment in Dukinfield, planting over 40,000 trees, and leasing a number of coal-mines, which brought in a large income for the estate (Hickey 1926, 17–18). Despite selling much land for industrial and urban development throughout the nineteenth century, in 1873 the Astley family estate still owned 1,140 acres of land in Cheshire, mostly in Tameside, which returned a gross yearly rental of £4,219 5*s.* 0*d.*, although they no longer lived in Dukinfield (PP 1874, lxxii).

The Hyde family of Hyde Hall, Hyde (Fig. 2.7), held *c.* 1,036 acres of land in Denton and Haughton, to the west of the Tame, (Young 1982, 21), whilst to

Figure 2.7 Hyde Hall in 1795. The home of the Hyde family, an ancient manorial family who had held the manor of Hyde since the early thirteenth century. By the eighteenth century the estates had passed by marriage to the Clarke family, who acquired extensive property not only in England, but also in the Caribbean. Edward Clarke bought a 6000-acre sugar plantation in Jamaica, worked by 570 slaves, and acquired lands in New York. The extent of the profits the family made from the North Atlantic trade of the eighteenth century can be seen from the medieval hall at Hyde, which was rebuilt in the fashionable classical style of the period.

the east in Hyde they held most of the 889 acres of that manor (Booker 1855, 133). They added significantly to their medieval estates during the seventeenth century, with the acquisition of the manor of Newton-by-Butley in the parish of Prestbury, and other lands in Brinnington and Romiley (Chester LRO DDX 16/1–5; Stewart-Brown 1935, 106). However, the family ran into debt at the end of the seventeenth century due to the profligacy of Edward Hyde, owing £700 to Lady Fowle and £3,200 to Reginald Bretland of Thorncliffe Hall (TLSL DD 161/2). To pay off the debt to Lady Fowle a large portion of the family estates were sold, firstly Norbury in 1690 (Earwaker 1880, 42) and other lands in north-east Cheshire in 1704 and 1706. The debt to the Bretland family remained and was added to by yearly interest. By 1721 the Bretland family, who had acquired the Lucy estates in Werneth in 1682 and were a powerful force in north-east Cheshire, were claiming the right to the title and lands of the whole Hyde estate. As a final desperate attempt to save the family lands Edward's son, also called Edward, conveyed his estate to his brother-in-law George Clarke for just £100 in that year. Indeed, these lands would have come to the Clarke family when Edward died in 1725, since Anne Hyde, who had married George Clarke, was Edward's sole heir (Ormerod 1882, III, 811). George Clarke had sufficient income to undertake a protracted law suite against George Bretland and his heirs, who were suing the Hyde family for the right to the title and lands of the manors of Haughton and Hyde (TLSL DD 161/2). The successful conclusion of this case in 1754 helped to restore the family's fortune and the Clarkes retained the estate intact until the end of the nineteenth century. George Clarke became governor of New York, and acquired extensive estates in north America. His son Edward settled in Jamaica, where he acquired a large sugar plantation of over 6,000 acres worked by 570 slaves (Ward 1973, 15). His nephew, George Hyde Clarke (1742–1824), divided his time between his American and north-east Cheshire estates until he settled permanently in Hyde in 1798/9. After his return to England he became a patron of Denton Chapel (contributing significantly to its upkeep) and in 1811 was appointed as a Justice of the Peace in both Cheshire and Lancashire. He helped to suppress the violent Luddite disturbances of that summer (Ward 1973, 20–1). The last male heir of the Clarke family, Edward Hyde Clarke, died in 1873.

2.4 The Archaeological Visibility of the Landholders

The archaeology of lordship

In the Tameside area there are a variety of monuments associated with the two dominant landholding families of the area, and the other landholders. Using the English Heritage and RCHME thesaurus as a common reference point for the classifications of archaeological monuments, and combining this with the extensive archaeological and historical work already undertaken within the Tameside area (Nevell 1991, 1992, 1993, 1994; Burke & Nevell 1996; Nevell & Walker 1998) it is possible to assign some of these sites to the lords or governors and maintainers of Tameside during the period 1642–1870 and these are; agricultural and subsistence monuments; civil monuments; defensive sites; domestic sites; education sites; monuments associated with gardens, parks and open spaces; those connected with health and welfare; industrial monuments; institutional monuments; religious, ritual and funerary sites, transport sites; and those monuments associated with water supply and drainage. The following discussion will be confined to the 29 new types of archaeological sites established during this period within these broad monument classifications.

Chronologically, the lords continued to establish new archaeological sites and expand existing ones, throughout the period studied, with five new type sites established in the seventeenth century, 12 in the eighteenth and 12 in the nineteenth century. Certain monument classes show a noticeable chronological concentrations of activity. In particular the establishment of new commercial, defence, public open spaces, health and welfare, and religious monuments were confined to the nineteenth century. In terms of the distribution of new archaeological sites amongst the three social groupings under examination, the lords were exclusively responsible for establishing new civil, defence, public open spaces, health and welfare, and institutional sites.

In the following sections we deal with four areas in which the relationships of the lords to the developments of the period are clearest both from the archaeological and the documentary evidence. Of the three most common archaeological sites within the lordships during the period 1642 to 1870, the new site types of the terraced house and the textile mill and the existing site type of the farm, only the latter saw substantial investment by the local lords, notable archaeological examples being the models farm yards at Hyde Hall, Denton and Hyde Hall, Hyde.

Manorial halls

The medieval hall had been the centre of the lord's estate and in Tameside these were amongst the largest structures built in the Ashton and Longdendale lordships prior to 1642 (Fig. 2.8). These halls, and those of the lesser lords, remained a focus for manorial activity during the transition to an industrial society, although changes in the role of the local lord were reflected in the design of these buildings. During the seventeenth and eighteenth centuries the architecture of the gentry house was strongly influenced by continental Europe. This resulted in ordered buildings of classical appearance, often on a massive scale, and within the North West region there are some very fine examples, including a group of sites in northern Cheshire which include Dunham Hall, Lyme Hall, Tabley Hall and Tatton Hall. The major Tameside halls were not rebuilt in this fashion because the lords of Ashton and Longdendale did not live in the area; indeed the Earls of Stamford rebuilt Dunham Hall rather than their other properties. Consequently Tameside has no buildings which can truly be considered as examples of this type, although the influence of the greater houses can be seen in a small group of buildings.

There were three halls in Tameside with classically inspired designs. Firstly, the now demolished Hyde Hall (Fig. 2.7), home of the Hydes which had an asymmetrical façade of seven bays with a raised ground floor and an entrance door approached via opposed flights of steps like Mottram Old Hall. Secondly, Thorncliffe Hall in Hollingworth, home of the prominent freeholding family of the Bretlands, and, finally, Dukinfield Lodge (Fig. 2.6), built in 1770 by John Astley as a replacement for Dukinfield Old Hall. Although the Lodge has been demolished the surviving photographic

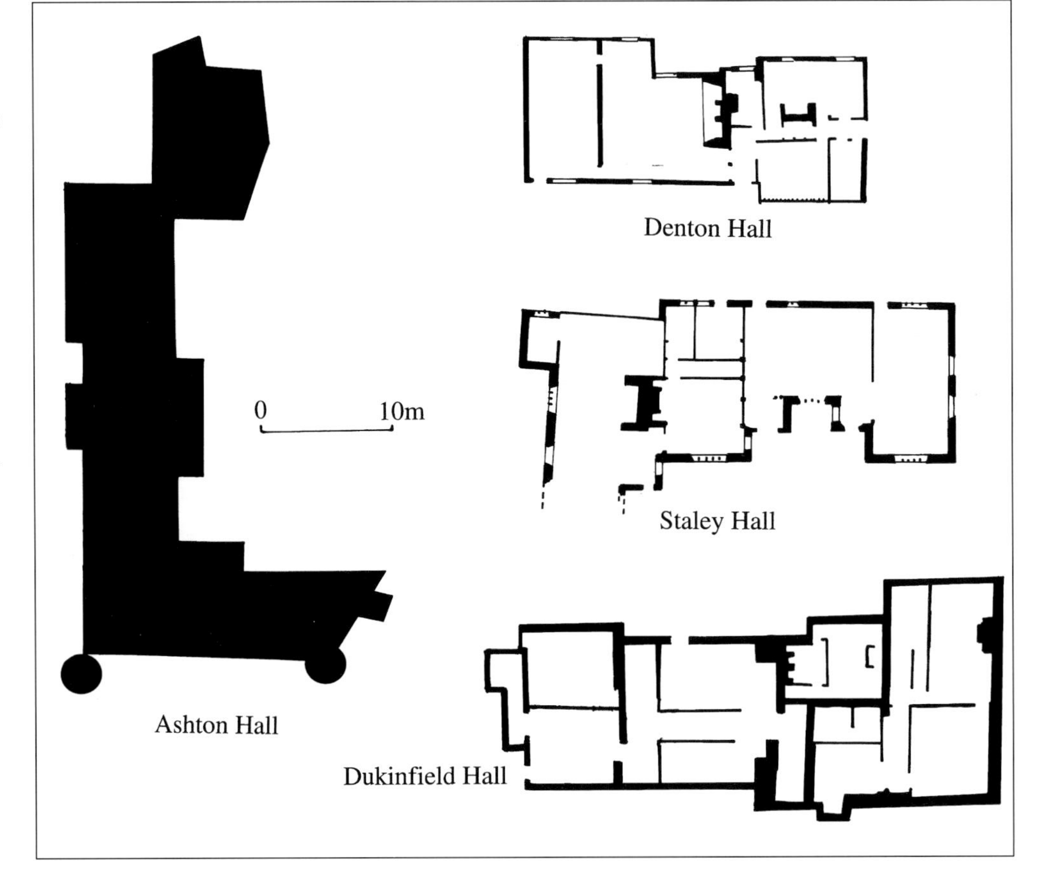

Figure 2.8 Plans of the later manorial halls of Tameside. These buildings were the biggest domestic buildings of their era, only being exceeded in size by the advent of the cotton spinning mill within the study area in the late eighteenth century. Their size and ornamentation indicate that they were important sites associated with lordly civil administration. Dukinfield Hall was the only property to be occupied by its manorial lord into the eighteenth century. As such it shows the most sophisticated plan-form development, with double depth rooms and a floor area almost equal in size to that of Ashton Hall.

Figure 2.9 Dukinfield Old Hall in the late nineteenth century. After the building of Dukinfield Lodge and the removal of the Astley family to their new country house Dukinfield Old Hall declined in status; first being rented as a farm, and then from the mid-nineteenth century as a series of three estate workers' cottages. This decline in status is reflected in the archaeological assemblage from the site, particularly in the pottery, and in the conversion of the hall grounds into allotments and gardens.

evidence depicts a striking building which was atypical of the symmetrical and classical form in vogue during most the period. It was an elaborate Gothic structure, with a façade comprising an arched loggia surmounted by a tower with a castellated parapet, with the castellation continuing around the main parapet. Most of the windows to this façade were also arched and contained traceried glazing bars. This exaggerated Gothic style was in the 'Strawberry Hill Gothic' mould, a term derived from the architectural alterations made by Horace Walpole to his home in Strawberry Hill, London. It is worth noting that Walpole was a patron of Astley's during the 1750s and this association may have influenced Astley's design of Dukinfield Lodge (Burke & Nevell 1996, 26).

The sparsity of new country house style buildings in Tameside after the seventeenth century reflects the decline of many local lords, and absence of the two largest landholders. The manorial occupants of buildings such as Ashton Hall, Denton Hall (Fig. 2.8), Newton Hall and Staley Hall either died out or moved away and these buildings became the homes of tenants, who were very often farmers. These new occupants did not have the same needs or requirements as their manorial predecessors and as a result the buildings often underwent substantial change. The new occupiers viewed their homes with a more functional eye and when renovation or rebuilding was required this was often carried out in brick, rather than in keeping with fashionable trends. Cinderland Hall, Denton Hall and Dukinfield Old Hall (Fig. 2.8) are all examples of timber-framed buildings which were substantially rebuilt or encased in brick. In the case of Dukinfield Old Hall the building was subdivided into three cottages (Fig. 2.9), whilst other halls such as Denton became so dilapidated that they were eventually demolished.

Town halls

Apart from the churches the major public buildings associated with civil administration in the area before 1642 were the Court Leet structures or rooms in Ashton and Mottram (Nevell & Walker 1998). The single largest structure was Ashton Hall which consisted of a double courtyard structure that contained a complex of rooms which contained, amongst other things, both a jail, a court and a public space. The south face of the Hall was remodelled in the fifteenth century in the latest French style.

During the nineteenth century a new series of civil administration structures were built by the new urban based local boards that were responsible for government. From the 1820s onwards, firstly through commissioners and subsequently through elected councillors, local government became increasingly sophisticated. A functional response to these changes was the establishment of a building to house the growing administration, the town hall. These buildings combined administrative office space with large functional areas which could be used by the public.

The town halls of Tameside form a range of building types which illustrate not only changing styles in town hall architecture and planning, but also the increasing statutory requirements of the new local government authorities of the nineteenth century. The earliest building in the Borough to become a town hall was at Stalybridge. Built in 1831, it was originally intended as a market hall but, during the design stage, came to incorporate committee rooms and a ballroom (Burke & Nevell 1996, 117–18). The only surviving element of this building is the Market Street entrance façade. This is a classical portico composed of two Tuscan columns supporting an entablature and a low pediment. The

Figure 2.10 Ashton Town Hall. This was the first purpose-built town hall in Tameside. Designed by Young and Lee in classical style the earliest phase (on the right) was opened in 1840 and the left-hand extension was opened in 1878. It housed the Ashton-under-Lyne Local Board and from 1847 was the headquarters of the new Municipal Borough, institutions which replaced the local court leet as the principal means of local government.

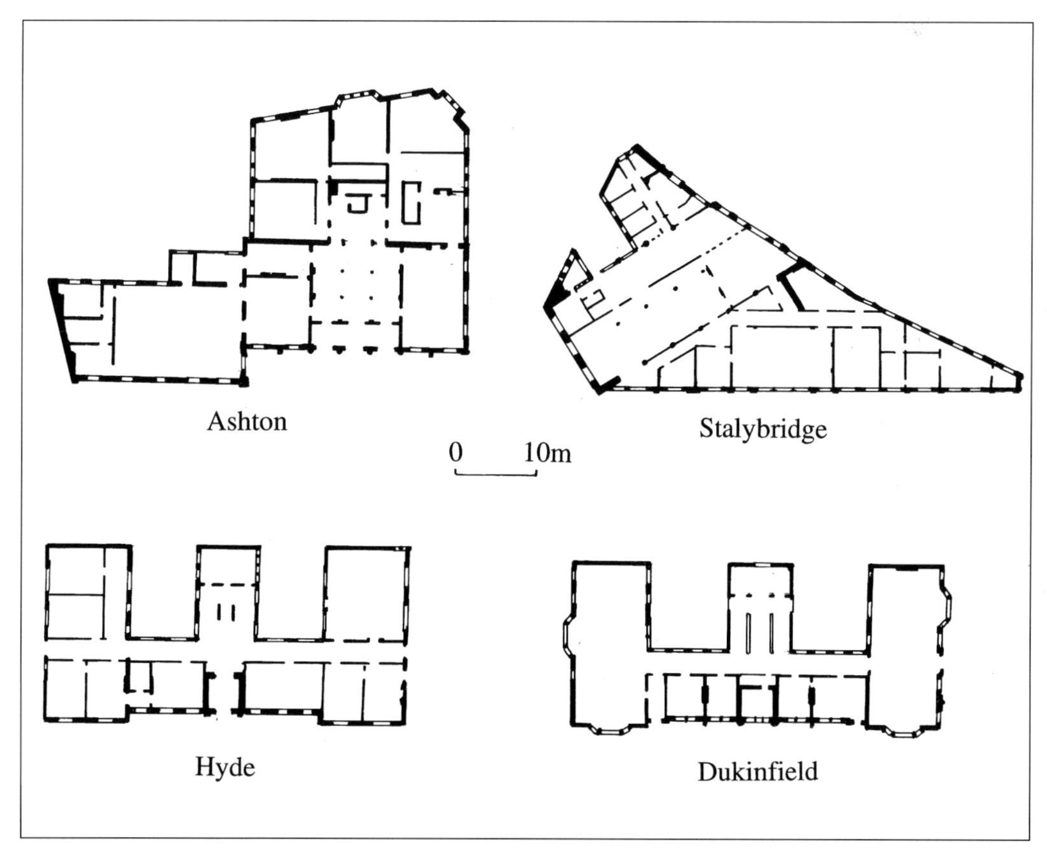

Figure 2.11 The town halls of Tameside. Nineteenth-century towns halls acted as the administrative centres of the new urban local governmental systems of the nineteenth century, in the same way that the manorial halls of the seventeenth century acted as estate centres. In size they were comparable. The town hall at Ashton, for example, is similar in overall area to Ashton Old Hall. As the requirements for local government increased during the nineteenth century, so did the size of the town halls.

neo-classical style of the market hall was in keeping with trends in public architecture of the early nineteenth century. Although at Stalybridge the expression of this style was limited to the entrance, it suggests an intention on the part of the town's commissioners to construct an imposing, fashionable building that would reflect Stalybridge's new found status as a town.

Classical composition was also used by the architects of Ashton town hall (Fig. 2.10), Young and Lee, in 1840. This building was the first purpose-built town hall in Tameside and the main façade looks on to the new market place, created in 1828, and is composed of a raised podium divided into seven bays; four attached Corinthian columns divide the central bays and support an entablature and a balustered parapet. The classical portico leads into a large entrance hall supported by Ionic columns, on one side of which was a committee room, and on the other the mayor's parlour. At the rear of the entrance hall is a grand staircase which divides into two flights at the landing stage giving access to a banqueting room or public hall which runs the full length of the building; similar features could be found in the larger country houses of the same period.

The towns halls at Ashton and Stalybridge were substantially enlarged, in 1878 and 1882 respectively. These changes were mirrored in town halls throughout England at that time and were a direct response to increasing administrative responsibilities. The extension at Ashton was designed by local architects John Eaton & Sons and continued the classical style of the 1840 building, although without the podium level and with Corinthian pilasters. Unlike the earlier building, the 1878 extension used stone for the façade only, the other elevations being built in brick. Thus while the extension retained a level of ostentation in its façade, its construction was tempered by a more functional approach which utilised cheaper building materials where possible. The two other purpose-built town halls in Tameside, at Hyde and Dukinfield, are relatively late constructions dating from 1883–85 and 1899–1901 respectively (Fig. 2.11).

The town hall extensions at both Ashton and Stalybridge housed court rooms, council chambers, police offices and cells; all features once overseen by the local lord of the manor. These larger and more elaborate structures which represent a fundamental break in traditional power structure of civil administration are generally built in the latest fashion as was Ashton Hall. In may ways both the older manorial halls and the new town halls were as similar as the common descriptive term 'hall' suggests. Within the town halls the most common reference back to the earlier system were prominently displayed coats-of-arms of the new civil authorities. The arms of Ashton were designed locally and not submitted for formal approval; they were based not upon the arms of the Stamfords but upon the earlier Assheton family (Bowman 1960, 647–8).

Schools

The establishment of new educational sites in the seventeenth and eighteenth centuries within the two lordships is an example of the continuing traditional role of the lord of the manor. By 1557 there was a schoolmaster in Mottram, based at the parish church in the centre of the Longdendale lordship. By 1623 a proper school house had been constructed with money from the local lords, the Wilbraham family, and a freeholder benefactor, Robert Garsett, a Norwich Alderman, with the right to appoint a school master alternating between them (Harris 1980, 242). This building was rebuilt in 1670 (Fig. 2.12), this time with money from the parishioners, including several local manorial families, and took the form of a two storey stone structure with coped gables and kneelers, a fashion common amongst Pennine farmhouses at the time.

A schoolmaster for the Ashton parish is mentioned in the will of John Cocke of Ashton in 1590 (LRO Cocke WS). A school house was built next to the parish church on land given by the manorial lords, the Booth family in the seventeenth century. This timber framed school was replaced by a new stone school in 1721, and in that year it was agreed that the local lord and the rector should have the joint appointment of the school master (Bowman 1960, 384). The 1721 building consisted of a three storey central range flanked by two storey wings. It included a dining room, parlour, kitchen, pantry, dormitory and bedrooms. There were two main teaching rooms; the 'Grammar School' and the 'Writing School' (Burke and Nevell 1996, 126–7).

Eventually control of the local schooling was to pass, like civil administration, from the lords to local government.

The coal industry

The development of Lancashire coal mining varied from area to area but in general terms it evolves from early lordly controlled pits worked by part time farmers to commercial companies operating deep mines worked by professional miners. In some areas, such as Colne, freeholders had the right to dig for coal whereas in others they had to pay. As early as 1527 the tenants at Burnley lost their free access to coal and it seems that for many years local lords were keen to maintain their overall control whilst working in partnership with experts to reach ever deeper seams (Philips and Smith 1994).

A detailed archaeology of the coal mining industry within the study area appears in Nevell (1993, 96–107). Coal digging using small surface pits was relatively commonplace in the seventeenth century from which developed an indigenous industry that broadly follows the wider trends within the Lancashire coalfield. The eighteenth-century coal industry saw two major technical developments which allowed coal seams at greater depths to be exploited and thus for production to be vastly expanded.

The first of these was the application of steam power to pump water from the coal shafts through the use of the Newcomen steam engine from 1733 (Flinn with Stoker 1984, 121–2). Lawrence Earnshaw, a noted inventor and tenant of Mottram, is said to have built a pumping steam engine in the mid-eighteenth century for use at a group of pits in the Longdendale lordship at Mottram, below the Hague (Aikin 1795, 467). A steam engine, possibly of the Newcomen type, was used for pumping at Denton colliery which was adapted in 1834 by Musgrave & Co. of Bolton, and continued to be used until the Denton Colliery Company closed in 1929 (Cronin & Yearsley 1985, 61). The earliest reference to such a Newcomen engine within the Ashton Lordship is a reference, in the Steward's notebook for the Earl of Stamford's estate, where one was used to pump water from a coal pit at Hurst, under the control of a Mr Lees, in 1788 (Bowman 1960, 470). The Steward notes specifically refer to 'using Mr Lee's Fire engine for drying his Lordship's Coals' (Bowman 1960, 470). This reference suggests that the Lord had some control over this activity and that far from being solely run by independent entrepreneurs this early technological introduction was shaped by the Lords influence. A similar pattern of closer control also emerges, as we have seen, from the rentals of the neighbouring Tollemache estate. Mr Lee's Fire Engine appears to have been the Newcomen engine that was used by the Fairbottom Coal Company (Fig. 2.13) from at least the 1780s, until about

Figure 2.12 Mottram Grammar School, 1670 (*left*) and Mottram Sunday School, 1832 (*below*). Although considerably different in age, Mottram School was rebuilt in 1670 and Mottram Sunday School was built in 1832, and in size these differences merely reflect elaborations over the intervening 162 years; Mottram was built for a few dozen boys and used a few times a week, whereas the Sunday School was built for several hundred children and later in the century was used as a day school.

1834 (Wilkins-Jones 1978, 20; Ashmore 1969, 109). There was a second Newcomen engine at another of the pits run by the Fairbottom Coal Company. This was at New Rocher pit, above the Park Bridge iron-works, where the engine, which had a waterwheel attached to the pump beam, was used as an extra power source for pumping, in case the water failed.

The second technical innovation was the use of steam power for lifting coal from the shafts. For most of the eighteenth century the lifting of coal was done either

Glass House Fold Colliery

During the summer of 1999 the University of Manchester Archaeological Unit carried out a programme of archaeological survey and excavation at Glass House Fold, Haughton Green, near Denton. The archaeological possibilities for this area were considered high as it contains the remains of a seventeenth-century glass making works with two of the earliest coal fired glass furnaces found in the country. The area also contains the two natural resources common to many early industrial sites, water and coal.

Glass House Fold lies on the west bank of the River Tame opposite the site of Hyde Hall the ancient home of the Hyde family who have owned part of Hyde, the township of Haughton and part of Denton since the thirteenth century. The Hyde family had utilised the potential of the River Tame at this point since medieval times by building the manorial corn mill on its east bank.

In the early seventeenth century a Huguenot family from Lorraine, possibly fleeing religious persecution, settled in the area. The Du Houx's had a long tradition of glass making on the continent and were given permission by the Hyde's to build the glasshouse from which this area takes its name. As with all industries choosing the correct site was very important and the availability of raw materials close to this part of Haughton Green would have been an important factor. There are a number of easily exploitable, good quality coal outcrops as well as nearby deposits of fireclay and quartz sand, materials essential to the production of glass. An additional incentive was the site was close to the expanding regional markets in Stockport and Manchester. The glasshouse seems to have flourished in the first half of the century but despite their well laid plans the Du Houx family could not control the political situation in the country. It seems that the glass house was destroyed in one of the many Civil War skirmishes that took place in the district from 1642 through to the Cheshire rising of 1659.

No structural remains which can be directly related to the glasshouse were found during the current survey, although it is quite possible that like the well preserved glass kilns excavated in the early 1970s other buildings dating to the early seventeenth century have been buried by the waste products from the extensive later coal mining in the area. Some evidence of the scale of the glass industry was revealed s during excavation of the buildings relating to the nineteenth-century coal mines at Glass House Fold when large amounts of waste material from the glass making process were recovered.

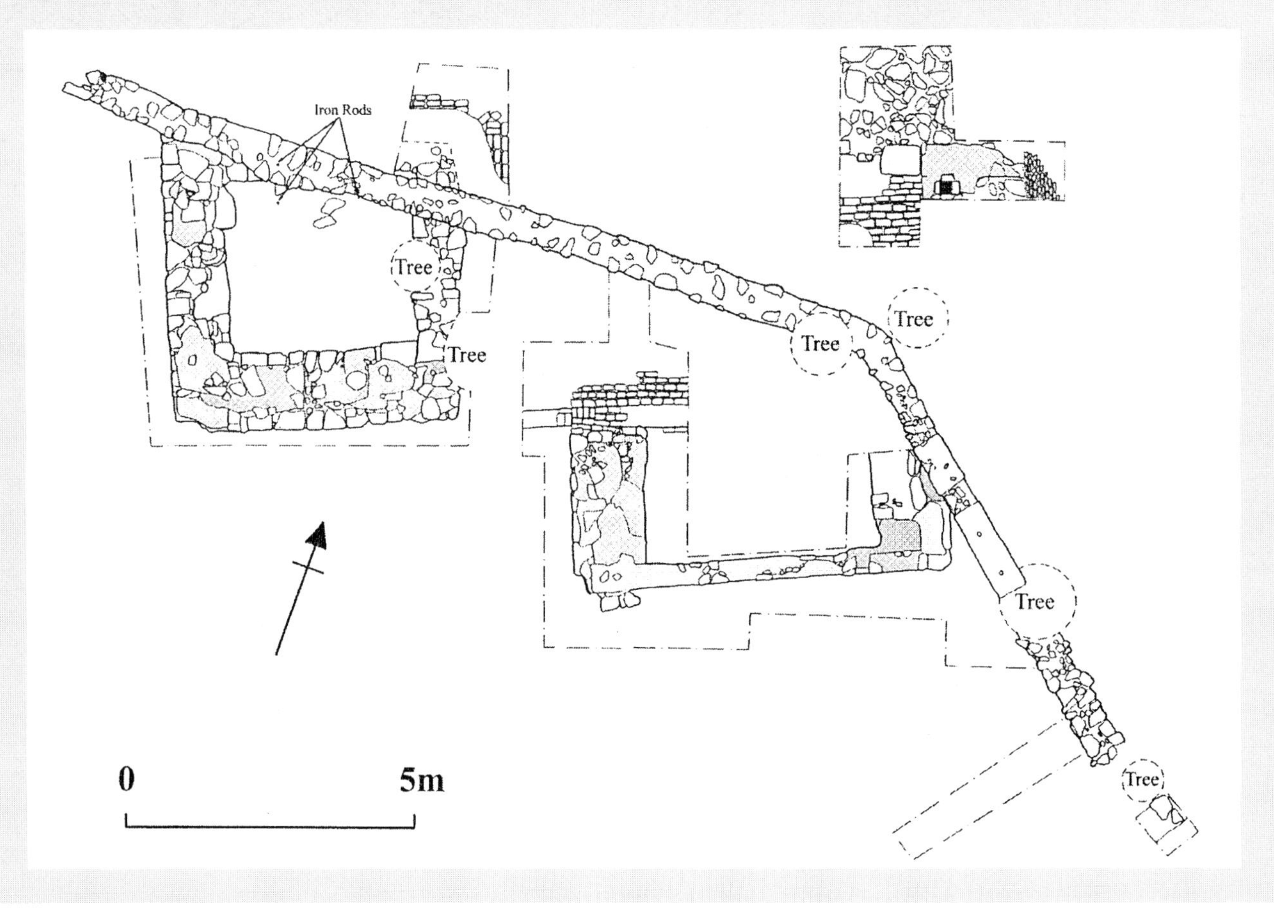

It is quite likely that unofficial mining was taking place at Glass House Fold prior to the building of the glass works and probably continued on this basis after its destruction; in 1743 it was recorded that a man 'was killed in ye colepit in Haughton' (Middleton 1932, 32,531). It was the rapid growth in the number of cotton mills in Hyde shortly after 1800 that triggered full scale commercial exploitation of the coal measures at Glass House Fold and soon subterranean Glass House Fold was a labyrinth of mine workings.

The remains of two buildings associated with this period of mining were found during the survey of Glass House Fold (*facing page*). The buildings sat side by side, the more westerly was a square structure measuring 5m by 5m (*above*). This building had substantial, stone walls between 1.10m and 1.40m wide which were bonded with a hard, white, gritty mortar. Protruding from the north wall were three, thredded, iron rods, possibly associated with machinery that may have stood in this building. The second building contained two short stretches of wall 2.50m long by 1.40m wide. The two walls ran parallel to each other, 5m apart, and were linked at their south ends by a 0.40m wide stone wall. Both buildings have a later wall cutting across them which appears to have been constructed from reused stone from the two buildings after they were demolished. Towards the north end of this wall are two stone blocks 1.20m long by 0.50m wide. One of these has a concave base and both have a number of deep regular holes drilled into them. There size and shape would suggest that they were used as machine beds. From their proximity to each other and the similarity in size and build of their walls it seems likely that the two buildings functioned together.
A mid-nineteenth-century map of coal mines from the Coal Authority Mining Records Office shows a mine shaft and other structures on the same site as the two buildings. This mine is called Glass House Fold Mine and is owned by E. H. Clarke ESQ but leased by Messrs Bradbury. On the 1845 Tithe the area of land in which the two buildings stand is marked as No 427. The accompanying apportionment list describes it as 'Dwellings, Outhouses and Colliery Ground, owned by Edmund Hyde Clarke (a local manorial lord)and occupied by George Stansfield and others". It seems that these buildings were associated with the workings of Glass House Fold colliery and given the substantial nature of the walls it is likely that they were part of an engine house. This would either have been a winding engine bringing coal to the surface or a pumping engine used to pump water out of the mine workings.

The archaeological survey revealed the remains of five other structures the most substantial of which was a rectangular building 15m long by 6m wide. The external walls are of stone with two brick built internal walls which divide the building into three equal parts. On the 1845 Tithe Map this plot of land is marked as No. 412 and is described as 'Dwelling, Outhouse and Yard owned by Edmund Hyde Clarke and occupied by Henry Ashton junior'. This building can also be identified as a house shown on a 1904 photograph of Glass House Fold. The photograph shows the house with two doors suggesting that by this date the house had been subdivided into separate dwellings. The function of the other five buildings revealed during the survey of Glass House Fold is unclear although the Tithe Map suggests that they all contained dwellings. At the location of one however the Tithe Map has a representation of a pond, this is on the same spot that Johnson's 1820 map of Manchester and it's environs shows a water engine. It is possible that this is the water engine that John Aikin, writing in 1795, says Mr Hyde Clarke had built and which belonged to some valuable coal mines.

What the 1999 archaeological programme of work has shown is that hidden amongst the woodland of modern day Glass House Fold are the extensive remains of a nineteenth-century community. Although the area at that time was one of increasing industrialisation many families continued to live there and the discovery of a brass miner's tally during excavation of one of the houses suggests that some at least worked there. *John Roberts*

Figure 2.13 Fairbottom Bobs around 1907 when it was disused. This was the first colliery in the Tameside area to have a Newcomen steam engine installed, some time in the 1780s if not earlier. Located at the bottom of the steeply sided Medlock valley, on wasteland on the northern bank of the river, this was one of the earliest collieries to be established in the Ashton Lordship and contributed to the dramatic rise in income from extractive industries during the mid-eighteenth century.

by hand-turned or horse-driven windlasses. This imposed a physical limit to the amount of coal which could be lifted each day and the depths of the shafts (Ashmore 1969, 103; Flinn with Stoker 1984, 99). The application of steam power to winding was first undertaken by Boulton and Watt in 1788, in a colliery at Whitehaven in Scotland, by which time the problems of rotary transmission had been solved (Flinn with Stoker 1984, 102). Aikin refers to the use of steam engines in Dukinfield, formerly part of the Longdendale lordship, for the winding of coal from great depths in 1795 (Aikin 1795, 457), although it was not until the 1840s that steam-powered winding gear became common in the Lancashire coalfield (Ashmore 1969, 103–4; Dickinson 1855, 71–2).

The introduction of these innovations within the Ashton and Longdendale lordships was funded by the later colliery companies not by the local lords (see *Glass House Fold Colliery*). The leases attached to these pits by the Earls of Stamford were very similar. They allowed the digging of pits, soughs, trenches and other holes, but not within 70 yards of any building, whilst proper roads had to built to the mines, which were required to be fenced. Whilst the estates did not increase thier direct investment in the pits during the eighteenth century the local lords were prepared to help with transportation problems.

A good example of this process can be seen in the promotion of the canal network in Tameside (see pp. 22–4), especially in the Manchester and Ashton Canal which cut across the southern part of the Ashton lordship, that was partially sponsored by the Earl of Stamford, as a way of speeding the transportation of coal from the Ashton collieries to Manchester. The use of canals in this manner, with the support of the local lord, had been popularized by the Duke of Bridgewater, who had financed the construction of the Bridgewater Canal in the 1760s as a way of boosting his income form the collieries at Worlsey (Preece 1981, 22–30).

The other centre of the coal industry in Tameside

lay in Dukinfield. The coal deposits at Newton Wood, Newton, were initially exploited by the Dukinfield-Daniel family, and their heirs the Astleys, who owned most of the townships of Dukinfield and Newton. Sir William Dukinfield Daniel, in his will made in December 1756, talks about 'my Coal Mines in Dukinfield, Newton, and Hyde' (CRO D 73). It is clear from this document that some of these mines were leased, and that all were mortgaged, perhaps giving an indication of their relative value at this early date. In 1795 Aikin could comment that 'Dukinfield is very valuable, abounding in mines and quarries that yield a considerable revenue. The coal-pits are from 60 to 105 yards in depth, according to the bearing of the strata ... One mile from hence is *Newton Moor*, under which coals have been got for ages at different depths. The water is pumped out and the coals raised by steam engines, which are now generally taking place of the former horse-machines' (Aikin 1795, 455, 457).

The earliest seams to be exploited by deep mine technology in Mottram were in the vicinity of Hague Carr. Hague Carr Colliery may have been established sometime before 1767 (Aikin 1795, 467). There were coal pits below the Hague which are shown on Burdett's map of 1777 and Aikin's map of Mottram in 1794 (Aikin 1795, 457). These may have been worked by Messrs Garlick & Co. who occur in the land tax returns form the period 1796–1801 owning Hague Farm, paying one of the highest land taxes in the township at £1 4*s.* 9*d.* (CRO QDV2/299). The 2,464 loads of coal got by Thomas Cardwell, probably the local mill owner who ran Arrowscroft Mill in Hollingworth, in 1803 may have been from this colliery. He got a further 1445 loads of coal in 1807 (CRO DTW 2477/A/1). The last record of the colliery occurs in 1837 when Hague Carr was put up for sale by a Mr William Thornely (Manchester Guardian 18/3/1837). There is evidence of coal workings between Hague and Carr Farms in the form of earthworks, but the area has been recently ploughed and much of this evidence obscured.

The largest mine in the township was Mottram Colliery, located in an area called appropriately the Mudd. The seam that this colliery exploited stretched across Warhill from Mottram Moor to Hurst Clough and had been exploited since the seventeenth century (Nevell 1991, 91–2). According to the parish records for Mottram in 1768 coal was discovered under the glebe lands near Parsonage Farm by a Mr Wray who 'dug for it and converted same to his own use' (CRO EDP 198/10). The Mottram estate records note that by 1771 Edward Kershaw was exploiting these deposits (CRO DTW 2477/A/1). Whilst in 1791 the vicar of Mottram, the Reverend Kinder, wrote to the Bishop complaining about the coal workings run by John Hadfield (CRO EDP 198/10). These were probably related to the shaft sunk by Hadfield and mentioned in the general survey of 1800 (CRO EDP 198/10). From about 1818 the colliery was worked by John and James Braddock and in that year 4,614 loads of coal were mined (CRO DTW 2477/A/1). The Braddock family ran the colliery for the rest of its life.

The coals got from the three collieries in the township were never extensive. For instance the Mottram estate accounts indicate that the Tollemache estate raised £10 in rent from the coalmines in 1771 (CRO DTW 2477/A/1). A general survey of the township in 1800 noted that although there were coals beneath the glebe, on Warhill, they were only of value when worked with the adjoining deep shaft colliery (CRO EDP 198/10). This may account for the modest rise in value of coals to the estate, which by 1801 had only risen to £16 5*s.* (CRO DTW 2477/A/1). Even so the steward of the Tollemache's Longdendale estate must have felt that there was money to be made from coal mining for in 1828 the estate was paying for prospecting in the Longdendale valley. However only a small coal seam not worth working was found near Waterside (CRO DTW 2477/A/1).

Husbandry

Despite the large incomes that could be garnered from coal mining some of the local lords continued to invest directly in agricultural production rather than only managing tenancies. Around 1700 there were 143 farms within the study area and this had increased by 1850 to 273 (Nevell 1993, 80–95). Only two of those farms consisted of a planned courtyard arrangement indicative both of significant capital outlay and a desire to implement the latest technical innovations (RCHME 1998). The two courtyard farms were at Hyde Hall Farm, Hyde and Hyde Hall in Denton and were both directly owned by local lords of the smaller manors. Some of the absentee, such as the Stamfords, also invested directly in new buildings but these are found within their directly farmed land clustered around their seat at Dunham.

Hyde Hall Farm was rebuilt in the early nineteenth century and before demolition consisted of a separate farmhouse with neighbouring farmyard. The farmyard consisted of a courtyard with gatehouse surrounded on four sides by a steam power house, barns, shippons and piggeries. The farm was owned by the local manorial lords the Clarke family of Hyde Hall. Extensive estate records and the diaries of John Clarke survive from the nineteenth century (TLSL DD 1/1/1–84) and these contain detailed accounts of the high farming regime employed at Hyde Hall in the 1840s, whilst the courtyard farm was in use. The extent of the demesne or home farm in 1845 included ten horses, one bull calf, six 'milch' cows, eight calves, two bulls, nineteenth 'feeding' cows, 79 ewes, three rams, 155 'feeding' lambs and thirteen other livestock. There were also 30 statute acres of wheat and 29 statute acres of oats, the latter used as fodder for the cattle and sheep. A detailed description of the farming year in 1842 indicates the emphasis placed on good husbandry (Nevell 1993, 85). From January to March the fields were manured with guano and lime, and the cattle kept inside, fed by fodder crops such as oats, potatoes and turnips. The estate was also kept in general trim, with repairs to walls, hedges and the installation of tile drains in fields by the river. April and May were spent sowing two acres of cauliflower, and a number of fields of barley. The cattle were turned out in these months. Turnips, carrots and cucumbers were also sown in the steam-heated hot house next to the hall. By June the farm workers were mowing ryegrass and 'soiling up' the potatoes, while August saw cheese making, more grass mowing and the start of the barley harvest. By September the crops were in and these fields were being ploughed and harrowed. The biggest events of October appear to have been the hatching of a clutch of 'game chickens', the sowing of wheat at the end of the month and the bringing in of the cattle. Finally, November and December were spent preparing the farm for winter, repairing hedges and fences and installing more tile drains (TLSL DD 1/1/38).

2.5 The Old and the New

Taking the histories of the local manorial lords presented here together with the role in creating certain of the new types of archaeological sites in the area it is possible to suggest an underlying pattern. As suggested by the study undertaken of the period between 1348 and 1642 (Nevell & Walker 1998) the local lords actively encouraged and fostered developments in the areas that fell within their traditional remit. In these areas they could be remarkably innovative taking a strong role in introducing glass working, steam power, deep coal mining, model farms, new forms of transport (see pp. 22–4), new urban housing and even schools. Where the innovation involved technology with which they were not familiar they frequently formed links with individual specialists and entrepreneurs. In many ways the lords' approach to change both in industry and agriculture seems to have been very uniform and conformed to the following rule; where a particular right could be exploited but required either capital investment or technical know-how then a 'partnership' was formed with a suitable person, engineer or tenant farmer, who provided the expertise or capital, and profit was then reaped through the rent or dues.

Throughout the period under study, 1642–1870, landownership determined a person's standing within the local rural community conferring on the individual governmental responsibilities ranging from being a local justice of the peace to a member of parliament (Scard 1981, 26–7). In return the landowner was expected to treat the local community fairly, promoting charities, fair rents and the rights of their tenants (Mingay 1989, 545; Scard 1981, 24–6). This social structure had its origins in the medieval period and by the mid-seventeenth-century society in Tameside was arranged on a pyramidal basis (Mingay 1989, 545–6; Nevell 1991, 63–7). At the top were the great landowners who held had more than 3000 acres (not all of it within the modern borough). In Tameside there were three such families during the period 1642–1870, the Stamfords, Egertons, and Tollemaches. Below them were the gentry, who individually held estates between 100 and 3,000 acres in the period 1642–1870 (mostly within the modern borough), and in Tameside included old manorial families such as the Duckenfields, Hollingworths and Hydes (Mingay 1989, 547–8), and freehold farmers such as the Bretlands, Highams and Reddish. At the bottom were the landless labourers.

There seems to have been one area of activity where

the lords' influence was very low, textile production. The Tollemache rent books are replete with references to textile shops and yet no additional rent seems to have been charged as a result of these developments. As we describe below these shops also seem to have developed physically not as a result of direct lordly influence but as a result of tenants' own initiatives. As described in the companion volume (Nevell & Walker 1998) this form of development continued on its own distinct trajectory controlled by other forces.

From the available evidence one might conclude that the survival strategy of the local lords (if they had such a thing) was to seize the opportunities presented by economic and technological growth to build on their traditional activities, often using 'partnership' arrangements, whilst eschewing activities that might, as we shall describe below, have lowered their social status such as trade and textile working.

By 1870 there had been a decisive shift in civil and social power within the lordships of Ashton and Longdendale. Power had was moved away from the court leet towards the new Victorian forms of local government. Halls had been replaced by town halls.

CHAPTER 3

The Freeholders

> The yeomanry, formerly numerous and respectable, have greatly diminished of late, many of them having entered into trade: but in their stead, a number of small proprietors have been introduced, whose chief subsistence depends upon manufactures, but who have purchased land around their houses, which they cultivate by way of convenience and variety.
>
> *John Aikin 1795, page 23*

3.1 Introduction

In chapter one of this study, and in the companion volume that looked at the proto-industrial transition in the Tameside area, we established that freeholders as a landholding group were distinctive, and that they used particular sites. It was noted their houses had a distinctive plan and form, which in the century before 1642

Figure 3.1 Mottram Old Hall. This was the home of the junior branch of the Hollingworth family from the fourteenth century, and was the centre of a small 100-acre estate on the western side of the manor of Hollingworth. The core of this building is a seventeenth-century hall with crossings, but this was rebuilt and elaborated in style in 1825 by the addition of this classically façaded southern wing. This refurbishment, however, was carried out by George Hadfield, nephew of Samuel Hadfield, a local millowner who bough the estate in 1800.

consisted of two storeys often with one or two cross-wings. We also suggested that our model of competing social groups or adaptive systems could explain the rise and fall in freeholder numbers within the lordships of Ashton and Longdendale. Since freeholders lacked the sources of power and income available to the holders of manorial rights we suggested that once the landscape had been filled and divided freeholder numbers would decline.

Theoretically during a time of spectacular economic growth in trade and industry anyone not active in those areas, either directly or indirectly, should be at a disadvantage and show, at the very least, a relative decline in prosperity. Whilst there was a growth in agricultural prosperity it was less than that in other sectors of the economy in this area. As we can see from the quote at the top of this chapter contemporary local observers noted a decline amongst traditional agricultural freeholders and a move to trade. From Aikin's comment it would seem that those without a freehold were socially inferior to freeholders a view implied by William Harrison some 200 years earlier in 1577 (Nevell & Walker 1998, 73).

Within the Ashton and Longdendale lordships a pattern of decline can be seen down to the end of the eighteenth century amongst the traditional freehold families. During the years 1780 to 1870 newly wealthy industrialists such as the Ashton family of Hyde, the Lees family of Park Bridge, and the Sidebottoms of Broadbottom became increasingly able to buy large areas of freehold land in Tameside. Their growing power in rural society is reflected in both the documentary record, such as the land tax returns for the period 1785–1830, and in the increased occurrence of a wider range of archaeological sites linked with these industrial freeholders.

There may have been another reason why the traditional freeholders declined, reproduction. As a group there were relatively few freeholders and many families simply disappear through lack of sons. An even smaller group was the manorial lords and they were also struck by the same problem. The difference between the two groups is that the lordships survive for a very long time whilst the traditional freehold estates disappear.

In the following sections we review the history of the freeholders and their estates more closely to try to describe and analyse the changes recorded by Aikin.

3.2 The History of the Traditional Freeholds

The old medieval freeholders of Tameside were still quite numerous in 1642, and could be found in both the Ashton and Longdendale lordships. As already noted they were distinguished archaeologically by the plan and form of their houses and the associated oval enclosures that represented their estates. As a group they relied heavily on agriculture as their major source of income.

The Hollingworths

The oldest surviving freehold family was the junior branch of the Hollingworths of Hollingworth who resided as Mottram Old Hall (Fig. 3.1). This lesser estate was not sold by the Hollingworths until 1800, when it was bought by a local millowner, Samuel Hadfield, who in turn passed it to his nephew George Hadfield, later owner of the neighbouring Thorncliffe Hall estate (Ormerod 1882, III, 871). Both estates descended to the Shellard family and when the last heir died in 1889 they were sold and split up (Earwaker 1880, 148; Nevell 1993, 90).

The Highams

The Higham family of Werneth were listed as freeholders in 1445 (Earwaker 1877, 17) and it seems that at this date the freehold property lay wholly within Werneth. By 1580 this property had been split between the manors of Werneth and Hyde, the latter becoming a tenant farm (Nevell & Walker 1998, 45). However the branch still resident in Werneth, at Lower High Farm, remained freeholders. The gentry status of this family is emphasised by the marriage in the late sixteenth century of Ann Hyde, daughter of Robert Hyde lord of the manors of Hyde and Norbury, and one of the most important families in north-east Cheshire, to John Higham, gentleman, of Lower Higham (Nevell & Walker 1998).

The Hydes of Denton

Outside the ancient lordships of Ashton and Longdendale the largest and most prominent freeholders were the Hyde family of Hyde Hall in Denton (Fig. 3.2); a junior branch of the manorial family of the Hydes of Hyde and Norbury. This junior branch of the family are attested in Denton from the late thirteenth century onwards (Farrer & Brownbill 1911, 315) and by the beginning of the seventeenth century the Hydes held around 299 acres in Denton (Young 1982, 21). In 1699 the estates passed through marriage to the manorial family of the Asshetons of Middleton and then, again through marriage, to the Listers around 1716. In 1762 the estate was sold to William Hulton of Hulton Park in Bolton, whose family had held a large freehold estate elsewhere in Denton since the fifteenth century. In their turn the Hultons sold the property to Francis Woodiwiss in 1813 (Booker 1855, 34–5). It passed to Charles Lowe in the late nineteenth century and was sold again in 1901 (Farrer & Brownbill 1911, 316). Despite these many sales in the eighteenth and nineteenth centuries the estate was one of the few freeholds to remain intact as an agricultural property.

The Bretlands

Perhaps the most successful of the old medieval freeholding families in Tameside was the Bretlands of Thorncliffe Hall in Hollingworth. A John Bretland occurs in the Cheshire list of freeholders for the early fifteenth century (Earwaker 1880, 146). The parish registers record that a descendant of his, John Bretland, married Ellen Barber in 1561 when he is described as a yeoman (Driver 1954, 61). The family figures in the Cheshire list of freeholders for 1579 (Driver 1954, 61; Earwaker 1877, 17–18). In the early seventeenth century the Bretland family of Thorncliffe Hall in Hollingworth were directly farming an estate that amounted to *c.* 241 acres (Stewart-Brown 1934, 78). His grandson John Bretland was a successful lawyer, and although his family estates were sequestered in 1647 during the Civil

Figure 3.2 Hyde Hall, Denton. This was the home of the Hyde family, a junior freeholding branch of the Hydes of Hyde and Norbury. Despite changes in ownership, this estate remained intact throughout the period 1642–1870. When the adjacent farmyard was remodelled in the mid-nineteenth century a new double depth, central staircase plan brick farmhouse was added to the east of the hall.

Figure 3.3 Hillend Farm, Mottram. This freehold was the home of the Reddish family in the late medieval period and the surviving farmhouse, a large two-storey structure, dates from the late sixteenth and early seventeenth centuries. However, by 1770 the estate had been bought by the Lords of Longdendale, the Tollemache family; like most of the medieval freehold properties in the Tameside area, it was unable to compete successfully with its manorial neighbours.

War, when they were worth £556 16*s.* 8*d.*, they were returned in 1654 (Morrill & Dore 1967, 67–74). Despite this upheaval the family prospered after the Restoration in 1660. His son, Reginald, followed him into the legal profession, becoming a serjeant-at-law and a wealthy man (Driver 1954, 62). According to a deed dated the 7 July 1682 the Werneth estates of Sir Fulk Lucy were sold by his widow Dame Isabell to Reginald Bretland. It was probably around this time that Reginald also bought the Lucy estates in Romiley (CRO DDX 67/5). Reginald Bretland's will, written in 1699 and proved in 1704, indicates that the family owned property not only in Hollingworth, Romiley and Werneth but also in Derbyshire and Lancashire (Earwaker 1880, 147; Nevell 1991, 122). Reginald was also responsible for lending the Hyde family £3000 in the 1690s, in payment for which his nephew George Bretland, who had inherited Thorncliffe, later tried to claim the Hyde lands in Haughton and Hyde (TLSL DD 161/2). When Tobias Bretland died in 1750 the estates were inherited by his daughters, who in 1768 sold Thorncliffe Hall, along with the manors of Romiley and Werneth, to the Egertons of Tatton, one of the biggest landholding families in Cheshire (Ormerod 1882, I, 871). They maintained the Bretland estates until the mid nineteenth century, only selling the Werneth lands as individual parcels in 1857 (Nevell 1993, 91).

Other freeholders

Other freehold properties within the Ashton and Longdendale lordships disappeared before the end of eighteenth century. These included the Hillend estate in Mottram (Fig. 3.3), home of the Reddish family, which had been bought by the Lords of the Longdendale, the Tollemache family, around 1770. The Cinderland Hall estate to the north of Ashton was purchased by the lords of Ashton, the Booth family around 1756. The Bostock family took over a small freehold property at Woolley bridge in Mottram in the 1690s. Centred on Broadbottom Hall, this estate was sold off in the early nineteenth century, much of the land being bought by the Sidebottom family. The Heyrod estate to the east of Ashton town (Nevell 1994, 64) and the Woolley estate in Hollingworth both appear to have been spit up and sold in the seventeenth and eighteenth centuries.

Only one of the eight traditional freeholds remained throughout the period as a coherent independent unit. The remaining four were amalgamated into larger holdings and three divided into smaller holdings, a survival rate that is considerably less than the manors.

3.3 The Rise of the New Freeholder Industrial Magnates

Whilst most of the old medieval freehold families of the Ashton and Longdendale lordships had disappeared by the end of the eighteenth century they were replaced, and sometimes their property acquired, by a new type of freeholder; the industrial magnates. Most of these families had begun as dual income tenant farmers in the seventeenth and eighteenth centuries and the most prominent of these, archaeologically, economically and politically, in the nineteenth century, were the Ashton family of Hyde, the Cheetham family of Stalybridge and the Hindley family of Dukinfield.

The Ashtons

In the seventeenth century the Ashton family were tenant farmers in Werneth and a Peter and a Robert Ashton are mentioned in the Werneth Manor Court Book for 1658 (Butterworth 1827, 304; CRO DAR/I/16). A Samuel and Robert Ashton are mentioned in the Land Tax Returns for 1713, and by the early eighteenth century Samuel Ashton (1674–54) was renting Gerrard's Fold, and other lands in Werneth and Bredbury amounting to 33 acres from John Gerrard, Surgeon

Figure 3.4 Castle Street Mills, Stalybridge. These were built by George Cheetham (1757–1826), a tenant farmer from Newton, in the period 1805–21. The success of the family was secured by the establishment of Bankwood Mill in 1832–34, the largest mill complex in Stalybridge. The family built Eastwood House, set in 20 acres of grounds in the late 1820s on the fringes of the town next to the Bankwood Mill complex, marking their arrival as the wealthiest of the Stalybridge cotton mill-owners.

(CRO DDX67/23). It was Samuel who rebuilt the Gerrards Fold. This is a large L-shaped, two-storey, brick farmhouse with a later one-storey crosswing. There is a datestone that reads 'AIS 1722' on the gable of the original crosswing, probably standing for 'Ashton Isobel and Samuel' and indicating that the Ashton family had moved here by that date. The later crosswing has a datestone that reads 'AIS 1723'. The windows have brick label moulds, and there are brick quoins at the corners of the building.

Samuel's son, Benjamin began as a linen weaver, selling his cloth in Manchester and later becoming a putter out for the Manchester merchants Touchett's (Ashmore 1982, 98; Bann 1976, 16). One of the earliest cotton factories in the Hyde area was built by his son Samuel at Gerrard's Wood Mill, on Gerrards Brook near Gee Cross, between 1780 and 1794 (Middleton 1936). This fine four storey six bay, water-powered mill, can still be seen and is one of the earliest cotton spinning mills still standing in Greater Manchester. Samuel Ashton died in 1812 but his seven sons continued to expand the family business in the early nineteenth century, establishing four further textile sites; Carrfield, Greencroft, and Newton Moor Mills, and the Newton Bank print works. When the brothers' partnership was dissolved in the years 1821–23, Samuel took Gerrard's Wood mill, later taking over the nearby Apethorn Mill, and building Woodley Mill in Stockport. John and James took over the Newton Moor Mills, founding the firm of J. & J. Ashton which later took over Lees Factory and the Lees Street Mills in Newton (Bann 1976, 20; Ashmore 1982, 98–9). Thomas took Carrfield mill, building Bayleyfield Mill in 1824, and extending the Flowery Field textile community in the 1820s and 1830s, he lived in Flowery Field House (built in the 1820s), a grand gothic style mansion set in its own grounds. The firm established by Thomas, Ashton Brothers, was to dominate the economic life of Hyde throughout the rest of the nineteenth century and for much of the twentieth century.

The Ashtons produced several mayors of Hyde; the first member of parliament for the new Hyde constituency in 1885 with the election of Thomas Gair Ashton industrialist and philanthropist (who became Baron Ashton of Hyde in 1911); and one of the leading women in the suffragette movement, Margaret Ashton (Nevell 1994).

The Cheethams

The Cheetham family owned the largest textile complex in Stalybridge and were a significant influence on the development of the town for over 100 years through the firm of George Cheetham & Sons, which lasted from 1805 until 1930. The family are recorded as tenant farmers in nearby Newton where, around 1784, George Cheetham (1757–1826) bought a carding engine (Hill 1907, 240–4). He moved to Stalybridge around 1794–95

Figure 3.5 Astley Cheetham Public Library. This was built with money donated by John Frederick Cheetham (1835–1916), and was opened in 1901. John represented the new industrialist freeholders at their most philanthropic. He was an active promoter of educational and cultural pursuits in Stalybridge as well as an MP.

Figure 3.6 Croft House, Stamford Street, Ashton. This large detached house in classical style was built for the wealthy Ashton mill-owner Samuel Heginbottom in 1810–12, and is the earliest of the surviving factory-owners' houses. Originally the house stood in its own grounds beyond the urban fringe of Georgian Ashton but in the 1820s it was swamped by new urban development along the middle and lower reaches of Stamford Street.

founding the firm of Lees, Leech, Harrison & Cheetham in a mill close to Shepley Street, known locally as the Bastille, after the French prison it was reputed to resemble (Preece 1989, 104; Sheppard 1984, 3). When their cotton mill was destroyed by fire in 1804 the partnership was dissolved, George then going on to build the Castle Street Mills (Fig. 3.4) between 1805–21 (Haynes 1990, 27). The fortune he raised allowed the next two generations of the family to expand their interests in politics, the arts and philanthropy. John Cheetham (1802–86), MP for Salford from 1864 until 1868 (Sheppard 1984, 7–8), extended the Castle Street Mills in 1827 and built Bankwood Mill in 1832–34 (Haynes 1990, 27, 32) and a new family residence known as Eastwood House, set in 20 acres of grounds, in the late 1820s (Sheppard 1984, 10). Outside his business interests he promoted the establishment of the Dukinfield Free Library and was a member of the General Council of the Exhibition of Art Treasures of the United Kingdom which was held in Manchester in 1857, underwriting any debts. This was the most prestigious art exhibition held in the north of England during this period (Preece 1989, 105–6).

The philanthropic interests of the family found their fullest expression in his son John Frederick Cheetham (1835–1916), who was a member of Parliament between 1885 and 1910. He was an active promoter of educational and cultural pursuits in Stalybridge, being a member of the Stalybridge school board from 1870 to 1880, governor of the district infirmary, a member of the Stalybridge library committee, president of the Stalybridge Mechanics' Institute, a justice of the peace for Lancashire and Cheshire, and from 1889 a member of Cheshire County Council. From 1894 he was a governor and from 1898 a member of the council of Owen's College, later to become the University of Manchester. His lasting legacy to Stalybridge was the founding the Astley Cheetham Library (Fig. 3.5), opened in 1901, and Eastwood House, the grounds of which became Cheetham Public Park (Nevell 1994, 72; Preece 1989, 107–11).

The Hindleys

The Hindley family lived in the Moravian settlement at Fairfield in Droylsden in the late eighteenth century. The family textile business was founded by Ignatius Hindley, who built a cotton warehouse in 1786 at Fairfield. This lay on the northern side of chapel square and can still be seen today, although it is now divided into two, three-storey, brick houses. The warehouse continued in use until around 1813 (Speake & Witty 1953, 138), even though in 1802 Ignatius bought the Chapel Hill Mill in Dukinfield, built in 1792 by James

Sandiford, as a cotton warehouse (Nevell 1993, 39–41). Around 1803, the Hindley family turned Chapel Hill into a cotton spinning mill. His son John took over the business and in 1815 bought a second mill, on Oxford Road, in Dukinfield. When John died unexpectedly in February 1819 the business was taken over by his younger brother Charles Hindley (1796–1857), who was later to become Ashton-under-Lyne's second MP and a noted social reformer (Nevell 1994, 31). Although he had no experience of the cotton industry the business prospered under the leadership of Charles, and he acquired Dukinfield Old Hall Mill in 1838. By this date the family were renting Dukinfield Lodge (Fig 2.6), the grand country house built by the local lord of the manor, Sir Francis Astley in 1770.

Lesser industrialist freeholders

There were many other tenant farmers who became successful industrialists, buying land and building there own workers communities and mansions, and thus having a significant impact of the landscape of the ancient lordships of Ashton and Longdendale. Amongst the better known of these are the Lees family of Park Bridge in the Ashton lordship. The Lees family are recorded as tenant farmers and blacksmiths in the Alt Hill area of Ashton from the late seventeenth century onwards (Nevell 1994, 38). Samuel and Hannah Lees founded the Park Bridge ironworks in 1786, on eight acres of land, which included Dean Farm, next to the river Medlock, rented from the Earl of Stamford. The first phase of the ironworks was built between 1786 and 1789 and comprised a water-powered iron forge. Samuel was described as a watchmaker in 1787 but by 1789 he was described as a whitesmith. By the time Samuel died in 1804 his estate was worth between £600 and £800. Although the business was left to his eldest son Edward, Hannah ran it in trust until Edward came of age. Thus, she was responsible for leasing a Copperas House and pyrites beds at The Park in nearby Bardsley in 1808. In 1810 she borrowed money to build a new weir and water-powered building, probably the roller-manufacturing shop and the new mill iron forge. By 1823 the family had built a small row of five workers cottages known as New Mill, bought the Dean farm freehold from the Earls of Stamford and built a new residence, Dean House (Nevell 1994, 41–3). As the firm expanded, more workers housing was added in the 1840s and 1850s, a set of stables in the 1860s and Dean House itself was rebuilt in the mid-nineteenth century.

The Hibbert family were prominent textile mill owners in Hyde during the eighteenth and nineteenth centuries. Randal Hibbert (1769–1849) was the first member of the family to enter the textile business, building Godley Mill in the late eighteenth century. Later the family ran Boston Mills and High Bank Mill. They built a substantial number of houses in the Great Norbury Street area of Hyde during the mid-nineteenth century. The family were active in Hyde politics during the nineteenth century, being supporters of the Liberal Party (Middleton 1932, 476–7). Along with the Ashtons and Sidebothams they formed a powerful controlling non-conformist influence in Hyde affairs throughout the nineteenth century.

John Chapman senior (1764–1819), was the founder of another of the new industrialist freeholder families of the nineteenth century. John came from Hurdsfield near Macclesfield, where his family had held a small tenement since the early eighteenth century. In 1802 he built the Hurst Mount Mill in partnership with his brother Samuel (Haynes 1987, 17–18). He left four children, John, William, Ann and Mary. His brother Samuel continued to operate the Hurst Mount Mill until 1834 when John's second son William took it over. John Chapman junior, the eldest son, went to Oxford where he graduated with an MA in 1838. In 1836 he married his cousin Annie Sidebottom, daughter of George Sidebottom of Hill End House in Mottram (see *The Sidebottom Family and Broadmills*). They had nine children, although only three survived into adulthood. He was a magistrate for Cheshire, Derbyshire, Lancashire and the West Riding of Yorkshire, High Sheriff of Cheshire in 1855 and MP for Great Grimsby from 1862–64 and again from 1874 until his death. He was also one of the original and largest shareholders, and later chairman, of the MS&L Railway Company. He is said to have financially supported the company at times of financial crisis during the driving of the Woodhead tunnel to Sheffield (North Cheshire Herald 21/7/1877, 8c). He promoted a fleet of ships for deep sea fishing on behalf of Grimsby (Hanmer & Winterbottom 1991, 113; Middleton 1907, 39–40; Middleton 1932, 322). He purchased the Carlecote estate in 1847 and added to his already extensive Longdendale estates by purchasing Hattersley manor from the Earls of Stamford in 1858, and later had extensive interests in property around Belle Vue in

Manchester, Stalybridge and Dukinfield (North Cheshire Herald 21/7/1877, 8c; Ormerod 1882, 864). He was a great benefactor and during the cotton famine he set up a soup kitchen at his home and supplied food and clothing to the textile workers of Mottram and Broadbottom who were without wages or work. Around 1850 he opened a lending library in Mottram and set up a Penny Savings Bank to encourage thrift (North Cheshire Herald 21/7/1877, 8c).

The Horsefield family of Hyde were important early pioneers of the textile industry in that area. Joseph Horsefield (1769–1838), a local tenant farmer, founded the family business, starting with a pair of jennies in Newton. He established Slack Mills in the 1790s, and later built Slack House near by, as well as a large amount of workers' housing around the mills (Nevell 1993, 176). This large complex later passed to his nephew Samuel Horsefield. Later in the nineteenth century the family bought the nearby Arden Hall estate. They took an active part in local politics, helping to found the Hyde Conservative Association in 1829 (Middleton 1932, 471–2).

3.4 The Archaeology of the Freeholder

The freeholders of the industrial period, whether they were the old medieval families or the new industrialists, were responsible for the introduction of 47 new archaeological site types across nine monument classes. These groupings were; agricultural and commemorative monuments, commercial, domestic and educational monuments, and industrial, recreational, religious, transport and water archaeological sites. Prior to 1780 only five new type sites were established by freeholders within the Ashton and Longdendale lordships. An analysis of these sites shows that they were related to improvements on the freeholders' estates (threshing barns, brick and stone farmhouses) and to expressions of their social status (memorial stones, datestones and chapels). The remaining monument groups, industrial, recreational, and water supply sites were introduced in the nineteenth century.

The Hyde Estate, Denton: a traditional agricultural freehold?

The Hyde family of Denton illustrate the archaeology of a successful freeholder in the seventeenth century. During this period the Hydes held 299 acres in Denton and although most of these lands were farmed directly by the family, two tenant farmers are known from 1645 (Young 1982, 20–1). They had their own family memorial in the chapel of ease at Denton and invested a considerable sum in renovating the buildings of their estate during the seventeenth century. Hyde Hall, Denton (Fig. 3.2), is a partially timber-framed and brick two storey building, T-shaped in plan. It has a two storey stone porch and a one bay two storey oriel style addition to the north-eastern elevation. The porch bears the inscribed date of 1625. The principal features of the interior are a large inglenook fireplace which backs onto a cross-passage which retains studded oak doors at each end. The hall, as well as the chamber above it is entirely panelled, in Jacobean and eighteenth-century styles. Immediately to the south-west of the hall is a complex of various buildings, the earliest of which is a two bay timber hay barn with an inscribed date of 1674.

The farm contains one of only two planned courtyards in the study area. The whole farm was re-organised in the mid-nineteenth century with various buildings, including threshing and hay barns arranged around a central courtyard. In the same century a brick, double pile, farmhouse was added to the eastern gable of the timber hall. This planned farm formed the focus for the old freehold estate which is the only early freeholding to have survived intact as an agricultural unit up to recent times. The planned farm is not the work of a freeholder but was built for the Woodiwiss family shortly after they purchased the holding.

After 1780 the number and range of archaeological sites associated with freeholders increased rapidly, especially in the form of domestic structures. Freeholders were also linked to commercial, educational and industrial archaeological sites, as well as recreational, religious, transport and water supply sites. In this period three types of monument typify the new freeholder industrialist; the factory owner's mansion; the textile mill, and the worker's house, the latter two representing two of the three most common archaeological sites in the period 1642–1870. Thus, in the nineteenth century the freehold estate can often be identified archaeologically by the juxtaposition of these three archaeological type sites.

Mansions of the Industrial Freeholders

Industrialists mansions from the period 1800 onwards can, in many cases, be viewed as comparable with the freeholder halls of the same period although they are larger and more complex in plan. The symmetrical and classical façade was the most popular form of architectural expression amongst the industrialists of Tameside. This style can be found at Croft House (Fig. 3.6) in Ashton, which was built in the years 1810–12 for Samuel Heginbottom; in what became West Hill High School

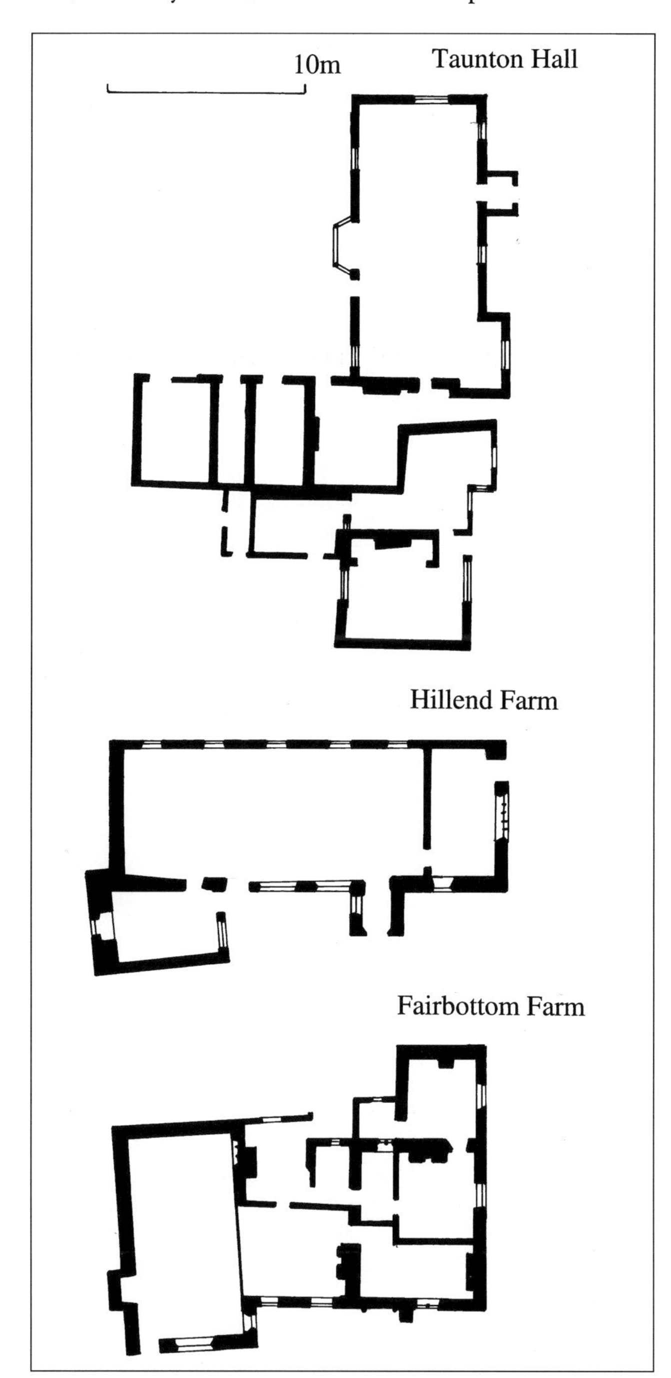

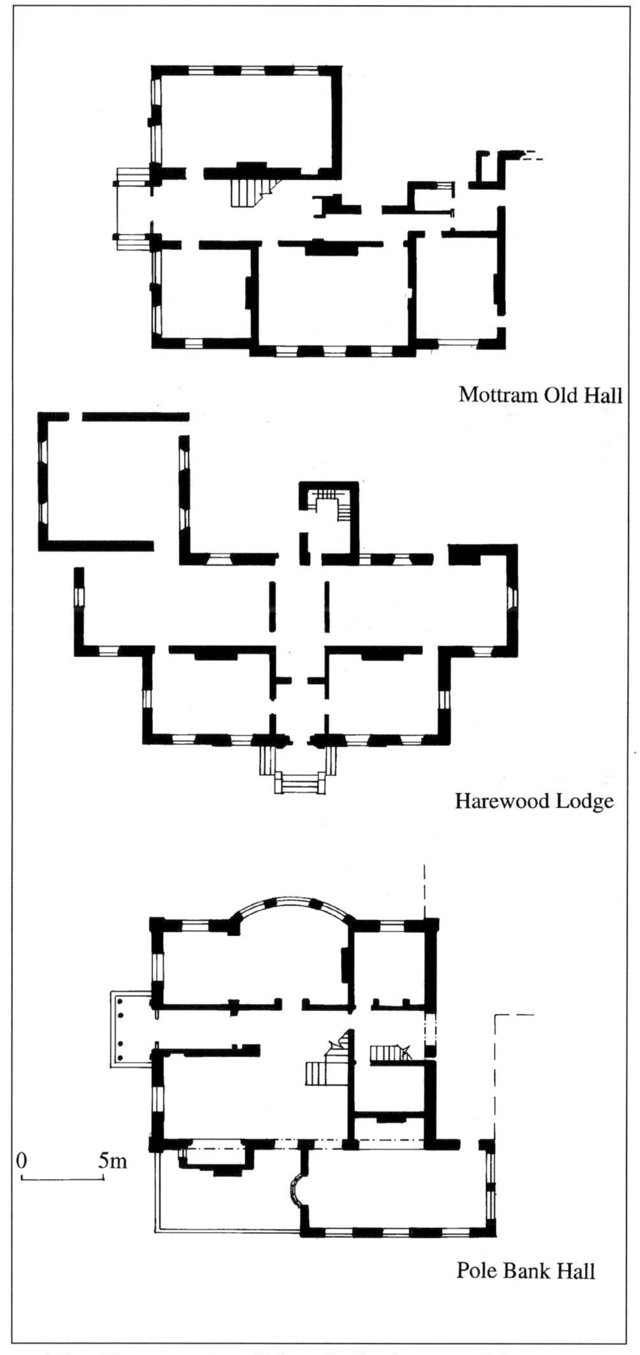

Figure 3.7 Comparative plans of freehold (*left*) and factory owners' (*right*) properties. Although the houses of factory owners were one of the new archaeological sites of the period 1642–1870, in spirit, design and size they are the successors of the sixteenth- and seventeenth-century freeholders' property. They had many of the same elements, such as centrally placed halls and wings. Their classically inspired designs, however, owed more to contemporary country house design and were larger than their seventeenth-century freeholder counterparts.

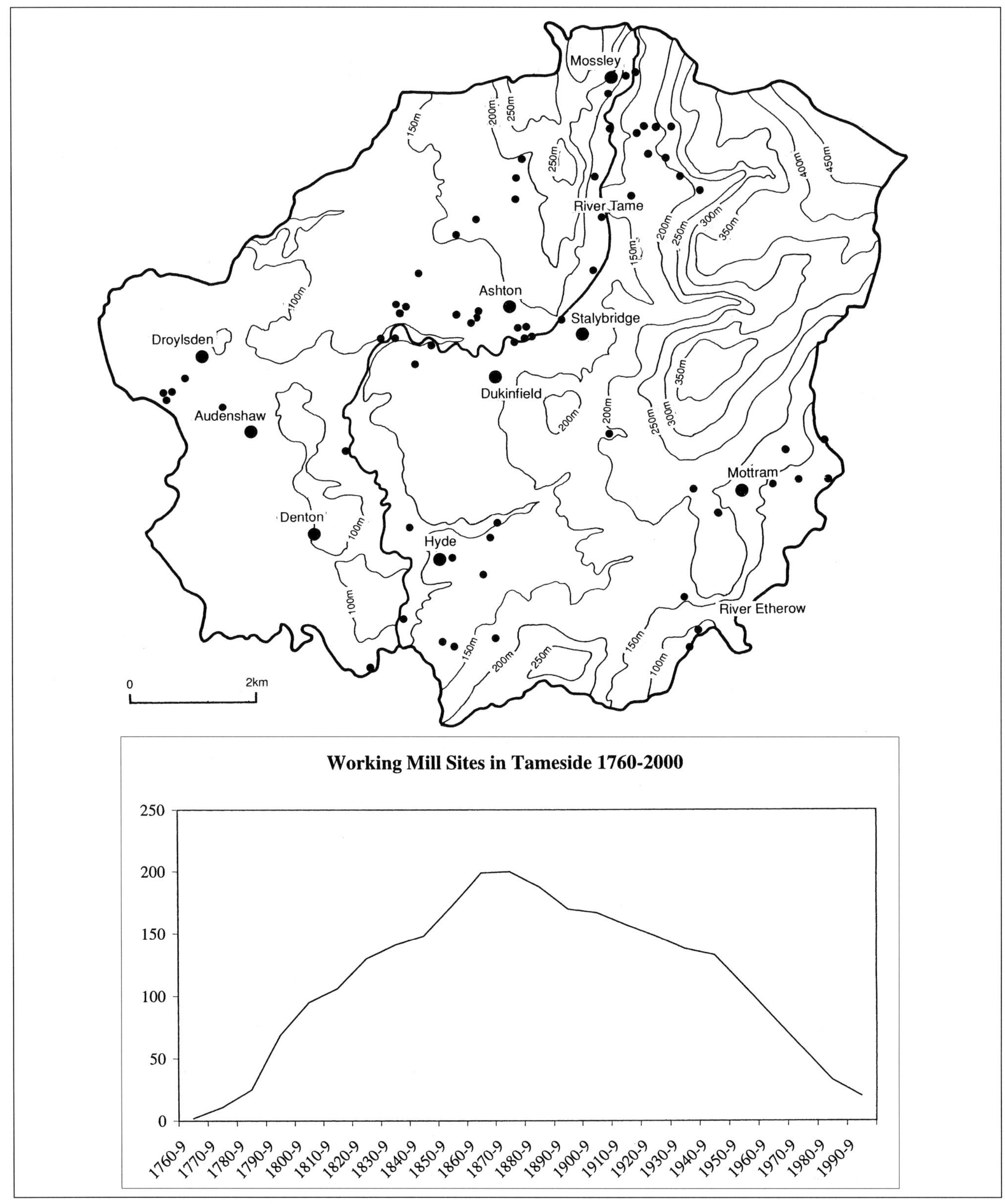

Figure 3.8 The Rise and Fall of Textile Sites in Tameside. The textile site, typically the cotton spinning mill, but also including the printing and dying works, and woollen mills, was the second most common site in the period 1642–1870, with 274 sites known within the Tameside area, 67 of which were established before 1800 (see map above), and over 1400 known in the Greater Manchester area. It was one of the type sites introduced in this period. Most were the property of the new industrial freeholder class by the mid-nineteenth century. This bell-shaped graph shows the rise and fall in the numbers of operating textile mills in the Tameside area between 1763 and 1999. This is a pattern of growth and decline that can be paralleled in other local areas, such as Oldham.

in Stalybridge, which was built in 1822 for William Harrison; Harewood Lodge, Broadbottom, built in the 1820s as the residence of the Sidebottom family (pp. 54–6); and at Pole Bank Hall in Hyde, which was built in the 1820s for the Ashton family (Fig. 3.7).

Croft House, which represents one of the earliest surviving examples, is in a reserved Georgian style, its Ionic columns to the porch being one of the few classical touches. It is situated at the western end of Stamford Street and lies within the heart of modern urban Ashton, although when built it lay on the edge of the Georgian planned town. Pole Bank Hall has palladian echoes, with large tripartite arched widows flanking the central porch, and in size rivals even such a large medieval building as Ashton Hall (Fig. 2.8).

When the new industrialists were able to buy existing freeholds they set about rebuilding the old freehold halls in the contemporary fashion. Mottram Old Hall in Hollingworth (Fig. 3.7), the seat of the junior branch of that manorial family, was bought by the successful industrialist Samuel Hadfield in 1800 and enlarged around 1825 by his son George. It contains many of the features which were very much in vogue across the country from the beginning of the eighteenth century onwards. The ashlar façade of the hall has a symmetrical appearance with a pediment spanning the central three bays of the five-bay building. It has a raised ground floor above a basement, with steps rising to a flat porch supported by Tuscan columns.

Textile mills of the industrial freeholders

The second most common building type in the area (after the terraced house), and the structure most associated with industrialisation in northern England, was the textile factory or mill. Some 274 textile sites were established in Tameside during the period 1763 to 1907 (Fig. 3.8), out of a total of 1,617 sites established across Greater Manchester. Most of the surviving examples in the region (some 1,112 sites when last reviewed in the

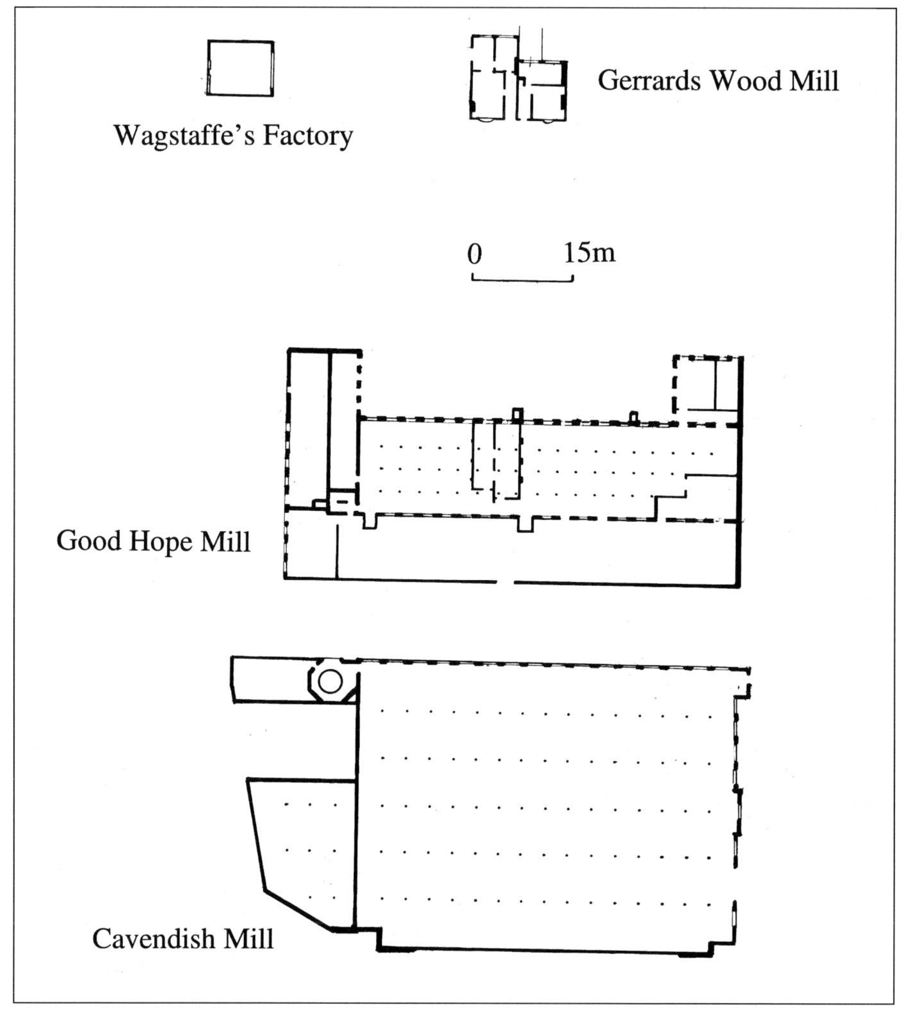

Figure 3.9 The changing shape of the mill complex in Tameside: mill plans from 1786–1906. The design of the earliest purpose-built cotton spinning mills was almost identical to that of the silk mills of mid-eighteenth-century Congleton and Macclesfield: that is a well-lit, uncluttered floor area large enough for the efficient accommodation of processes and storage. The small scale of these initial structures allowed the wealthier tenant farmers of the study area, such as the Wagstaffes (Wagstaffe's Factory, *c.* 1786) and Ashtons (Gerrards Wood Mill, early 1790s), to invest in their construction. However, the introduction of new power technologies such as bigger water wheels and steam power (Good Hope Mill, 1824–50), put these complexes beyond the financial reach of the farmer by 1820. Thereafter, the elaboration of mill design was driven by changes in cotton machinery design and changes in construction techniques, which meant that mills got bigger and bigger (Cavendish Mill, 1886).

The Sidebottom Family and Broad Mills

The Sidebottom family were the wealthiest and most influential of the new industrial freeheolders in Longdendale valley. The founder of the Sidebottom textile empire was John Sidebottom (1727–1803), a nailer from Stayley Wood. John married Elizabeth Kelsall in 1759 (CRO MF 41), whose brother Henry was later to become a partner in Best Hill Mill with John Marsland on the Derbyshire bank of the River Etherow in Broadbottom and ran Dog Kennel Mill in Hollingworth. At the death of his son John in 1782 he was described in the parish registers as a clothier from Stayley (CRO MF 41) but by 1789 he had built Millbrook Mills on Hollingworth Brook (CRO QDV2/217). John and Elizabeth had six sons, William (b. 1760), James (b. 1762), John (b. 1767), George (b. 1769), Joseph (b. 1780) and Thomas (b. 1784), as well as four daughters, Sarah (b. 1764), Mary (b. 1772), Betty (b. 1774) and Ann (b. 1777). Four of the sons became involved in the cotton industry.

William and George founded Broadbottom Mills (later Broad Mills) in 1801–2, their younger brother Joseph joining the business later on. This branch of the family was responsible for the construction of Broadbottom village, a small textile community on the northern bank of the River Etherow in Mottram township. In 1820 William and George bought the Hillend estate in Mottram and with it the small cotton-spinning block known as Lowe's Factory, on Hattersley Brook. James took over the running of Millbrook Mills when his father died in 1802/3, and in 1820 took over Waterside Mills in Glossop (CRO MF41/1–9; CRO QDV2/217; Hanmer & Winterbottom 1991, 111). The second generation of the family continued the expansion of these various businesses, building Bridge Mills in 1856, and Reservoir and Crystal Palace Mills around 1858 (Hanmer & Winterbottom 1991, 112).

The textile village of Broadbottom, on the River Etherow near Mottram, is a fine example of the impact on the landscape of the new textile mill freeholders that sprang up around Manchester in the late eighteenth and early nineteenth centuries. At the heart of this village was Broad Mills, originally Broadbottom Mills, founded by the Sidebottom family. It was the largest of several textile works that were established in and around Broadbottom. This industry, coupled with the drive of the Sidebottom family, was largely responsible for transforming a rural landscape into the extensive village of today. The attraction of the area to early textile entrepreneurs lay in the natural resource of the River

Figure 1 The Broadmills complex at Broadbottom, showing the Old Mill on the left (with the 1824 mill behind it), and the weaving shed on the right. Behind can be seen the village built by the Sidebottom family in the first half of the nineteenth century, and the viaduct of the Manchester to Sheffield Railway built in the 1840s.

Figure 2 A Reconstruction of the Old Mill at Broadmills. This was built in 1802 and was originally water powered; the tail race can be seen leaving the building through an archway. The one-storey building on the right is probably a weaving shed added in 1850.

Etherow which, when harnessed through the construction of weirs and leats, provided a power-source for their machinery.

In 1801 William Sidebottom and his brother George began building a cotton spinning mill on land bought from John Bostock, a local freeholder who resided at Broadbottom Hall. A second mill was added in 1814, the two buildings comprising the substantial structure later known as the 'Old Mill'. In 1824 a third spinning mill was added to Broadbottom Mills. In 1820 George and William Sidebottom bought the Hill End estate from the local lords of the manor, the Tollemaches. During the 1820s George and his brother Joseph, now a partner in the business, built Harewood Lodge as their local residence. William died in 1826 but the firm continued under the name of W. and G. Sidebottom and Company until about 1830.

By 1834 water-power was supplemented by steam at the mills and by 1836 George and Joseph had further expanded their activities to include both cotton spinning and weaving. George Sidebottom died in 1843 and his brother Joseph in 1849, having passed the business in the previous year to his son John. In 1849 John bought more land from the Bostock family and built a large new weaving shed. John's gambling habits led him into massive debts and he continued to run Broadbottom Mills only with the financial support of his mother.

The 1860s were a disastrous decade for Broadbottom Mills and their workforce. In 1861 1200 hands were employed here. However, the American Civil War stopped the importation of cotton and led to the closure of the mills. In 1871 Alfred Kershaw Sidebottom sold Broadbottom Mills to John Hirst and sons, woollen manufacturers and merchants of Dobcross in Saddleworth; they continued the spinning and weaving of cottons at Broadbottom. In 1884 the company changed to the Broadbottom Mills Co. Ltd. Although the number of spindles in the mills remained at about 60,000 from this date until the turn of the century, weaving capacity increased with the number of looms rising from 850 in 1884 to 1,197 in 1887. In 1904 Broadbottom Mills Co Ltd was replaced by Broad Mills Ltd, an amalgamation of Broadbottom Mills and the nearby Lymefield Mill. In 1908 there were 1,442 looms at Broad Mills. Textile production ceased on the site in 1937 when Broad Mills (1920) Limited sold the Broad Mills complex. The buildings were subsequently used for a variety of industrial purposes until 1949 when fire damage led to the demolition of most of the site.

Today only fragments of the walls of the 1850 weaving shed stand to any great height. The long interior wall still shows the outline of its 'saw-tooth' roof. However, a programme of excavation and conservation carried out since the 1980s has revealed a number of key elements within the mill complex. These include the late nineteenth century gas holder, the sluices and channels which fed the water-wheels of the early spinning mills, and the remains of an engine house of the 1830s.

Of these remains the oldest are those of the Old Mill

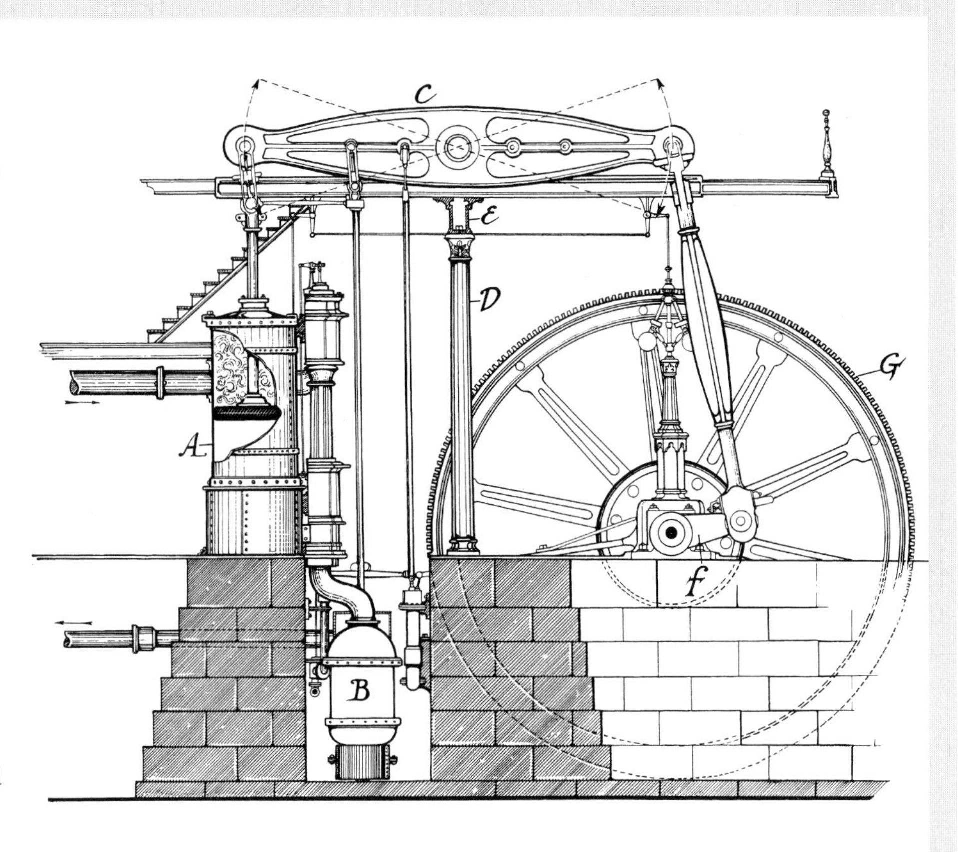

Figure 3 The Mill, 1824. This was originally powered by a water-wheel but in the early 1830s an engine house was added to provide a supplementary source of power. It contained a beam engine such as the one shown here, the typical form of steam-engine in mills of this period. Steam, generated in an adjoining boiler house, was fed into a piston-cylinder and cooled in a condenser to raise and lower a pivoting beam, approximately 21 feet (6.4m) long. This beam was connected via a crank shaft to a flywheel, the rotary motion of which was transmitted by a series of gears, shafts and belts to the machinery in the mill.

was built in the years 1801–2, with the foundations of the 1850 weaving shed visible on its southern side. The five storey Old Mill comprised two separate mills; the earliest of these was the original mill of 1801–2 and the second mill added in 1814. The final structure was over 300 feet (91m) long, divided into 34 bays. Both phases were built for cotton spinning, carried out on 'mules'. Power was provided by one or more water-wheels situated in the mill basement. The arched opening was the water outflow into the river. When, in the mid-1830s George and Joseph Sidebottom diversified into weaving it is likely that at least part of the Old Mill complex was given over to power-looms.

The basement of the 1824 contains the remains of one of the latest cotton mill water-wheels to built in the Greater Manchester area. The mill stood five storeys above the basement and was used for carding and spinning cotton. Carding, a process in the initial preparation of raw cotton, was usually carried out on the ground floor of mills of this period; spinning took place in the upper storeys. Both processes were carried out by machinery, powered during the early working life of the mill by water.

The remains of an engine house can be seen along the southern gable-end of the carding and spinning mill in 1824. This mill was originally powered by a water-wheel but in the early 1830s the engine house was added to provide a supplementary source of power. It contained a beam engine, the typical form of steam-engine in mills of this period. Steam, generated in an adjoining boiler house, was fed into a piston-cylinder and cooled in a condenser to raise and lower a pivoting beam, approximately 21 feet (6.4m) long. This beam was connected via a crank shaft to a flywheel, the rotary motion of which was transmitted by a series of gears, shafts and belts to the machinery in the mill. The remains of the engine house include the stone mounting block for the piston-cylinder (the position of the cylinder is marked by a circular depression and four holding-down bolts) and a second, centrally placed, mounting block (also with holding-down bolts) for the two columns which helped to support beam. The position of the flywheel, approximately 25 feet (7.6m) in diameter, is marked by two deep scour marks in the lower part of the mill wall and curved iron 'barring-rack' which was used to lever the flywheel into its starting position. This beam engine probably remained in use until the early twentieth century when a new and larger engine house was built at the south-eastern corner of the mill. *Tom Burke, Michael Nevell and John Walker*

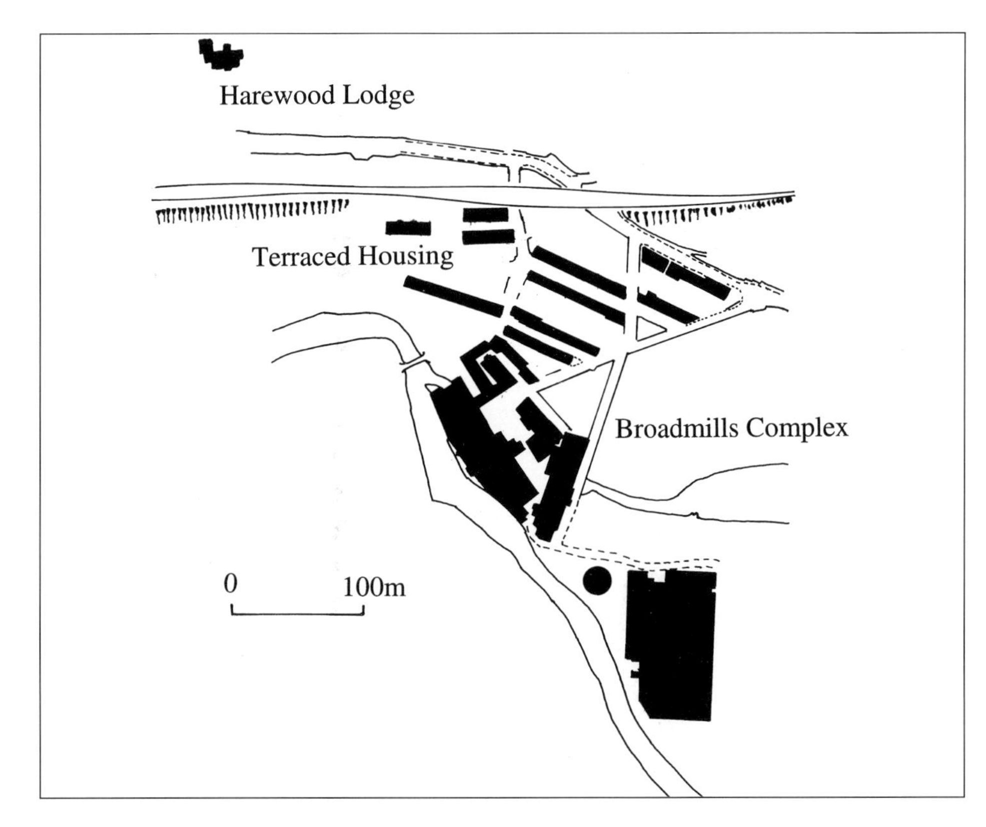

Figure 3.10 Plan of the Broadbottom industrial community. The economic and social dominance of the new industrialist freeholders can be seen in many of the new urban communities they created. Broadbottom textile village is a typical example. It was built by George and William Sidebottom in the years 1802–27, on land bought from the Bostocks of the nearby freehold of Broadbottom Hall, and comprised a series of two- and three-storey terraced houses clustering around the eastern edge of the Broad Mills complex. George and William lived in the nearby purpose-built Harewood Lode, a grand country mansion.

late 1980s; Williams with Farnie 1992) belong to the mid-nineteenth to early twentieth centuries and are associated with the cotton spinning industry. However the origin of the textile factory lies in the early eighteenth century and is associated with another branch of the textile industry: silk production. The first successful textile factory in Britain was Lombe's silk mill in Derby. Built in 1721, it was a five-storeyed building 33.5m long by 12m wide and 17m high, contained Italian-style silk throwing machinery copied by Lombe in Italy, and was driven by an undershot water wheel 7m in diameter (Calladine & Fricker 1993, 24–5). Lombe's machines were covered by a patent which did not expire until 1732. Of the seven silk mills erected in England between 1732 and 1769 and housing Italian-style throwing machinery of the Lombe type four were in Cheshire; Logwood Mill in Stockport built in 1732, Button Mill in Macclesfield in 1744, Old Mill in Congleton built in 1753 and an unknown Macclesfield mill, probably Townley Street, which was erected by 1769 (Calladine & Fricker 1993, 25; Arrowsmith 1997, 97–101). Of these buildings only the brick built hand-powered Old Mill in Congleton (the oldest standing textile mill in Britain) survives. The water-powered Sunderland Street Mill in Macclesfield, built in 1769, probably also contained Italian throwing machinery. These mills had the 'essential elements characteristic of all factory building: a well-lit, uncluttered floor area large enough for the efficient accommodation of processes, and adequate accommodation for ancillary processes and storage. Architectural embellishment and amenities for employees did not feature in these buildings' (Calladine & Fricker 1993, 22–3, 29–30).

In the late eighteenth century the earliest textile factories were on a small scale and were as likely to utilize an existing building as a purpose-built structure, thus allowing local tenant farmers to enter the business. One of the first textile buildings in the Tameside area was the 'Soot Poke' in Stalybridge which was established, around 1776, in an existing building which was described as 'no bigger than a cottage house' (Burke & Nevell 1996, 90). The small scale of even some of the earliest purpose-built factories is shown by the surviving example of Dry Mill in Mottram (Fig. 3.9), which was built in the 1790s by a local tenant farmer and in the early nineteenth century was converted to cottages; its name arose from the fact that it was not water-powered.

Textile mills were essentially functional and utilitarian buildings, whose form was dictated primarily by the processes they were intended to contain. As the machines changed in size and newly mechanised processes added to the industry so mill architecture changed. Up until the early nineteenth century the mills in the area were spinning mills providing yarn to looms operated by the local tenants. In the 1820s the Ashton family in Hyde, encouraged the development of mills to provide efficient accommodation for powerlooms.

An important influence on mill form was the development of new methods of construction, enabling ever-larger structures to be built such as Cavendish Mill (Fig. 3.9) in Ashton, built in 1886 and one of the first mills to have concrete floors, and Saxon Mill in Droylsden, a steel framed building erected in 1906, and thus permitting economies of scale in operating costs. The contrast between the non-fireproof timber-floored mills of the late eighteenth century, usually financed and built by one individual. In the 1870s some family firms, such as the Ashtons, became limited liability companies and started the trend towards the emergence of the fully commercial companies. The much larger steel and concrete-floored mills of the early twentieth century were erected by these textile companies and the output of the area peaked in the 1920s.

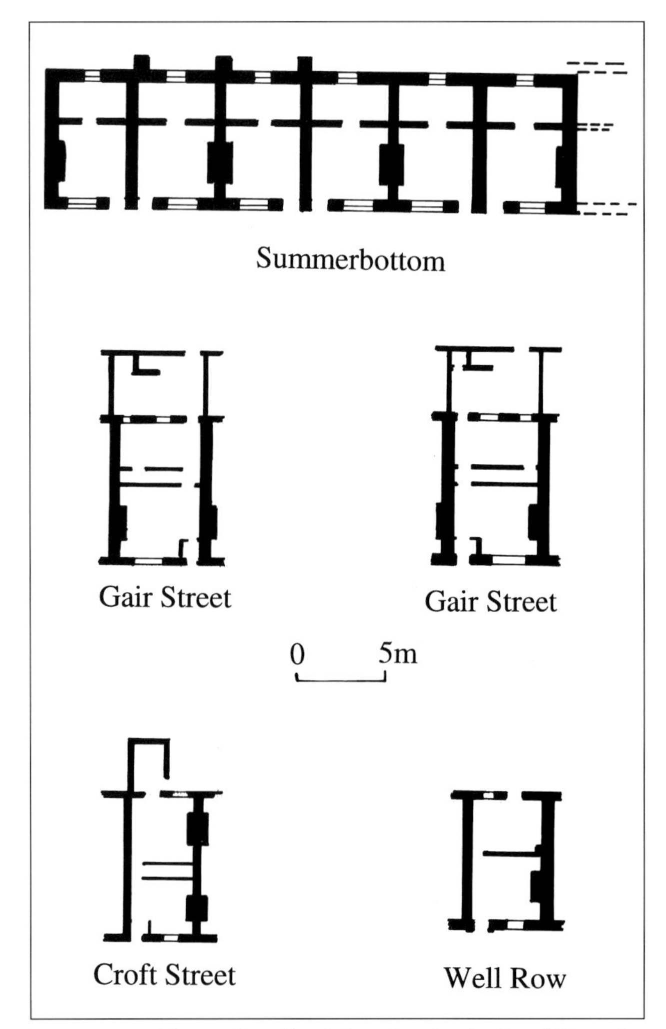

Figure 3.11 Plans of workers' housing in the Lordship of Longdendale. The worker's house was the most common archaeological site within the study area. Although individual types can be regarded as new innovations during the period 1642–1870, the size and layout of such properties remained little altered from their seventeenth-century ancestors. The major change in this period was the emergence of the terraced house with two storeys, but with seldom more than four rooms, built by the new freeholder industrialists and later by property speculators. These properties remained the smallest domestic dwellings in our area.

3.5 The Freeholders' Strategy

The freeholders traditional strategy for maintaining their social and economic position in the proto-industrial period had been to maximise their income through the intensification of their agricultural estates. In the period 1642–1870 most of the old freeholder estates disappeared either because they were split up or because they were bought by local manorial lords. The occasional success of a traditional freeholder family such as the Bretlands was due to the family having access to a second source of income; in this case money made from the legal courts in London.

The new freehold estates of the period 1780–1830 were owned and created by wealthy local industrialists who had risen from the tenantry. Many of these new estates comprised little more than the textile owner's house set in grounds ranging from two to 20 acres, lying next to the textile factories. Most successful freeholder industrialists, such as the Ashtons, Cheethams and Sidebottoms (see pp. 54–6) bought large tracts of land and built not only extensive housing for their factory workers but new mansions for themselves which in some cases exceeded the size of the old freehold 'halls' (Fig. 3.10).

There was a clear distinction in the number of freeholders between those townships where there was extensive industrialisation (witnessed in the archaeological record by the emergence of textile mills, market places, town halls, workshops, and workers housing without attached farmland; Fig. 3.11), and those townships which remained substantially rural, at least down to 1830. In the industrial heartlands of Tameside, Ashton, Dukinfield, Hyde, and Stalybridge (CRO QDV

2/148, 217, 231, 393) there was a rapid increase in the number of owners of freehold land and property. In Dukinfield, for instance, there was a five fold increase in freeholders during the period 1780–1830 (CRO QDV 2/148, 217), whereas in Hollingworth during the same period there was only a doubling. In 1790 Francis Dukinfield Astley was the major landowner (CRO QDV 2/313) in the township of Newton but by 1830 the majority of land was split between four landowners, Lord Astley and the mill owners George Goodier, Joseph Lees and the Ashton family. A similar pattern can be seen in the township of Staley where in 1780 the major land owner was the Earl of Stamford, but by 1820 he had been joined by 22 other significant freeholders, many of them such as George Cheetham, Joseph Harrop and Able Hyde, wealthy millowners (CRO QDV 2/393). All of these new freeholders were drawn from the rising mill owners of these townships.

Those Cheshire townships which remained largely rural in the period 1780–1830, such as Hattersley, Matley and Mottram, show little fragmentation of landownership in this period. Mottram is particularly noteworthy in that it was one of the early centres of the cotton industry in Tameside during the late eighteenth century (Fig. 3.8), yet throughout the period 1780–1830 most of the township was owned by the Tollemache family. Even though the Hillend estate was sold to the Sidebottom family in 1820 and the Hague estate to Samuel Marsland in 1841, both local millowners, Lord Tollemache still held over half of the land in the township in 1870 (CRO DTW 2477/B/10; Powell Collection).

The success of these new industrialists appears to have rested on their dual income. Most began as tenant farmers but found financial success and social advancement through a second source of income. In the lordships of Ashton and Longdendale this was usually through the textile industry. Why these tenant farmers were allowed to exploit so successfully this second source of income and the lack of competition from either of the two land holding groups (the lords and freeholders) is the subject of the next chapter.

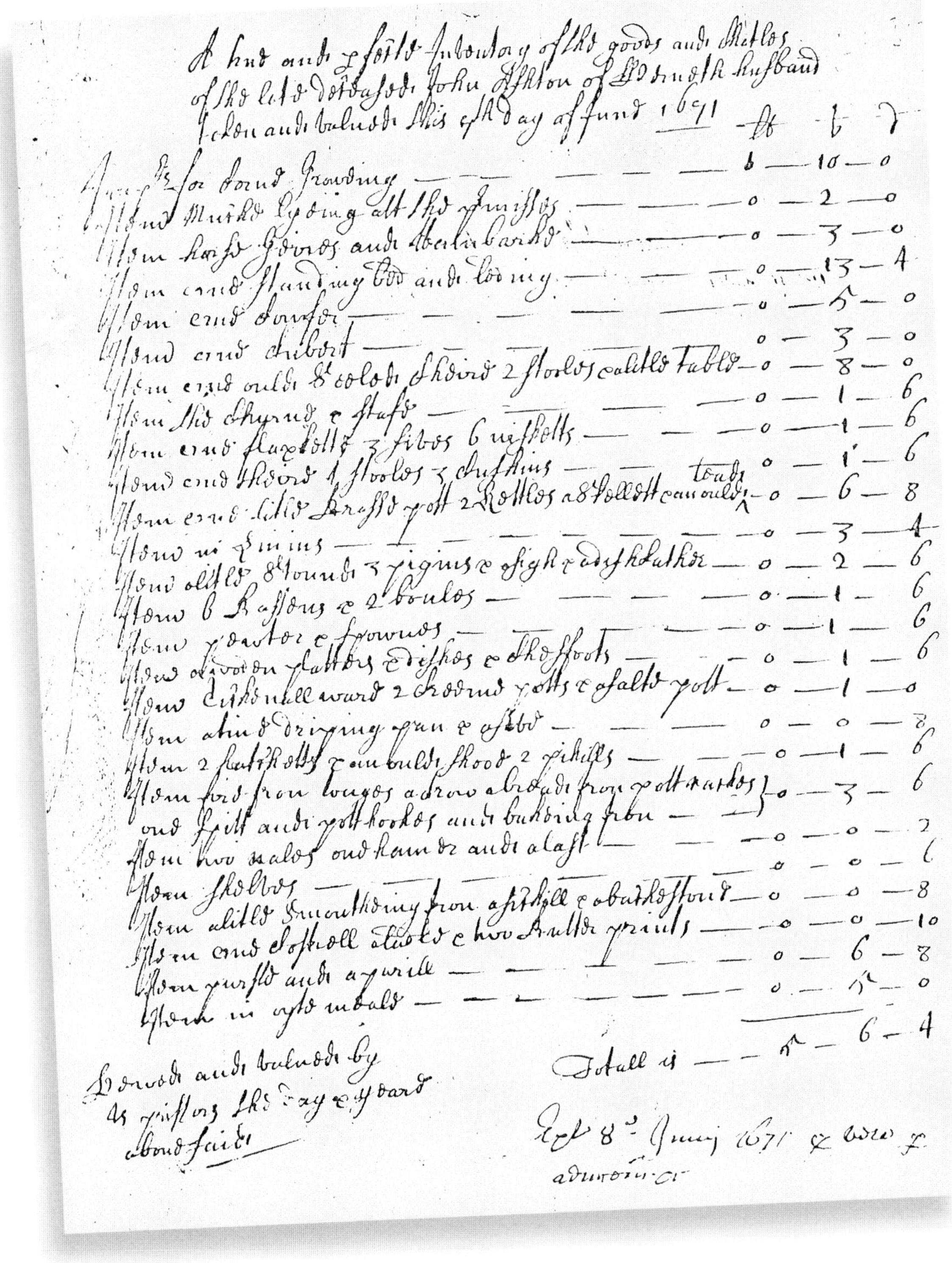

Figure 4.1 The inventory of John Ashton, husbandman, of Werneth, taken in June 1671. Wills and inventories are one of the few documentary sources in the period 1642–1870 which were written by the tenants. As such they can reveal a great deal about the economic basis of the local family unit and the social linkages between families, at least until the making of inventories falls out of fashion in the mid-eighteenth century. This document, for instance, is a typical inventory of the Longdendale lordship from the late seventeenth century in its range of personal goods it mentions, from basins to kettles. John was a member of the Ashton family which later came to dominate the textile industry of Hyde. (*Reproduced with the permission of the Cheshire Record Office, Chester*)

CHAPTER 4

The Tenantry

The farms are commonly small ... The smaller ones are let very high; nor could the tenant pay such prices but for the industry of himself and family, who are in general weavers, hatters or cotton spinners, and sometimes all in the same house. The chief article of the farm is a roomy house ... The old farm houses are nearly all built of stone, with heavy flag-slate roofs.

John Aikin 1795, page 472 on the tenants of Mottram

4.1 Introduction

This chapter attempts to explore the role of the tenant in promoting the industrialisation process during the period 1642–1870. *Lands and Lordships* defined the tenantry as those people who did not have freehold land and consequently whose 'land and other rights were easily subject to pressure from other groups' which in Tameside were the lords and freeholders (Nevell and Walker 1998, 95). Prior to the nineteenth century the majority of the population in the Tameside area were tenants who lived and worked in the countryside. In the middle of the seventeenth century there were only three urban centres within the lordships of Ashton and Longdendale; Ashton town with a population around 550 people, Mottram village with a population of roughly 240 and Tintwistle with a population of approximately 280 (Burke & Nevell 1996, 51; Nevell & Walker 1998, 85). By the late nineteenth century the majority of people lived and worked in the new industrial urban towns of the area; Audenshaw, Broadbottom, Denton, Droylsden, Dukinfield, Gee Cross, Hollingworth, Hyde, Mossley and Stalybridge (Nevell 1993, 12). According to W. J. Garnett, the mid-nineteenth-century social commentator, industrialisation 'created a market for Labour and skill far beyond anything the farmer could offer, and the consequence has been that all who were anxious to "get on" in the world ... have been drawn into the great vortex of trade, and now people the large towns of Liverpool, Manchester, Bolton, etc.' (Garnett 1849, 2). The archaeology of the tenantry shows that in the eighteenth century they were far from merely passive victims of the inevitable progress of industrialisation; but rather amongst the main instigators of the process in the area.

4.2 A History of the Tenantry, 1642–1870

Prior to the nineteenth century the documentary records of the tenantry are far more restricted than those for either the lords or freeholders. The majority of the tenants in the Ashton and Longdendale lordships appear in documents of the period that relate to either estate management (most commonly court leet records), legal cases (quarter session and local government records) or religious activities (parish records). Only rarely do we glimpse the tenantry as little more than a list of names as, for instance, in the exceptional circumstances of the Civil Wars of the 1640s which left a range of evidence from pamphlets to letters touching on the lives of the local tenantry.

There is one type of record that provides minute details about the tenantry, albeit for only a small proportion (perhaps as little as 9% in seventeenth century; Nevell 1991, 67), and this is the material supplied by the surviving wills and inventories from the period 1642–1870 (Fig. 4.1). Inventories are invaluable for analysis of agricultural practices, the distribution of wealth

Figure 4.2 Hartshead Green Farm. This was one of the new farmsteads established in the seventeenth-century Ashton lordship. Like many of the new tenant farms during this period it was built in stone and was of three bays with a central inglenook fireplace and lobby entrance. Changes in fashion and needs over the next two centuries led to an elaboration of this basic plan.

and industrial activities, whilst wills can be used to assess the patterns of inheritance and the size of families. This analysis is not a straightforward task, for there are many pitfalls and problems of interpretation. Used with care probate records are an indispensable asset to the study of the seventeenth- and eighteenth-century tenantry.

If we combine the documentary evidence from wills and inventories with the archaeology of the tenant a new vision of the history of this group emerges for the years 1642–1870; one of a group that is innovatory, dynamic and amongst whom are individuals who acquired substantial wealth which they were able to invest in areas outside of agriculture.

The rural tenantry to 1770

The wills, inventories and manorial records of the lordships of Longdendale and Ashton show that these areas lay across the boundaries of what were in the seventeenth century the woollen, fustian (a cotton and flax mix) and linen (flax) producing areas. The 143 tenant farms of this period (Fig. 4.2) were not large, although there were notable differences in both the size and the economic emphasis of the holdings in the Ashton and Longdendale lordships.

In Ashton the average farm tenancy size was 28.5 statute acres (roughly 13 customary acres) spread amongst 310 rural tenants in 1618 (Butterworth 1823, 155–66). By 1702 this figure had risen by over 15% to 34 acres per holding amongst a 5% larger tenantry at 330 individuals (Nevell 1993, 89). It was probably in this period that the number of farms in the lordship reached its maximum. The increase in farm size at a time of increasing tenant numbers is atypical for the Tameside area and can probably be best explained by continued internal colonisation of non-agricultural land within the Ashton lordship. There were two potential new sources of agricultural land in seventeenth-century Ashton. Firstly, on the edges of Ashton Moss where the 7m deep central basin was surrounded by an area of shallower peat 1m or less deep to the north and south-west at Littlemoss and around Audenshaw. Secondly, Lyme Park, a deer enclosure established in the Bardsley area on the north-western edges of the lordship in 1337 which appears to have been turned over to farming in this century (Nevell 1991, 58–9). Most farms in the Ashton lordship relied on a mixed farming strategy of cereals and cattle rearing. Flax production is also suggested by later field names, especially around the town of Ashton (Nevell 1991, 84–5).

In the Longdendale lordship between 1570 and 1680, farms had an average size of 33 acres which was mostly given over to grass for cattle and sheep production. Within the central manor of Mottram the number of rural tenants steadily increased during the seventeenth and eighteenth centuries, rising from 20 in 1600 to 25 in 1727 and reaching 40 tenants in 1799 (CRO DTW 2477/B10; Nevell 1993, 89–90). At the same time the average farm size was falling since, unlike the lordship of Ashton, almost all of the available land in Mottram had been turned over to agriculture by 1600. Thus by 1785, when the number of farms in the township appears to have reached its peak, the average farm size had fallen to 25.8 acres and as a result of the growth of multiple tenancies the tenancy size was only 13.6 acres (Nevell 1993, 89). Within the Longdendale lordship as a whole cattle keeping was most common in the hill areas around Tintwistle, Mottram and Staley, where the tenants had access to the high moors for summer grazing, but the herds, with an average of nine animals, were small, and during the first half of the eighteenth century grew smaller still falling to an average of six (Nevell 1993, 81). In seventeenth-century Longdendale

Figure 4.3 Dukinfield Old Hall Chapel. Although built in the late sixteenth century as the private chapel of the Duckenfield family, it was used in the 1640s and 1650s as a Congregational chapel, the first Independent church to be set up in England and in 1647 the location of the first sermon by the founder of the Quaker movement, George Fox. Although the pastor, Samuel Eaton, was Robert Duckenfield's personal chaplain, the congregation was largely drawn from the local tenantry.

40% of the tenants owned sheep, mostly in small flocks, although Nicholas Sykes, who lived at the upper end of the Longdendale valley east of Tintwistle, had 356 sheep in 1608.

Even in the seventeenth century many tenants had a second income from domestic textile production, with 29% of the Longdendale inventories from the period 1570–1680 containing some item of textile equipment (Powell 1976, 27), and a similar proportion from the inventories of Ashton in the years 1660 to 1680 (King 1987). There was a notable expansion in references to textiles after 1660 in both the inventories of the two lordships and in the parish records of the area. For instance, in the Ashton parish registers for the period 1701 to 1710 34% of all those giving an occupation put the textile trade as their primary form of work, as opposed to 36% for agriculture (Nevell 1993, 83).

As a group the tenants of the seventeenth-century farms displayed a remarkable independence of thought and action. In 1642, during the first English Civil War, 24 tenants of William Davenport of Bramhall Hall, in Stockport, petitioned him to lead them into action on the side of Parliament. Disappointed by his rejection the tenants enlisted in the regiment of Edward Hyde of Hyde a neighbouring Parliamentary manorial lord. This incident shows the tenants initially following the established order of marching under their manorial lord, but when he failed to move they over threw protocol and followed the nearest pro-Parliamentary lord (Nevell 1991, 77). In 1645 most of the tenants of Ashton-under-Lyne, on the other hand, refused to join the Parliamentary forces of their lord, Sir George Booth, even though he invoked ancient covenants in their leases. In 1644 and 1645 pro-Parliamentarian tenants in Colonel Robert Duckenfield's troops deserted in part to defend their homes from looting by pro-Parliamentarian Yorkshire forces, and in part because they had not been paid (Nevell 1991, 77). In Werneth between 1640/1 and 1657 when disruption arising from the Civil Wars led to a lack of manorial oversight the tenants went so far as to hold their own court and compile their own record. Once the proper manorial court was re-established in 1658 they seemed unwilling to pass their court manor book to the new local lord (Nevell 1991,78).

In each of these cases we can see the tenants, in times of stress and confusion, devising their own solutions which, whilst they followed the basic established order of things, contained innovations (Fig. 4.3). As a group they seem to have wanted to promote Parliament but their immediate needs came first.

Indicative of this independent, self-reliant, attitude was the most famous of all the local tenants in the period 1642–1770, the inventor Lawrence Earnshaw (*c.* 1707–67). Earnshaw lived in Lawrence Croft opposite Mottram Moor Farm which was rented from the Tollemaches. This simple three storey building had two rooms on each of the lower floors with a top floor reached by an external wooden staircase. The top floor was Earnshaw's workshop which contained, according to his will, an extensive range of simple hand tools. It was here that Earnshaw built musical instruments, designed new spinning machinery and pumping steam engines, and built the astronomical clocks for which, within 20 years of his death, he became nationally famous (Nevell 1994, 26–8) (Fig. 4.4).

The farming tenantry after 1770

For those tenants who remained on the land in the period from 1770 to 1870 the biggest issue was one of rising farm rents. In both Mottram and Werneth the national rise in rents during the Napoleonic wars can be traced through contemporary estate records of the local lords, Tollemaches and Egertons. In both townships rents had been rising before the 1790s. Davies has estimated that the usual rent per statute acre on the Tatton estates in Werneth between 1743 and 1768 was 10 shillings, compared to the average rent per acre in the years 1768–71 in Lancashire of 22*s.* 6*d.* and in Cheshire during the same period of 16*s.* (Mingay 1989, 1112). After 1768 the rents rose to 15 shillings per acre, and by 1780 they were 20*s.* or £1 (Davies 1960, 50). This contrasts with the rent of the new holdings from the residual common on the Low, near to Cheethams Smithy, which had small rents of 8*d.* to 12*s.* per annum during the eighteenth century (Davies 1960, 33). In Mottram the average rent per acre in 1785 was 23*s.* ½*d.*, but by 1799 this had nearly doubled to 42*s.* 2*d.* (CRO DTW 2477/B/10). However, rents per acre of farmland were still around the 42*s.* level in 1826 (CRO DTW 2477/B/13).

The map evidence suggests that farm numbers in the Manchester area reached a peak in the years 1845–72 (Nevell 1993, 84). Closer analysis of the archaeological and documentary record for the Tameside area, and in

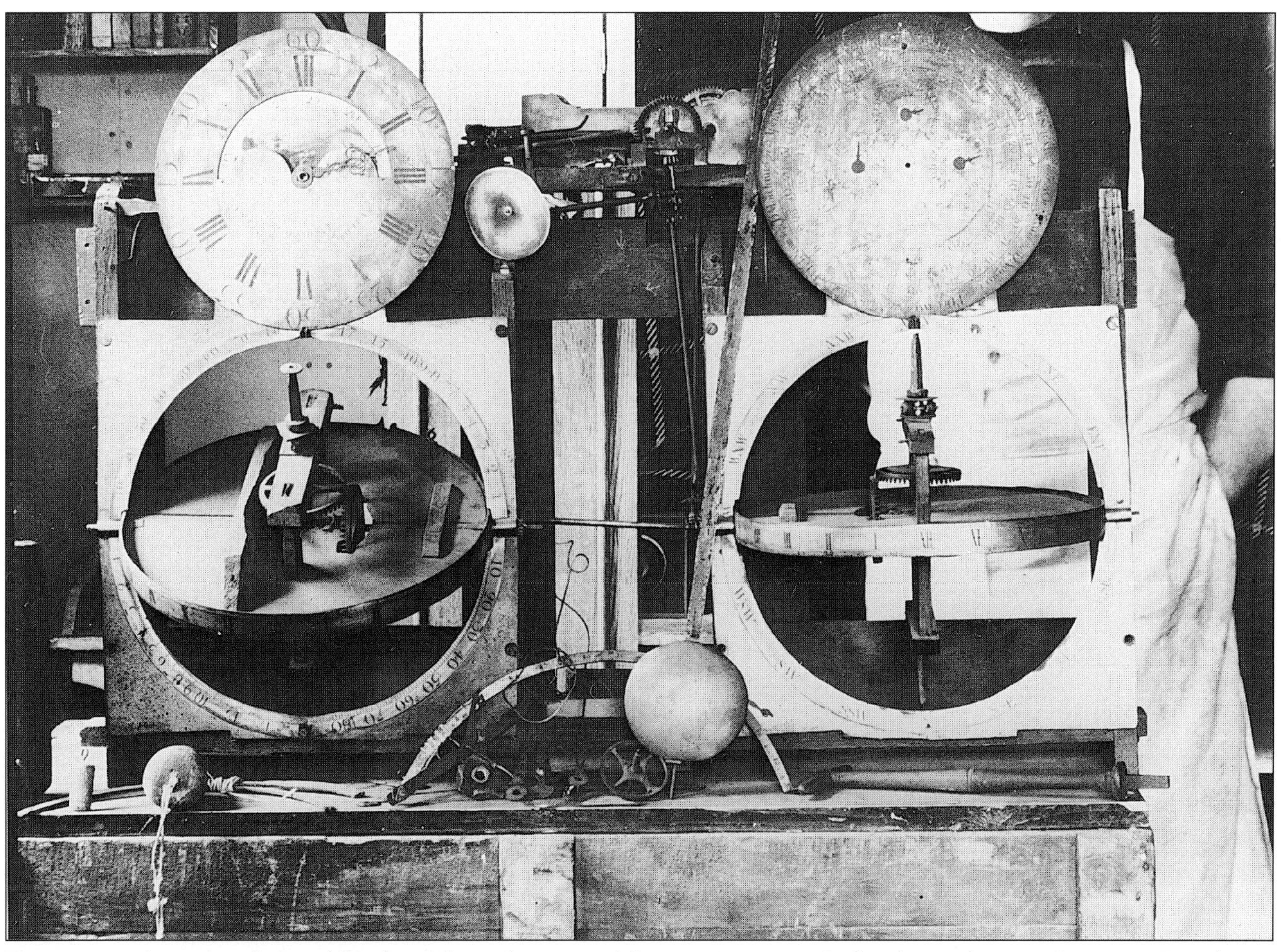

Figure 4.4 An orrery designed by the eighteenth-century Mottram inventor, clockmaker and tenant Lawrence Earnshaw (*c.* 1707–67). Earnshaw was one of the more prominent examples of the independent, self-reliant, attitude of the tenants of the Ashton and Longdendale lordships during the seventeenth and eighteenth centuries.

particular for the manors of Ashton, Mottram and Werneth, indicates that the peak in absolute farm numbers occurred at the end of the eighteenth century. From the 1800s increasing agricultural efficiency, coupled with the lure of employment in the new industrial urban centres, meant that the number of farmers and farms began to fall. In Mottram the peak of the growth curve appears to have been reached in the years 1785–1841 when the size of farms and the amount leased per tenant remained remarkably stable. Between 1785 and 1799 there were 19 farms and two crofts leased to 40 tenants, the average farm size being 25.8 customary acres, and the average tenancy size being 13.6 acres (CRO DTW 2477/B/10). By 1826 there were 23 farms, the average size being 25.9 acres, but fewer tenants so that the average tenancy rose to 15.3 acres (CRO DTW 2477/B/13). In 1841 262 acres of Tollemache land were unsuccessfully offered for sale, comprising seven farms at an average of 26.2 acres each, or 9.7 acres per tenancy. Between 1841 and 1919 there appears to have been a general consolidation of the Tollemache farm holdings in Mottram, with a significant reduction in the number of tenants and farms. When the Tollemache holdings in the township were finally sold in 1919 there were just ten farms, the average farm size was 36.1 acres.

In Werneth the pattern of expansion, followed by consolidation and the decline was also repeated. A survey of the manor of Werneth undertaken in 1658 records 26 tenants (CRO DAR/I/16), a number which had grown to 45 in 1713, 55 in 1785 and by 1816 had peaked at 64. The farms on the Tatton estate in Werneth during the eighteenth century were larger than those in Mottram, perhaps reflecting the greater overall elevation of the township and the existence of a sizeable sheep farming industry. Here too the absolute numbers of farms peaked in the late eighteenth century, and thereafter declined. During the eighteenth century there were very few farms above 50 acres, the majority being between 20 and 30 acres (Davies 1960, 50). By the time the township survey was taken in 1816 the average farm size was 35 acres and the number of tenants had reached 64, with multiple tenancy, as in Mottram (Powell collection) the norm. Yet the first half of the nineteenth century saw a sharp fall in the number of tenants in Werneth and the virtual disappearance of the multiple tenancy, so that by the time the Egerton family sold the estate in 1857 there were 24 tenants on their land occupying 20 farms, with an average farm size of 51 acres whilst the average tenancy was 42.5 acres (Powell Collection).

4.3 Tenant Families and the Dual Farming Economy

These broad trends in the development of the tenancies do not fully reveal the activities of the tenants and their relationship to an overall pattern of growth in wealth. The preceeding chapter outlined how some local families, such as the Hindleys, Hibberts and Ashtons, rose from the tenantry to become industrial freeholders. The patchy survival of the documentary evidence makes it difficult to follow the histories of all the tenant families but in the following cases we explore the activities of three families who remained as tenants in the period 1642 to 1870.

There is the Ashworth family, local farmers who became innkeepers; the Heap family who supplemented their income with domestic textile production; and the Wagstaffes who began and ended as tenant farmers but along the way made a failed attempt to establish themselves as textile mill owners.

The Ashworths of Mottram

The Ashworth family first occur in the Mottram parish registers during the late sixteenth century. Their residence, the Pack Horse Inn (Fig. 4.5), at the corner of old Market Street and Ashworth Lane in Mottram, stood on the main pack horse route from Stockport to Yorkshire. The Inn lay at the centre of a large farm holding of roughly 30 acres which ran from the western side of Ashworth Lane down to Hattersley Brook. In the Mottram-in-Longdendale rental of 1600 this tenancy was leased by Robert Ashworth where he is described as holding 'a Tennement with XXVI acres good land arable & meddowe & pasture valued to be yerely worth XII Xs. his yerely rent – XIIIs Xd' (CRO DTW/2477/B/9), A Robert Ashworth also occurs in a rental of January 1618 renting his farm at the same price but also for one heriot (CRO DTW 2406/12). This lease was renewed in January 1623/4 for a further 21 years at the same yearly rent, when Robert was described as a husbandman (CRO DTW 2477 J/1 a). This lease also lists some of the extra services required by the Lord of the Manor, Sir Richard Wilbraham. These included two capons 'at the usual time', presumably Christmas, 'customary services' for digging tor stone, slate and coal, and a requirement to plant yearly four trees of either oak, ash or elm. Robert or his son of the same name, died in 1662, leaving a will and an extensive inventory which gave his occupation as innkeeper and clearly indicates that the family now drew two incomes, from the farm and from the inn (CRO WS Ashworth 1663).

In Robert's will the lease for the Pack Horse Inn was transferred to his wife until his son John reached 21 years of age, when he was to receive the tenement. John Ashworth occurs in a renewal of the farm's lease in September 1684. This lease was almost identical to that of 1623, being for 21 years for a messuage now worth yearly £120 at an annual rent of 14*s.* 4*d.*, only a shilling more than in 1623 (CRO DTW 2477 J/12). John was described as a tenant rather than an innkeeper, although this may merely reflect the official view of his landlord as to his chief occupation rather than John's own assessment of the importance of his two occupations.

In 1727 a John Ashworth, possibly the same John as in 1684 or more likely his son, was renting the Pack Horse Inn and its farm land from a Mr Davenport of Manchester, who was in turn leasing the tenement from Lord Tollemache at an annual rent of £14 10*s.* This represents a substantial increase on the annual rent paid by the family in the seventeenth century, and in part reflects a general rise in rents in Mottram township shown by a comparison of the leases renewed in 1683/4 with those given in 1727. It is not clear when the Ashworth family died out, but a lease of 1789 indicates

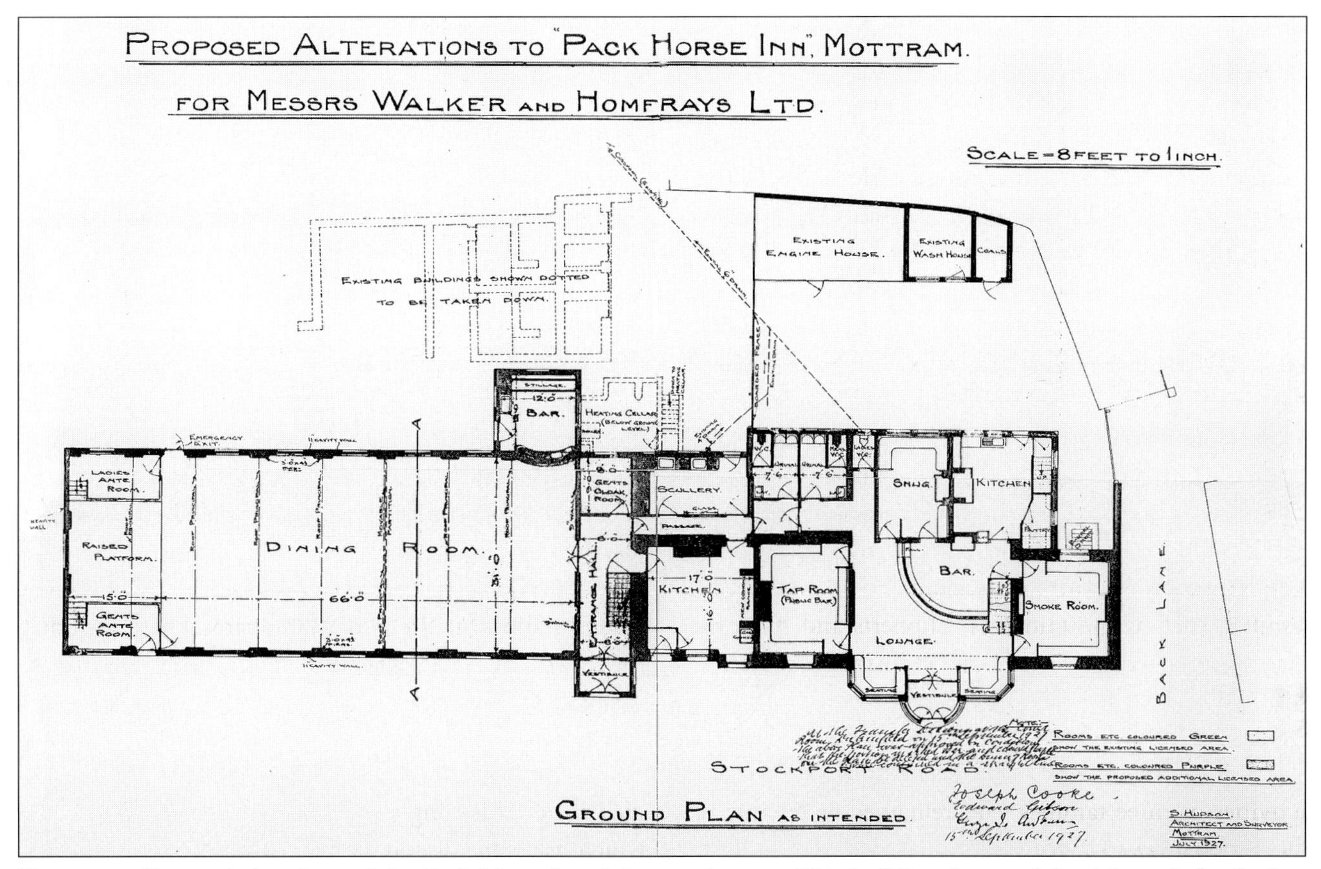

Figure 4.5 Plan and elevations of the Pack Horse Inn, Mottram in 1937. This building, home of the Ashworth family for nearly two hundred years, began as a two-bay, central-fireplace farmhouse, but as its role as an inn increased in importance it was expanded to include stabling for pack horses (later the Dining Room), and additional rooms were added. The property is still a public house in 1999. (*Powell Collection*)

that the Cook family had taken over the farm by this date, and the lands were split between the new family, who also took the inn, and the Wagstaffes of what is known as Old Post Office farm (CRO DTW 2477/I/12–18).

Like many of the tenant farmers of Tameside the Ashworth family of Mottrarn combined farming with a second business in an attempt to supplement their agricultural income. Such dual occupation was very common in the upland areas of the borough, particularly east of the River Tame. In the Ashworth's case they were innkeepers as well as tenant farmers, supplying the pack horse trade from Stockport, Manchester and further afield that flowed through the Longdendale valley into Yorkshire from as early as the fourteenth century (Nevell 1991, 60–1; Cunliffe-Shaw 1958, 15–17).

The importance of the inn trade to the family is indicated in the 1663 will and inventory of Robert (CRO WS Ashworth 1663). The livestock and crops associated with his farming activities are listed first but, in a perfunctory manner. He had five kine, one red cow and two calfs worth £18, one horse worth £3, and three swine valued at £1 13*s.* 4*d.* He also had hay and corn worth £4 10*s.* and 'husbandryware' to the value £1 9*s.* In contrast the furniture and equipment within the house is given in some detail, and there seems little doubt that most of this was associated with Robert's second trade, innkeeping. The most obvious items relating to this occupation are the 'stronge drinke and bread in the house at his decease' valued at £2 and the inn sign worth three shillings. It seems likely that most of the fourteen cushions, thirteen chairs and stools, eight forms, seven beds and six tables listed were used in the innkeeping business rather than for domestic use.

Out of an inventory worth £83 9*s.*, there were £16 2*s.* 0*d.* in debts owing to Robert, £28 12*s.* 4*d.* in farming livestock and goods, and £38 14*s.* 8*d.* worth of goods in the house, most of which were related to the innkeeping trade. Judging by this inventory the importance of innkeeping to the Ashworth family was at the very least equal to that of farming, if not of prime concern.

The Pack Horse Inn is still used as a public house, although the façade fronting Ashworth Lane was extensively rebuilt in 1927 (Nevell 1991, 140). Robert Ashworth's detailed inventory from 1663, which names several rooms, allows the farmhouse and inn of the mid-seventeenth century to be reconstructed. Nine rooms are mentioned in the inventory; the buttery, kitchen chamber below, parlour below, firehouse, new little chamber, new chamber and 'the house'. The oldest part of the surviving structure is a building of double depth with four bays and two storeys. A large stone barn lay immediately to the south, divided from the farmhouse by a cross-passage and forming a longhouse. The importance of this building is indicated by its size, with a kitchen and a buttery and by the presence of two parlours, one which was on the second floor.

The Heap Family

The Heap family of Staley township were tenant farmers cultivating farmland on the upland fringes of the borough, who supplemented their income through textile production. Their history indicates the struggle that such small tenant farmers had in coping with an agriculturally marginal upland area, even if they tried to increase their income by undertaking a second trade such as money lending, and later textiles.

The family may originally have farmed a small holding in the southern part of the township at a farm known as Heap's on the edge of Hollingworth Moor. The earliest occurrence of the family in the township

Figure 4.6 Moorgate Farm. This property, the centre of a small upland holding of 36 acres, was rented by the Heap family from the end of the seventeenth century to the mid-nineteenth century. In the early eighteenth century the family turned to clothmaking as a way of supplementing their income from stock rearing, and these three-storey weavers' cottages were built next to the farmhouse.

can be found in the parish registers. A Henrie Heape was baptised on 27 July 1563. The earliest will to survive is that of Joan Heap, Spinster, dated 1571, whilst her son Thomas Heap, tenant, is known from a will and inventory of 1623. However neither documents gives a specific location within the township and although many Heap family members occur in the Mottram parish registers from 1570 onwards none are associated with Moorgate in Stayley until after 1679, perhaps suggesting that the family moved to this new farm sometime in the mid-seventeenth century (CROWS Heap 1678/9). Moorgate Farm was rented from the Stamford Estate and today is an area of west facing rough pasture over 180m above sea level (Fig. 4.6).

A Thomas Heape occurs in a will and inventory of 1623/4, worth £469 *6s. 3d.*, describing himself as a tenant farmer (CRO WS). The inventory of his goods was modest, totaling only £68 *1s. 8d.* However, he had very large sums of money owing to him, amounting to £401 *4s. 7d.* From the list of the debts owing to Thomas it is apparent that the family's main income in the early seventeenth century arose from money lending to the other farmers in Mottram parish and the neighbouring parishes of Ashton, Glossop and Stockport. For instance, he had nineteen kine of which sixteen were 'in keeping of', that is rented to, thirteen other farmers, mostly in Staley, but including individuals in Arnfield, Hartshead, Mottram, Mossley and Saddleworth. Other debts owed to him came from farmers in Dukinfield, Hadfield, Heyrod, Highstone, Hollingworth, Luzley, Matley, Micklehurst, Ridge Hill and Tunstead.

The first member of the family who occurs at Moorgate farm in Staley is Robert Heap, and his will of 1678 states that Robert acquired Moorgate from a William Gaskell. Under the terms of Robert's will the family holdings were split in two, his eldest son Robert and his grandson, also called Robert, each received half of Moorgate farm. A Stamford rental of 1702 records a Robert Heap tenant and a Robert Heap 'cloathmaker', possibly Robert's son, as jointly renting 17 customary acres of land at 13 shillings per annum (John Rylands Dunham Massey MSS, Accession 8/5/92 Box 4/1).

Robert had three other sons but none of these seem to have received much from his will. The fate of such landless younger siblings who were forced to make their own way is indicated by the inventory of one of the sons, Daniel Heap, proved in 1694 when his estate was valued at only £22 *19s.* (CRO WI Heap 1694). Amongst Daniel Heap's goods and chattels were 'Cloath, yarn et wool' valued at £8 *9s.*, 'Looms, warping wools and Creeles' worth £1 *5s.*, and 'Comms and wilskits, whiles, cards and other metterals belonging to the trade', that is of clothier, worth £0 *14s. 6d.* It seems that Daniel had relied heavily on textile working to compensate for the shortcomings of his small tenantcy. Daniel's brother Joshua's goods were somewhat more when he died in 1708, at £38 *10s.* This presumably excluded any land he rented for the will was not declared Infra, or worth below £40. Joshua felt sufficiently wealthy to be able to will 'that the poore of this parish have fourty shillings given to them as my executor thinks fitt' (CRO WS Heap 1708). No will has survived of the last of these three younger sons, Samuel.

The low point in the fortunes of the family was reached on Robert's death in 1733, when 'the Goods and Chattels of the said Deceased did not exceed the sum of three pounds in common form of Law' (CRO WI Heap 1733). Yet, despite this low valuation, and the absence of a detailed inventory, it is clear from Robert's will that he alone was renting the Moorgate tenement from the Stamford Estate. He explicitly stated in his will that the he left 'all my Tenement and premises with the appurtenances, sittuate, lying and being at Moorgate afforesaid, Together with all my Right, Tide, Interest, and Claim therein and thereto whatsoever, and to Compound with the Lord for a new lease' to his two sons William and Daniel. Daniel's will survives from 1774, by which time the family fortunes had sufficiently recovered and although no inventory has survived internal evidence from his will suggests that the Heap family estate was now worth more than £68 (CRO WS Heap 1774). Daniel had four sons and two daughters, and his will indicates some of the provisions frequently made for the safeguarding of such a large family. The three youngest sons received Daniel's own house in which they could live until the lease expired, whilst the eldest son Daniel received the rest of the Moorgate property, on condition that he distributed £68 amongst his relatives (CRO WS Heap 1774).

The clothier element of this family's economy now appears to have become the dominant economic force. Despite inheriting the majority of the farm Daniel Heap described himself as a woollen clothier in his will of 1806 (CRO QDV2/393; CRO WS). His son Joseph, who inherited Moorgate, also described himself as a clothier in his will of 1829 (CRO WS). Furthermore,

Daniel's younger brother Robert, appears to have set up a thriving business as a clothier and by his death in 1790 his estate was worth £90 (CRO WS Heap 1790). It is not clear from these documents whether the Heap family were just textile spinners or whether they acted as middle-men in the putting out system.

Joseph Heap's estate was worth under £100 in 1829, and was left to his wife. Only after her death was Daniel Heap to receive 'the leasehold of Moorgate' which his father held for three lives (CRO WS Heap, 1829). The family had moved from Moorgate by 1840, for in that year the tithe award for the township did not list them amongst the occupiers of Further and Nearer Moorgate. A John Heap was resident at Boar Fold in the southern part of the township (CRO EDT 366), but it is not clear how he was related to the Moorgate branch of the Heaps. A clue as to the fate of the family is provided by the will of a Daniel Heap woollen clothier of Stayley proved on 24 January 1835 (CRO WS Heap 1835). This gives the family's home as Brun, a settlement slightly north of Moorgate. There is no mention of any property rented from the Stamford Estate, so that if this is the will of Joseph's son the family seem to have given up their holding completely in the early years of the 1830s, when home weaving was dying out because of the competition from mechanised loom weaving in the mills.

The physical extent of the tenancy can be partially recovered from the Staley tithe award of 1839/40. The Moorgate farm holding was split between Further and Nearer Moorgate, then in the hands of George and Joseph Hyde, and Hugh Henshall, these two parts totalling just fourteen acres (CRO EDT 366). This compares with the seventeen acre leased by the family in 1702.

The character of the farm in the seventeenth century is indicated by the inventory of Robert Heap, husbandman, in 1679. This was worth £135 19*s.* 0*d.* and included 'horses, kine, sheepe, and hog' valued at £51 16*s.* 0*d.*, 'corne and Hay' worth £10, and 'ploughes and harrows and Husbandry Geares' worth £1 16*s.* 0*d.* (CRO, WS Heap 1678). It is not clear from the inventory what if any crops were grown, although comparison with other Mottram parish inventories would suggest that the ploughs and harrows were used in the production of fodder crops for the farm's livestock (Powell 1976, 15–16). Robert also had debts owing to him worth £47 10*s.* 0*d.* which suggests that the family was continuing to lend to the local farmers of the parish. Joyce Powell has noted that Staley township contained the most moneylenders in the parish of Mottram whereas the highest number of borrowers lived in Godley (Powell 1976, 24–5).

The success of this family is reflected in the surviving farm complex, much of which dates from the eighteenth century. The oldest element of the complex is formed by a central farmhouse, now No. 3, dating to the seventeenth century, which is of two storeys in water-shot stone and squared rubble, with mullion windows to both floors. The eighteenth-century additions include at the western end a range of two, two storey cottages again with mullion windows, which suggest that the top floor may have been used for spinning. At the eastern end there is a shippon and a barn with an arched entrance.

The Wagstaffes of Mottram

The Wagstaffes first appear as farmers in Mottram township in 1694. In that year Nicholas Wagstaffe and his wife Martha built what is now known as Post Office Farm (Fig. 4.7), a two storey, stone building with mullioned windows, coped gables and a two storey porch in the style common in the southern Pennines at the time, on the western side of Market Street. This building was one of many new farmhouses created during the seventeenth and eighteenth centuries in the lordships of Ashton and Longdendale and the new farm holding was carved out of the neighbouring Angel Inn and Pack Horse Inn farm. The size of this holding was large at over 30 acres, and was a compact parcel of land lying to the east of Market Street, in the area known as the Pitses. In 1727 their son John, who also described himself as a tenant farmer, held the tenancy, which was still around 30 acres. He had two sons, John born on 19 November 1752 and James born on 2 November 1758. By 1799 the family had added to this holding by renting a large part, roughly ten acres, of the former Ashworth tenancy, which lay immediately south of the Post Office Farm land, making it one of the largest tenancies within Mottram during this period (CRO DTW 2477/B/10).

Although principally tenant farmers they were involved in the domestic spinning of textiles during the eighteenth century. During the boom of the 1780s and 1790s many of the farmers in the Mottram area took

Figure 4.7 Post Office Farm, Mottram. Built in 1694, this was the home of the Wagstaffe family until the mid-nineteenth century. The farm itself appears to have been a new creation of the late seventeenth century carved out of two neighbouring holdings.

to building housing for hand loom weavers (Nevell 1993,46). As well as building such loomshops, local farmers also set about converting barns or erecting new sheds to house the hand-powered spinning jennies. Perhaps the foremost of these farmers in the Mottram area to speculate in the cotton industry was John Wagstaffe (Nevell 1991, 43). In 1786 John Wagstaffe decided to convert a barn on his land into a horse or hand-powered spinning Jenny mill (Fig. 3.9). This was on the western side of Back Lane (SJ 9929 9556) immediately south of Old Post Office Farm and was known as Wagstafe's factory (CRO DTW 2477/B/10). Around 1797 the land tax returns indicate that he had a second cotton factory opposite the first, this one being known as Dry Mill (CRO QDV2/299), though whether he ran both together is not clear (Fig. 4.8).

Dry Mill was erected on land opposite Wagstaffe's first factory, for a lease of 1804, mortgaging the site to Robert Newton of Heaton Norris, describes the factory as a 'new building and workshop lately erected' (CRO EDT 281). It is a stone built two storey building, three by two bays, with a ridge slate roof and chimneys. The west elevation has a door with a small single light to its right on the ground floor and a modern window. The first floor has a four-light flat faced stone mullion window. The eastern elevation has three windows all with stone sills and lintels.

The mill was probably built in the mid-1790s. A lease of 1799 to John Ashton of Hollingworth indirectly mentions the mill, when it describes a plot of land for building a house on boarded on the northern side by the cotton factory of John Wagstaffe, on the eastern side by Mottram (Market) Street, on the western side by Back Lane and on the southern side by land belonging to Thomas Cardwell (CRO DTW 2477 F/12). Although the land tax returns do not mention the site by name until 1799, the plot of land concerned, valued at 3*s.* 4½*d.*, can be traced in entries for 1798 and 1797 (CRO QDV2/299). In 1796 the Land Tax Returns record John Wagstaffe as owning a cotton mill in Mottram, assessed at the higher rate of 3*s.* 9*d.* but it is possible that this referred to Wagstaffe's factory established in 1786. This suggests that Dry Mill may have been built in 1796/7 as a replacement for Wagstaffe's factory, although it is possible that the earlier site was included in other lands owned by Wagstaffe in Mottram.

The factory did not last very long and was soon converted to cottages. This had probably occurred by 1813, for the Mottram rental of that year does not mention the cotton factory by name, although it could have occurred as early as the remortgage in 1805 (CRO DTW 2477/B/12). In this regard it is worth noting that James Wagstaffe, who is described as a shopkeeper from Mottram in three leases from the period 1792–94 (CRO D 3553/19–21), was called a cotton spinner in a lease and re-lease dated the 16 September 1806, perhaps suggesting that he had taken over Dry Mill from John Wagstaffe (CRO D 3553/24). The family's fortunes declined in the mid-nineteenth century for by 1845 the land rented by Robert and Margaret Wagstaffe only covered 18 acres. Since the family now had seven houses, four shops (it is not clear from the tithe award whether these are retail shops or workshops, but probably the former; CRO EDT 281) and a barn besides the farmhouse itself, it may be that they had found a new source of income from renting property to supplement that from farming.

Figure 4.8 Dry Mill, Mottram. Dry Mill was one of the earliest purpose-built cotton textile mills in the Ashton and Longdendale Lordships. It was erected in the 1790s by the local tenant farmer John Wagstaffe. He already had one textile factory in the village, in a former barn on Back Lane, which he had converted in 1786. The machinery in these buildings was either horse- or hand-powered, but no evidence survives at Dry Mill as to the power source. During the 1780s and 1790s dozens of such small-scale factory buildings were established in the Longdendale valley. However, by 1800 they were being superseded by the larger water-powered textile mills and all had gone by 1820. Dry Mill itself was converted to cottages by 1813.

Dating Standing Buildings 1: Bricks

The growth in the use of bricks in vernacular and polite buildings during the period 1642–1870 is one of the most obvious changes in the archaeological record, and approximate dates can be assigned to particular bricks depending on their shape, size and finish. Many of the improvements in yeoman accommodation used brick in the alteration of existing structures or for new features, such as fireplaces, within new timber-framed houses. The most obvious use of brick was in the construction of hearths and chimney stacks, both in the middle and at the end of houses. The heat resistance of bricks was better than that of stone so that consequently they were used often in stone farmhouses. The other main use of brick in existing structures was as a replacement for wattle and daub or timber studding in timber-framed buildings, and as wall sills where it was used as a permanent replacement for timber or stone (i.e. Denton Chapel). Brickworks developed on the edges and around many of the towns of seventeenth- and eighteenth-century England. Large houses set the fashion for brick production, forcing producers to make bricks of high quality, fostering skills among the brickmakers and encouraging the use of permanent rather than clamp kilns. By the eighteenth century brick building was the norm in most areas and the brick-making industry begin to be focussed on specific areas, such as Bedfordshire where large permanent kilns were developed.

Bricks consist of mainly baked clay and sand and many of their characteristics vary with the type of clay and firing process. Their rectangular block shape results in small end faces known as headers and long side faces known as stretchers. Prior to 1850 bricks were hand-made in wooden moulds. In the seventeenth and early eighteenth centuries bricks tended to be long and thin, with irregularities in the shape, surfaces and edges giving a relatively rough texture. During the eighteenth century bricks became shorter and deeper, as legislation was passed restricting their size in 1725, 1784 and 1803, as well as more regular and smoother. After 1850 machine made bricks of uniform, regular, shape and finish reached a maximum depth and largely replaced hand-made bricks.

Brick colours depend chiefly upon the clay and firing temperature. Most traditional buildings in the Manchester and Tameside areas are built in red brick. The older bricks tend to be dark red-brown but during the eighteenth century brighter red-orange bricks were sometimes used. In the late nineteenth century harsh Accrington bricks or Ruabon bricks with more pink and purplish variations were widely used.

Strong walls in traditional buildings were generally achieved through thickening and sound bonding and jointing. Walls were normally solid and consisted of two, three or fours widths of brick giving 9″, 13″ and 18″ thick walls. The bricks were bedded in mortar and were also overlapped or bonded. The three most commonly used bonds in this period were English (*c.* 1650–1700), English Garden Wall (*c.* 1642–1870) and Flemish. (*c.* 1700–1850).

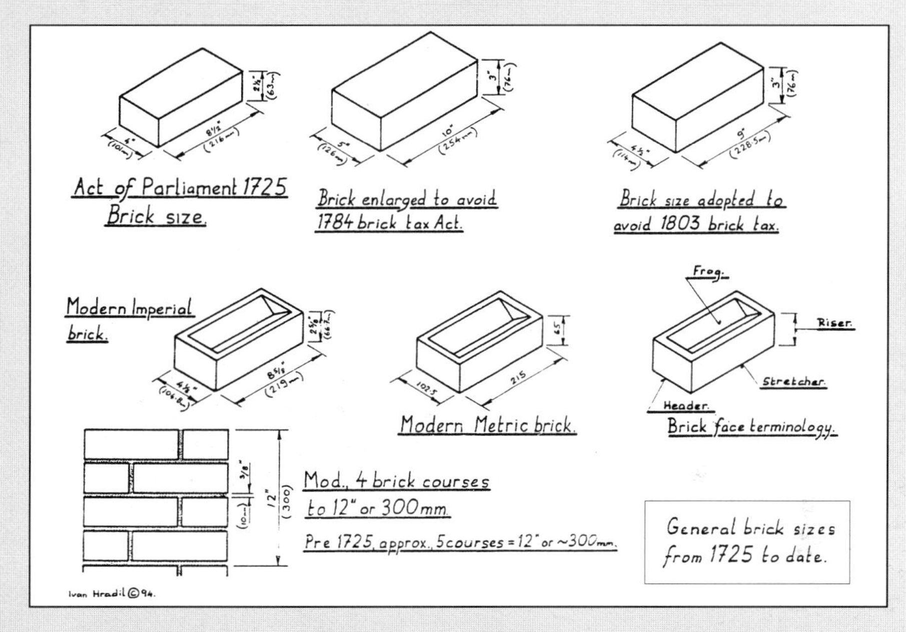

Occasionally decorative bonding such as herringbone may also be found in traditional buildings. The heads of window and door openings were often finished with a timber or stone lintel of brick arches bridging the openings as an important structural element. Seventeenth and eighteenth century arches were often formed from soft, carefully cut and shaped, bricks with very fine joints. Bricks could also be projected slightly in front of the face of the wall, especially in the mid to late seventeenth century, to form decorative shapes, bands, string courses, initials, numerals and labels (drip moulds) above doors and windows. Projecting bands of three bricks depth continued to be used into the early eighteenth century.

Ivan Hradil, Michael Nevell and John Walker

Dating Standing Buildings 2: Doors

The domestic dwellings are the most common archaeological sites of the period 1642–1870. Many of these buildings contain features that date to various periods within this era and these can be identified and dated by their style and material. Amongst the most readily dateable house features are doors and doorways.

Medieval and sixteenth-century doors
Early doors were defensive in character. Heavy oak planks, smoothed with an adze, were fastened on to horizontal boards. The two faces were connected with wooden pegs or iron studs. Strap hinges were hung from iron pins seated directly in the stone or timber surround to the door against which the door closed directly with no intervening door frame. Security was of paramount importance and was achieved by using an internal draw-bar, with no handle or knob on the outside.

Figure 1 General door styles; sixteenth to nineteenth centuries. *Top left* sixteenth century; *mid left* seventeenth century; *bottom left* late seventeenth to early eighteenth century; *top right* eighteenth century (Georgian); *middle right* early nineteenth century; *bottom right* late nineteenth century.

Seventeenth-century doors
Whilst the overall construction techniques did not change, the number of vertical planks in each door increased as the planks themselves became narrower. The arch at the top of the door was often shallower. Many old houses have stone or heavy timber lintels over the door, sometimes carved with the date, or the initials of the original builder. Defence gave way to decoration and external fastenings were introduced, normally in the form of a heavy iron ring-pull. In some buildings there was still no separate door frame, whilst in others the door closed flush against a heavy timber frame.

Batton and braced doors – seventeenth to nineteenth centuries
This was the most widespread type of door in use during this period and evolved from the heavy plank doors. Instead of a double layer of timber the vertical boards were supported by three batons on the internal face. The diagonal braces gave additional strength and rigidity. Simple strap hinges connected the flush face to a rebated timber door frame. Strap hinge details varied over the centuries and their position moved from the outside to the inside of the door. Planks were originally butt-jointed and gradually evolved to the tongue and groove door we know today. Simple metal Suffolk-type latches were the most common type of fastening.

Eighteenth-century doors
The revival of interest in the architecture of Greece and Rome known as the Renaissance period produced a sophisticated and elegant architectural style. Panelled doors became the norm. The panels are jointed into the surrounding timber, either with a moulded stile or a separate 'bolection' moulding. Some panels are flush with the stiles and rails. Details of the panels vary widely, the six-panelled version being the most common. Hinges had to be obtrusive, so as not to spoil the effect and often H and L shaped hinges were used. Internally, the door no longer opened into a main room but into a smaller hallway and fanlights over the door allowed light to reach this internal space. The classical doorcase, with columns and a wide variety of pediments,

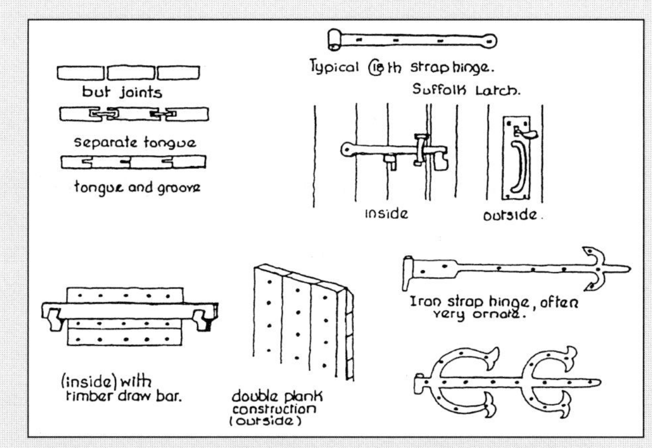

Figure 2. Common fixtures and fittings on doors from the sixteenth, seventeenth and early eighteenth centuries.

Figure 4. Doorways to the hatting factory of Joseph Howe & Sons, Annan Street, Denton. This building, dating from the foundation of the factory in 1868 was designed so that it could be converted to terraced housing should the business fail. The plain brick rounded headed doorways are typical of terraced properties of this period.

Figure 3. The stair tower at Post Office Farm, Mottram. This door is a copy of the original 1694 structure which was of the plank and batton type would have had hand-forged strap hinges and handles.

emphasised the social significance of the door. Door furniture became more elaborate with knockers, door knobs and eventually letter-boxes, all normally made of brass. Boot scrapers outside the door protected the polished floors and rugs inside. The details of the newly introduced terrace house, including the doors, were intended to demonstrate the unity of the block; uniformity not individuality was the aim.

Nineteenth-century doors

During this period the number of panels diminished until four-panelled doors became the norm. One large raised and fielded panel at the bottom was not, however, uncommon, particularly in the latter part of the century. Overall the effect was chunkier and more solid than the elegance the eighteenth century. Fanlights became simpler, with plain rectangles or arches replacing the delicate tracery of the earlier doors. A greater variety of door furniture was used, with iron and on occasion glass or porcelain added to the familiar bras. The door was hung with butt hinges similar to those still used today. Terraces remained an architectural unity during this period, with matching doors, windows and other details, the elaboration of which reflected the social standing of the houses' occupants.

Ivan Hradil, Michael Nevell and John Walker

The new urban tenantry

Between 1770 and 1831 the parish records for Ashton and Longdendale and, from 1801, the census show that the population of the area expanded rapidly, between 1801 and 1831 it rose from 28,565 to 81,302 (See *Population Growth*). The majority of this increased population was housed in the new industrial towns of the two lordships and formed a new urban tenantry. The largest of these urban centres was the old town of Ashton, which had whose population rose from around 2,859 in the mid-1770s to around 14,900 in 1831. By 1831 Ashton had been joined in size by Stalybridge and there were other new, smaller, urban centres at Broadbottom, Compstall, Denton, Dukinfield, Gee Cross, Hollingworth, Hyde and Mossley. These new urban centres and their urban tenantry were based around the textile mills and the factory system. Wadsworth and Mann in their review of the contemporary descriptions of weavers (1931, 320–1) described the early nineteenth-century weavers of Lancashire as consisting of two classes, the landless, often immigrant, urban weavers living in poor-quality dwellings (Fig. 4.9) and the rural weavers with a few acres held at high rent.

Below the urban tenantry were the really poor. Urban almshouses for these people had been erected in Ashton as early as 1684 (Bowman 1960, 519) although the poor could also be housed out in the country. In 1701 the overseers of the poor of Ashton built a cottage at Audenshaw for a poor family having obtained 'the

Figure 4.9 Terraced housing in Denton. This aerial view of the terraced housing around the junction of Manchester Road and Ruby Street was taken in 1923. The townscape is dominated by the most common building type of the Industrial Revolution: the terraced house. Most of these houses were two-storey, four-roomed, terraced properties, and all were rented from either local mill-owners or local property speculators. Moore's hat factory can be seen on the centre left-hand edge of the view.

Consent of the Lord of the wast' (Bowman 1960, 519). By 1731 Ashton had a form of workhouse which was replaced in 1850 by a structure that now forms part of the local hospital (Burke & Nevell 1996).

Prior to 1770 tenant families worked at home, or in small community groups, and were in control of their own hours and conditions (Fitton 1965, 2). In contrast the new urban based textile industry established in Tameside during the period 1770–1830 imposed a harsh discipline on people's lives and broke up the family work unit. The hours were long; during the 1820s the textile mills of Ashton worked a fourteen hour day from 5am to 7pm, so that home became merely a place to sleep (Kenworthy 1929, 53–5). Within the textile mills there was quite a strict gender division; spinners were nearly always men since it was perceived that spinning was a highly skilled job, whilst weaving by power loom was seen as less skilled and was thus normally undertaken by women (Cotton 1977, 14–23). Each spinner employed a big piecer and a little piecer to mend broken threads, as well as a scavenger to clean around the machinery. These jobs were filled by the spinner's children whenever possible. Before the advent of the factory system spinning had been a female occupation, whilst handloom weaving had been generally done by men (Fleischmann 1973, 199–201).

Children were an essential part of the mill economy and by the late eighteenth century mill owners had learnt that children could operate certain machinery as well as an adult, whilst they could be paid considerably less (Cootes 1982, 58–9). According to Aikin during the 1790s children in the cotton mills of Dukinfield were treated especially badly, leading him to comment that the new textile industry had 'debilitated the constitutions and retarded the growth of many, and made an alarming increase in the mortality. This effect is greatly to be attributed to the pernicious custom, so properly reprobated by Dr Percival and other physicians, of making the children in the mills work night and day, one set getting out of bed when another goes into the same ...' (Aikin 1795, 456; Haynes 1993). Such practices led to demands for legislation, initially to improve the working conditions of children (Cootes 1982, 119–20).

By the late 1840s wages and working conditions were much improved, as can be seen from Angus Reach's tour of 1849. He visited two mills in Ashton, those of Messrs Redfern at Bank Field, and those of Hugh Mason, the Oxford Mills. He was offered no specific details as to the wages of the operatives at Bank Field Mills. However, Hugh Mason furnished Reach with a list of weekly wages for each type of employee, who worked twelve hours a day. Spinners earned 42*s.* a week, whilst the average of all employees, both skilled and unskilled, was 22*s.* 5*d.* per week, although Reach noted 'that piecers are not included in the calculation' (Aspin 1972, 77). In 1849 there was a widespread system of fines, stoppages and payments in kind, or truck, which meant that workers were often paid less than they expected. This was despite the passing of the Truck Act in 1831 which aimed to stop the practice. Dr McDouall, for instance, in 1838 angrily denounced the great mill-owning Ashton family of Hyde; 'Mr Ashton has always a book very neatly balanced, showing a certain number of men to have received so much money. Now that money Mr Ashton knows never was paid, because he deducts his charges, as a landlord, for house, coal, water, and 2*d.* per week for a Sunday School, besides other drawbacks in fines etc'. (Middleton 1932, 94).

Factory conditions continued to improve in the second half of the nineteenth century, as further legislation was passed. Even so cotton factories remained hazardous work places. Spinning required a high humidity so mills were low, poorly ventilated, and had high temperatures, often up to 100 degrees Fahrenheit for spinning the finest cottons. These conditions made operatives susceptible to the cold, the carding room being particularly unhealthy because of the air-borne fibres which could cause severe bronchial illnesses (byssinosis), as well as stomach and eye complaints. As late as 1872 the cardroom and blowing hands in John Mayall's textile mills in Mossley asked for an advance of 15% of their wages, 'on the grounds that the work they undertook often led to attacks of asthma, consumption, and other respiratory diseases due to the inhalation of dust' (Eckersley 1991, 22). Efficient air extractors and filters were not made widespread until the end of the century, after the introduction of appropriate legislation. The Factory Act of 1867, which consolidated all previous factory acts, required the installation of fans to extract dust and gases from industrial premises, as well as proper sanitary facilities (Richardson 1986, 232).

4.4 The Archaeology of the Tenant

The archaeological sites associated with tenants during the period 1642–1870 were far fewer and more restricted in range than for either of the other two groups, the lords and freeholders. Consequently, the archaeological profile of the tenants as a group is quite distinctive.

There were just five monument classes which saw activity by tenants; agricultural sites, commemorative sites, domestic sites, industrial sites and transport sites. The chronological distribution of these sites is the same for the lords and tenants, each showing a peak of activity during the eighteenth century, whereas those sites associated with the freeholders peaked, and are concentrated, in the early nineteenth century. Most of the tenant's activity during this period was concentrated in two areas; domestic sites and above all industrial sites.

In the seventeenth century the archaeology of the tenantry was typified by the 143 farmsteads, a figure which had grown to 273 by the period 1842–76. By the end of the period, in the mid-nineteenth century, the archaeological sites typical of the rural tenantry, were the farmstead, the weaver's cottage and the industrial

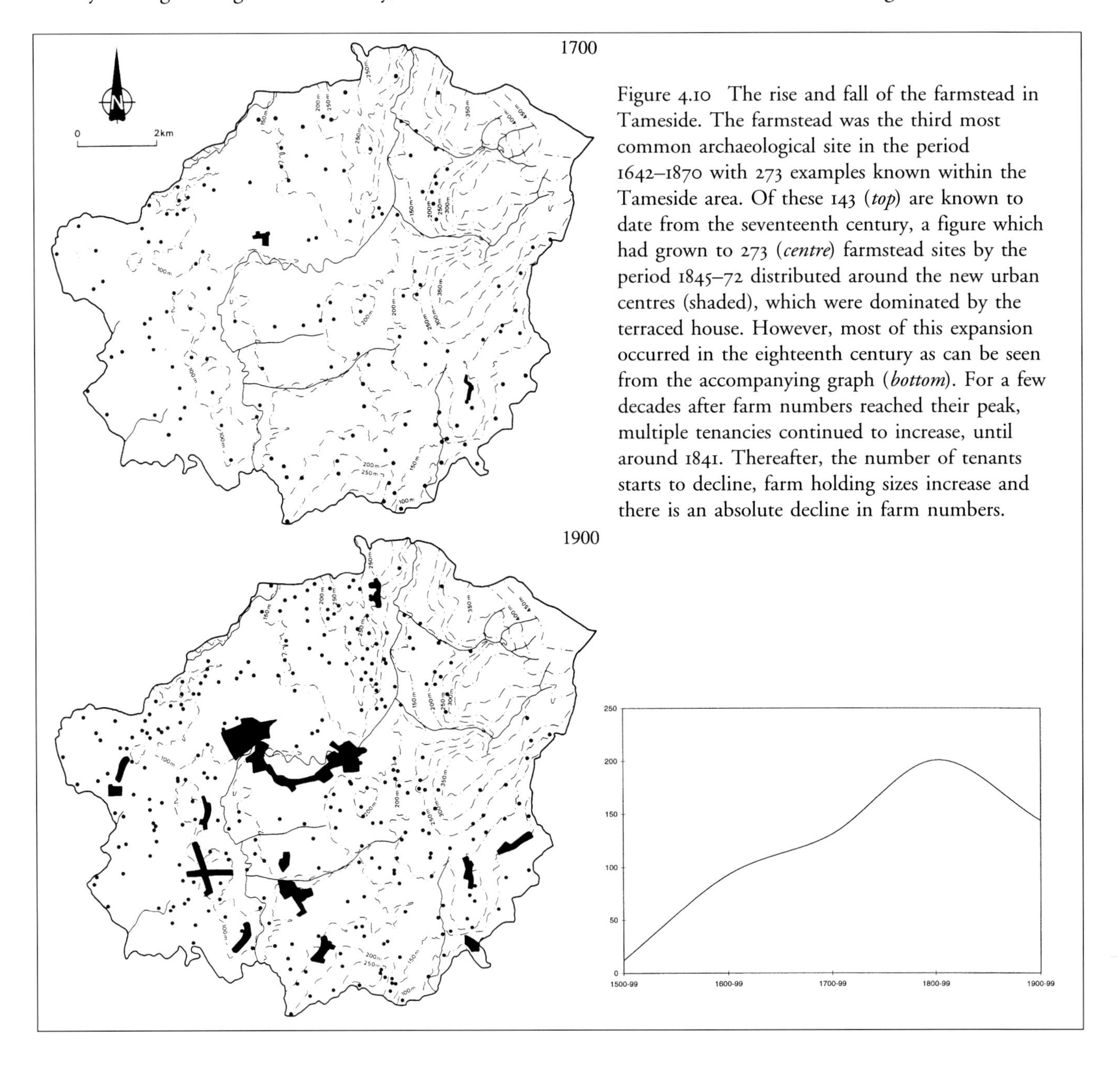

Figure 4.10 The rise and fall of the farmstead in Tameside. The farmstead was the third most common archaeological site in the period 1642–1870 with 273 examples known within the Tameside area. Of these 143 (*top*) are known to date from the seventeenth century, a figure which had grown to 273 (*centre*) farmstead sites by the period 1845–72 distributed around the new urban centres (shaded), which were dominated by the terraced house. However, most of this expansion occurred in the eighteenth century as can be seen from the accompanying graph (*bottom*). For a few decades after farm numbers reached their peak, multiple tenancies continued to increase, until around 1841. Thereafter, the number of tenants starts to decline, farm holding sizes increase and there is an absolute decline in farm numbers.

site, usually a single mill. Although the most common archaeological site of the period, the workers houses, would at first site appear to be intimately associated with the tenants within the towns, this type of site was generally built and owned by the lords and freeholders.

The farm

The most numerous monument group prior to the late eighteenth century were the farmsteads (Fig. 4.10). The tenants were responsible for only two new types of agricultural site within the Ashton and Longdendale lordships during this period; the cow-shed and the laithehouse. The most common archaeological site during the seventeenth and eighteenth century was the farmhouse. Across Greater Manchester over 1,800 farm sites are recorded and the period of greatest increase appear to be the eighteenth and nineteenth centuries, when 550 and 689 new sites are first recorded. The evidence from Tameside indicates, on the other hand, that most of the local farms had been occupied by the end of the eighteenth century, if not earlier. Most of this expansion representing colonisation of common lands within the lordships (Fig. 4.11).

In the previous volume we saw how during the seventeenth century the house of the tenantry could be distinguished archaeologically by their size, usually of less than 200 square metres, and their plan, usually two or three bays and no more than one and a half storeys. During the seventeenth century the effects of the Great Rebuilding can be seen on the houses of the tenantry. The new farms of this period were mostly either timber-framed structures, usually in the lowland areas such as the Ashton lordship, or stone-built, more typically in the upland areas such as the Longdendale lordship.

The stone-built houses, in particular, provided the tenant with the opportunity to make a visual statement about his wealth and social status that has often survived (Fig. 4.7). The emergence of datestones is a particularly good example of this. Many of the farms within the area bear such stones which usually record not only the date of construction but also the initials of the individuals, often husband and wife, for whom the house

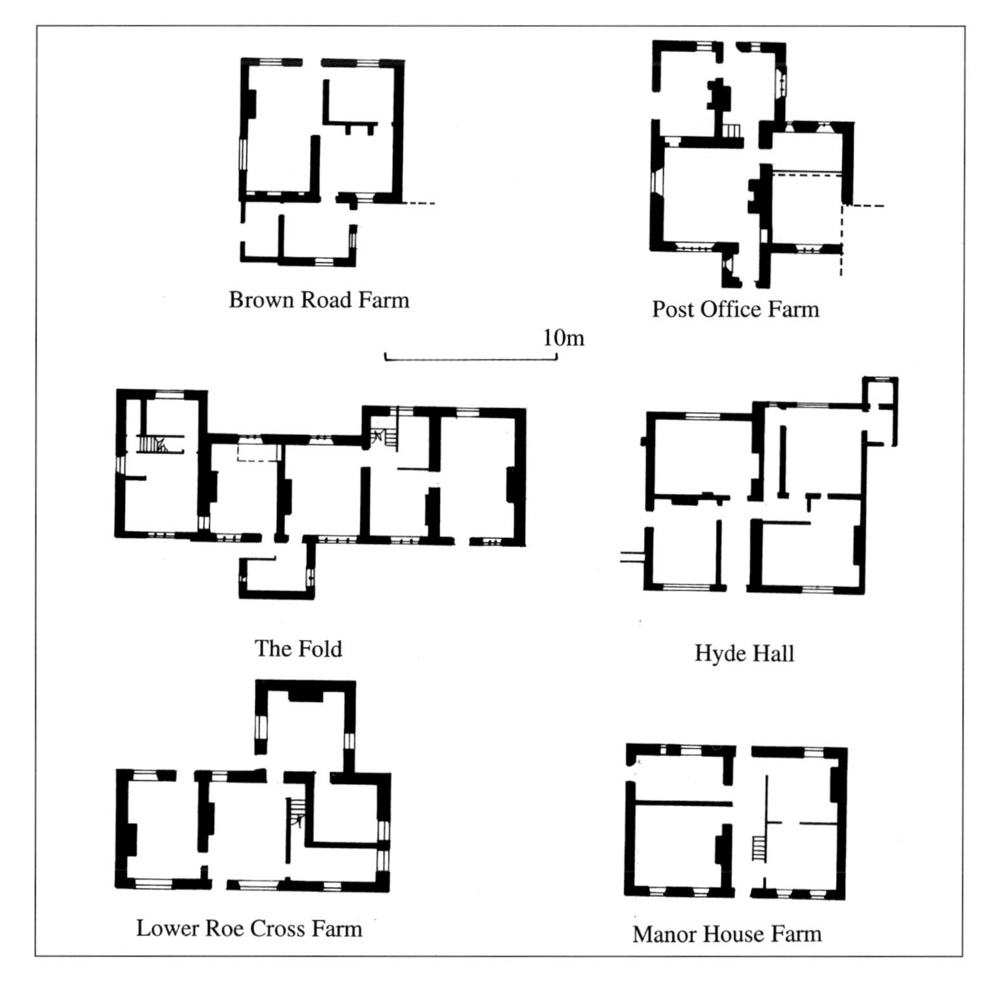

Figure 4.11 Plans of seventeenth- and eighteenth-century farmhouses. These farms show some of the stylistic development of farmhouses in the Ashton and Longdendale lordships during the period 1642–1870. Of particular note is the emergence of the double-depth, central-staircase plan farmhouse, often with a symmetrical façade. In size, as in the mid-seventeenth century, the tenant farmhouse of the eighteenth and nineteenth centuries remained two to three times the size of the average worker's house or cottage, but was considerably smaller than the houses of the new industrialist freeholders and lords.

was built. The earliest surviving example is at Hillend, Mottram, which simply bears the date 1604 (Fig. 3.3). Among the more decorative examples are those at Lower Fold Farmhouse in Ashton and Godley Hall. The windows and doors of the tenant's stone farmhouses were embellished, the former with hoodmoulds and the latter with chamfered mullions and surrounds. Another feature of the stone-built tenant house was the porch, usually of two storeys and sometimes containing a dovecot in the attic. The gable frontage of a porch provided a canvas for further architectural embellishment such as projecting corbels, known as 'kneelers', and finials. In the early houses of the tenantry the desire for a symmetrical façade was not a consideration, but by the early eighteenth century it had become an increasingly important concept (Fig. 4.12) and the porch was readily integrated into this.

Timber-framed exteriors do not survive in anything like the same number as those which were stone-built, either because of deterioration and demolition or because they have been masked by later rendering. Even with the much smaller corpus of examples it appears that timber-framed construction did not lend itself to the same level of decoration as stone. The decorative panelling and coving found on the halls of the lords and freeholders does not appear to have been adopted by the tenantry. However, one example in Tameside does suggest that some timber-framed farmhouses may have included a form of decoration which in most cases has been removed through the course of time. This decoration is known as pargetting and survives in a now enclosed gable at Lower Fold Farm, Ashton. Pargetting is a form of rendering, whereby plaster is applied to a wall surface and then decorated with incised and relief patterns. The example at Lower Fold Farm is, therefore, of some significance. The area of pargetting is in the western gable of the seventeenth-century farmhouse and its survival is due to the fact that in 1710 a wing was built across this end, enclosing the decoration within its roof space. The incised decoration comprises an unsophisticated geometric pattern which includes semicircular and triangular motifs.

Although much less common than stone or timber framing as a constructional fabric, brick began to be used as a building material in Tameside during the Great Rebuilding (see page 73). Within the Borough the outstanding example of a brick-built tenant farmhouse of the seventeenth century is Buckley Hill in Littlemoss. With hoodmoulds and raised lozenge and square panels, the exterior displays a variety of brick embellishment.

Whatever building material was used, the decorative treatment of the tenant house also extended to the interior, with ceiling beams, wall panelling and internal doors all showing an attention to detail. As in the houses of the gentry, the staircase became an important feature within the house; that at Lower Fold Farm is a particularly fine example.

Until the mid-eighteenth century tenant houses were of two storeys and had a main room, which was usually referred to as the housebody and in contemporary documents was often called simply the 'house'. This room can be compared with the central hall of the larger houses of the freeholders and gentry in that it was where the main source of heat was situated and where most of the activities of the household took place. Unlike the hall the housebody retained its functional importance, probably because the tenant could not afford to indulge in the level of privacy exhibited by the other two social groups. The heating source in the housebody usually took the form of an inglenook fireplace which was situated at one end of the room. Smoke from the fire was channelled out of the house by a plaster-lined, wattle and daub funnel, known as a firehood. The firehood was supported by a timber beam or bressummer, spanning perhaps three-quarters of the room's width. At one end this beam was built into a side wall of the house; the other was supported on a partition wall or 'heck' within the housebody. The inglenook fireplace often occupied almost one third of the length of the housebody and was usually lit by a small window, known as a fire window, set within the inglenook. Most of the cooking operations were carried out within the inglenook. A common feature of these fireplaces are salt boxes located in the back wall; these took the form of square-cut recesses in which salt was placed and kept dry by the warmth of the fire.

A second room common to the majority of tenant houses was the parlour, which was usually situated adjacent to the housebody. It was originally unheated and used as the primary bedroom within the house, although this function later changed as the bedroom was moved upstairs and the parlour became a private sitting room.

Other ground-floor rooms within the tenant house had a service function. These usually included a buttery

Figure 4.12 Oakdene Farmhouse, Mossley. This farmhouse, built in 1755 by the Hadfield family, is one of the earliest Tameside examples of the new double-depth, central-staircase, symmetrically façaded house which was introduced in to North West England around the beginning of the eighteenth century. Only the wealthier tenant farmers could afford to rebuild their homes in the current fashion. The Hadfields were renting 65.5 acres from the Stamford estate in this period, one of the biggest tenancies in the Ashton Lordship during the eighteenth century, and were also involved in domestic textile production.

and a pantry and which served as storage areas for food and other household items. Sometimes a service room is referred to in contemporary inventories as a kitchen. In the seventeenth century this did not necessarily imply a place where food was cooked, but rather was an alternative name for a storage room. The construction of lean-to buildings, or outshuts, to the rear of houses was a common secondary phase to a tenant house and these outshuts usually served as additional service-room space. The continuous outshut at Lower Fold Farmhouse, Ashton, includes a large dairy room where butter and cheese would have been made. A small nineteenth-century addition to Jeremy Cottage probably served as a dairy, while an addition of 1642 may also have had a service-room function.

The first-floor chambers within the tenant house were principally used for storage as well as sleeping areas. Usually the principal room on this floor was the chamber over the parlour, with the chamber over the housebody being of lesser importance, often because of the obstructive and somewhat unsightly firehood rising through the room.

The earliest forms of the tenant house, like the contemporary halls of the freeholders and lords, were restricted to a single-depth plan. Within this general parameter, however, several variations in layout have been recorded. One of the first discernible and most common variations is a linear arrangement of three rooms, with a through-passage dividing two of the rooms. The origins of the through-passage plan may lie either in the development of the medieval screens passage plan, which divided the hall from the service end of the house, or as an evolution of the cross-passage long-house. Tenant examples of this arrangement include Apethorn Fold in Werneth and Lower Fold Farmhouse and Limehurst Farmhouse in the Ashton lordship.

Although a common plan, the through-passage was not a feature found in all tenant houses. There are many examples in Tameside which demonstrate a different arrangement. Jeremy Cottage, Ashton, in its original form was a two-bay house to which a wing was added in 1642. The house contains a housebody with an inglenook fireplace but there is no through-passage. The wall forming the back of the fireplace represents the original gable end of the house, and the original entrance to the housebody is also in this gable wall, to the side of the heck. The other bay of the original house was divided into two rooms, probably a parlour and a service room. A similar arrangement can be seen at Warhill Cottages in Ashton and at Hartshead Green Farm in Ashton.

The evolution of the post-seventeenth-century tenant house displays a continuing change in attitude to room use (Fig. 4.11). The construction of an outshut at Lower Fold Farmhouse probably coincided with the change of use of the former service room into a second parlour, thereby maintaining service-room capacity but improving the quality of rooms within the house.

The most important change to the tenant house was concerned with the centralisation of rooms. At Old Post Office Farm (Fig. 4.11) the original arrangement was a central lobby or baffle-entry house, with access available into either the housebody or the rear parlour immediately upon entering through the central doorway. At some time during the early eighteenth century a rear wing was added to this building which squared rather than elongated the overall plan, ensuring that from the housebody there was direct contact with all other ground-floor rooms.

Elsewhere within Tameside by the early eighteenth century new farmhouses were adopting a more compact layout from the outset. This was in the form of a double-pile plan, two rooms deep, such as at Brown Road Farm in Mottram (Fig. 4.11). Here the adoption of this new plan can be seen to coincide with other significant changes, which included the demise of the firehood and its replacement by the stone or brick stack. This new form of vent allowed greater flexibility in the position and number of fireplaces and also enlarged the available room space. Earlier buildings, such as Jeremy Cottage and Lower Fold Farmhouse, which formally had firehoods, now acquired solid stacks placed within the inglenook. A result of the introduction of the solid stack was that first-floor rooms could be heated for the first time. The obtrusive firehood in the chamber above the housebody was removed, thus raising the quality of this room as a bedroom.

The arrangement of rooms within the double-pile plan, such as that at Manor House Farm in Denton (Fig. 4.11), or the early nineteenth-century double-pile farmhouse built at Hyde Hall, Denton, typically consisted of two rooms at the front of the building, with entry into the building either via a central hallway or directly into the housebody. These front rooms were typically the housebody, or principal living room, and a parlour. Two further rooms were positioned at the rear of the building and were normally a kitchen (which by this date had adopted a function more closely associated with the modern meaning of the term) and a secondary service room. The rooms at the rear of the house were usually divided by the stair leading to the first-floor rooms, which by this time would have been used as bedrooms. As well as greatly improving circulation, the double-pile plan also harmonized with the increasingly popular appeal of the symmetrical façade, as exemplified by Oakdene, Mossley (Fig. 4.12). The popularity of the double-pile house amongst the tenant class reflects a similar trend to that of the freeholders and lords. To a lesser extent the appeal of classical decoration also filtered down to the tenant house (see pp. 74–5). Fairbottom Farmhouse, Ashton, is a stone rubble building which contains a former door (now a window) with Tuscan columns supporting a pediment. Four Winds, Ashton, similarly has a pedimented Gibbs door surround, above which is a window with an architrave surround.

Workers' housing

The workers' housing of the study area is very similar in appearance to large areas of the southern gritstone Pennines in Lancashire and Yorkshire. In 1986 the Royal Commission on Historic Monuments and West Yorkshire County Council published Caffyn's (Caffyn 1986) extensive survey of the architecture and history of workers' housing. As well as showing that workers' housing could vary with the nature of employing industry the survey also revealed a general trend in urban workers' housing. That trend showed, in West Yorkshire, four distinct phases. First, existing urban plots were infilled with small houses. This phase was then followed by a wave of speculative building funded either by local builders or building 'clubs', later societies, run by prosperous tenants. In the third phase workers' housing built by the owners of the new urban factories

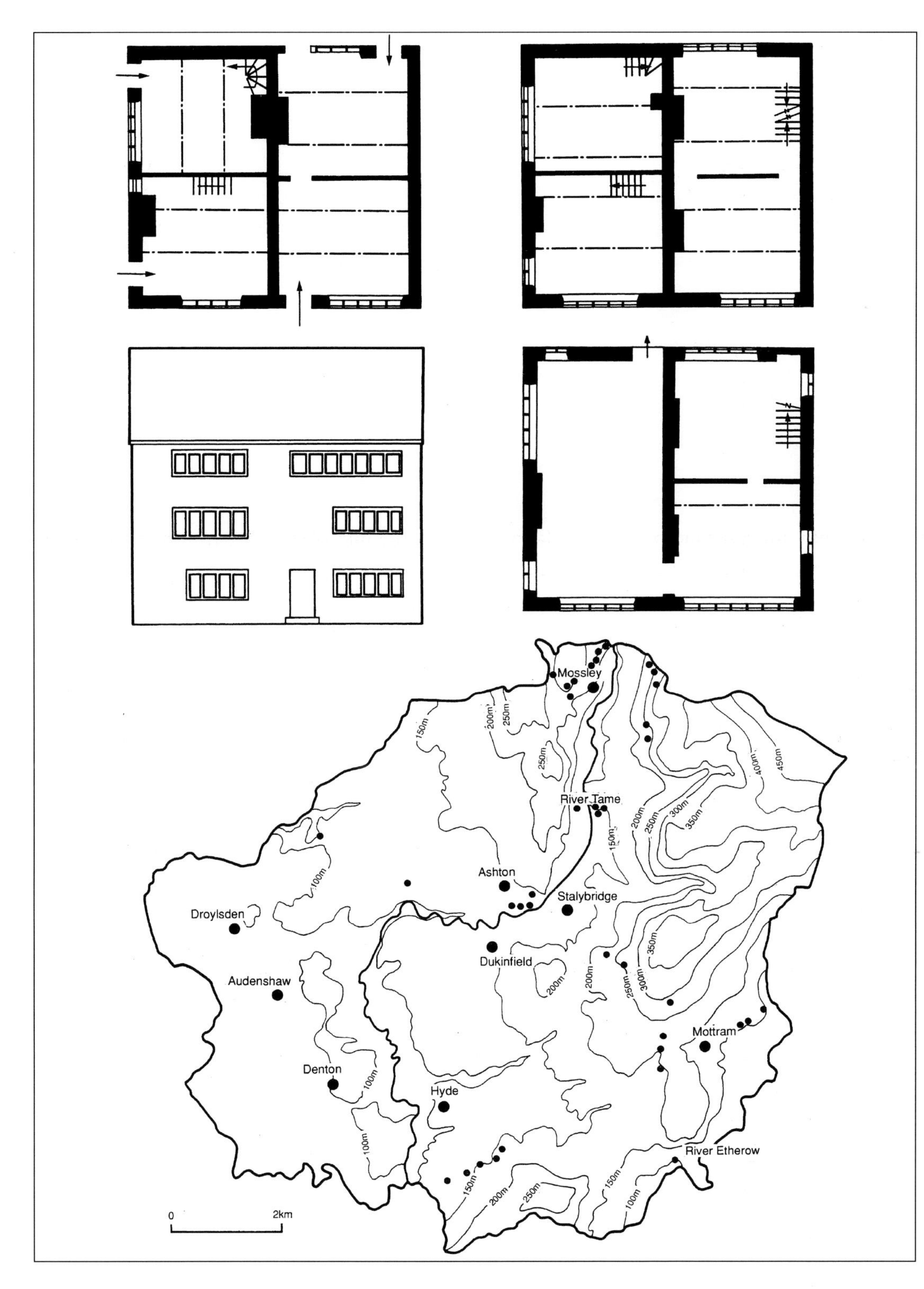

Figure 4.13 Plan of weavers' cottages at No. 18 Carrhill Road, Mossley and (*inset*) the distribution of weavers' cottages in Tameside. The plans of this building show the typical layout of the new archaeological type site for the region. The earliest dated examples in Tameside are a pair of cottages built in 1772 on Wednesough Green in Hollingworth, but the earliest example known from the Manchester area may be a building in Cheadle built by a shoemaker around 1705.

became commonplace. Finally, from the middle of the nineteenth century workers' housing gradually fell under the control of the local councils. This broad pattern of development has also been found immediately to the south of the study area in Stockport, where unlike Ashton, building clubs seem to have been quite common (Arrowsmith 1997, 174–6).

Burke & Nevell's (1996) survey of the buildings of Tameside revealed a broadly similar picture but there were some subtle differences. There is no clear evidence of separate workers' housing being built in the area prior to the seventeenth century. From the middle of the century there survive some cottages such as War Hill and Jeremy Cottage that are so small and simple

Figure 4.14 Weavers' cottages: (a) The Gunn Inn, Hollingworth; and (b) Stalybridge Road, Mottram. The three-storey height and multi-light mullion windows are characteristic features of handloom weavers cottages, 63 examples of which can still be found within the Lordships of Ashton and Longdendale. In the Mottram area there are three notable groups. Firstly, the row of three, double-depth cottages adjoining the Gunn Inn at Wednesough Green, Hollingworth. These were built by John and Ann Morehouse, of the Gunn Inn in, according to a datestone on the buildings, 1781. Land Tax returns in the late 1790s and early 1800s list the occupants of the cottages as cotton workers. Secondly, a further row of three double-depth cottages, on Stalybridge Road in Mottram. These are notable as probably the last such cottages to be built in the area, being erected between 1810 and 1832.

in comparison to the tenants' farmhouses that they may represent workers' houses (Nevell & Walker 1998, 78).

In the eighteenth and early nineteenth century the new building that characterized the more dynamic tenants was the domestic house with an integral workshop; in the lordships of Ashton and Longdendale this was usually referred to as the handloom weaver's cottage (Fig. 4.13). The wills and inventories of the Ashton and Longdendale lordships, and the parishes in the Bolton, Bury, Rochdale and Saddleworth often refer to 'shops', that is workshops, being used for textile, shoe or some other form of domestic industry by tenants from the late seventeenth century onwards.

It was not until after 1700 that combined 'shops' and domestic structures were being built in the general area, typically of three storeys, with two rooms on each of the lower domestic floors and a single workshop on the upper floor, lit by a long row of multi-light mullioned windows. Occasionally this pattern was reversed with the workshop on the ground floor. Such a large window frontage is one of the hallmarks of a weaver's dwelling, its function being to allow as much natural light as possible into the working area. Access to the workshop was through the house itself via an internal stair, but often the upper floor included an external taking-in door to facilitate the movement of materials. Stone-built cottages of this type can be found in many of the upland parts of Tameside, often as a pair of semi-detached buildings or a short terraced row (Fig. 4.14).

One of the earliest such buildings in the Manchester area is a brick three storey cottage built in Cheadle around 1705 by a shoemaker. In Tameside, however, these buildings do not appear until after 1760 and appear to have been used exclusively for domestic weaving. Despite the mechanisation of the spinning side of the textile industry, weaving was not successfully mechanised until after 1820. Consequently there was a boom in the construction of these dwellings (Smith 1971). There are 63 examples known from modern Tameside with notable concentrations in the upland areas of Mossley, Staley, Mottram and Hollingworth. Those examples with datestone range from a pair of cottages built at Wednesough Green in Hollingworth in 1772 to a row of four, three storey, cottages on Staley Road in Mossley dated to 1802, although the range is undoubtedly wider than this (Fig. 4.13).

A variation on the weaver's cottage with its individual workshop is provided by Summerbottom in Broadbottom built by the tenant, John Swindells. This consists of a terrace of six cottages erected in 1790, with later additions of the mid-nineteenth century at one end. The terrace, which is built into the valley side, is of three storeys. The ground- and first-floor levels consisted of two-storey cottages a single room wide and possibly originally only a single room deep, heated by a fireplace in the side wall. The second floor comprised a loomshop, which was divided into three intercommunicating rooms. The front of the terrace is south facing and at second-floor level contains several multi-light mullioned windows. Access into the loomshop was provided not from the cottages but via three entrances at the rear of the terrace. Because of the slope in the hillside, these are virtually at ground-floor level. One is now approached by steps, another by a stone bridge, and a bridge may also have provided access to the third.

An enigmatic example of late eighteenth-century workers' housing was the Circus in Dukinfield. This was a circular arrangement of two brick-built terraces, each comprising ten, three-storey, single-bay houses, some of which had a single-storey extension to the rear. They were built by John Astley, who inherited the manor of Dukinfield in 1762 and who died in 1787. The Circus plan may have influenced later developments in neighbouring Ashton. According to Aikin the houses were built 'for the accommodation of industrious inhabitants'. Both documentary and excavation evidence have failed to clarify what work was carried out by the original occupants, but it is possible that, for all their idiosyncratic arrangement, these houses represent the brick-built equivalent of the three-storey stone-built weavers' cottages of the uplands of the Borough. By 1800 double-pile handloom weavers cottages were also being built (Smith 1971), a fine example being the set of three such cottages on Mottram Road in Gee Cross.

The advent of the urban factory system around 1820 created a concentration of labour and with it the growth of new working-class communities. Much of new urban workers housing, at least before 1850 was built by the new industrialist freeholders to house their workforce. This housing was a direct development of the workers' cottages that can be found on farmsteads of the seventeenth and early eighteenth centuries. These were built for those individuals who had no land and who relied for shelter on others, and included not only the landless labourer but also the infirm and elderly.

Like their rural predecessors these houses were only two rooms deep, the main room being roughly 15 feet square and the second room half that size, although some had two or even three storeys. The earliest such group attested in the Tameside area was a row of ten stone-built two roomed cottages, known as Red Pump Street built by Nathan Sidebotham in the period 1784–95 (Nevell 1993, 158).

By the middle of the nineteenth century hundreds of two room deep cottages, or terraced houses, were being built across Tameside, as terraced housing saved on the cost of building materials. The typical layout was the through house, with both a front and back door, a very small individual yard and a shared privy at the back (Fig. 3.11). At ground-floor level they had a heated living room and a second room for the wash-house or scullery. A stair rising from the scullery led to two bedrooms, with only the front one usually heated. Examples of such dwellings can still be seen in the textile communities at Well Row in Broadbottom and Gair Street in Flowery Field, Hyde, but were also built by speculators in areas such as Hyde.

The external treatment of the terraced house tended to be simple presented a monotonous aspect (Burke & Nevell 1996, 61). The rising cost of building and the temptation to save money on building materials led to dangerous buildings, such as back-to-back and even cellar dwellings, which led to the spread of disease. As a consequence bye-laws and building control regulations administered by the new forms of local government were introduced into Tameside after 1870 (Burke & Nevell 1996, 63–5).

The single textile mill

The first cotton mills in Tameside were established in the 1770s and the last, Ray Mill in Stalybridge, was constructed in 1907. Between these dates the textile industry came to dominate the landscape of the borough and the lives of its people. Of the 274 textile sites known to have been in operation between 1770 and 1907 it is estimated that a little over 100 are still standing (Fig. 3.8).

Mills and other textile works were primarily functional buildings, constructed and run with profit as the overriding motive. Their form and appearance were related to the processes which they housed, and any attempt at architectural pretension was very much a secondary consideration. Because of their commercial importance, the design of these buildings underwent a continual process of development centred on improvements in both their construction and operation.

The first purpose-built textile buildings were constructed by enterprising tenant farms in both the lordships. These were water-powered fulling mills, associated with the woollen industry. By the late eighteenth century the fulling process, whereby woollen cloth was washed and pounded, had been mechanized for several centuries and the presence of fulling mills on rivers and streams was well established. The earliest fulling mills in Tameside are attested at Ashton, and possibly Stalybridge, in the fifteenth century. By the later date of 1712 William Kenworthy, a tenant of the Earl of Stamford's estate in Mossley, had established a fulling mill at Quickwood. 'Hodg Mill' on the River Etherow in Mottram (later the site of Hodge Print Works), first recorded in 1763, was possibly fulling mill.

The second half of the eighteenth century witnessed a succession of major innovations, notably Hargreaves's spinning jenny (1764), Arkwright's water frame (1769), his carding engine (1775) and Crompton's mule (1779), which revolutionized the preparatory and spinning processes and led to the establishment of textile factories. These brought several machines together under one roof. While jennies remained hand-powered, other forms of the new machinery were driven by an external source, initially by horse or water, and later by steam. The term mill came to be used of textile factories precisely because so many, like the earlier corn mills and fulling mills, were water-powered.

In Tameside the earliest textile factories were often on a small scale and re-used exiting structures; this was the key to their rapid adoption by the tenants of the lordships of Ashton and Longdendale. One of the first was the 'Soot Poke', in Stalybridge, which was established in 1776 by a local farmer Neddy Hall in a rented building later described as 'no bigger than a cottage house'. It contained a water-powered carding engine as well as spinning jennies. At Fairfield a Joseph Mallalieu used a horse gin to drive textile machinery, probably carding engines, in a house he rented in the Moravian settlement in 1786. The small scale of even some purpose-built early factories is shown by the surviving example of Dry Mill, Mottram, which was built in the 1790s by the local tenant farmer John Wagstaffe, a two-storey stone structure roughly 10m by 5m in size (Fig. 4.8).

The largest of the early textile mills of Tameside were purpose-built, water-powered structures, the first of these probably being Throstle Nest Mill on Cock Brook, a tributary of the River Tame in Ashton, established in 1779 by a small group of local farmers cum fustian manufacturers (Nevell 1993, 36). Although these mills also housed preparatory processes, such as carding, they were predominantly used for spinning, with power being provided by the river or stream alongside which the mill was sited. Typically these buildings were several storeys high and rectangular in plan.

By the early nineteenth century mill-owners in Tameside were erecting factories on a much larger scale, moving the factory beyond the means of the average tenant farmer. Among the first of these was Old Mill, part of the Broadbottom Mills complex (see pp. 54–6). This building was six or seven storeys in height and was probably constructed in two phases between 1802 and 1814 by William and George Sidebottom who had inherited capital from their father's estate which included the late eighteenth-century textile mill at Woolley; which in its final form was over 90m long. The advent of steam power also increased the cost of mill building beyond that of the average tenant farmer. By the 1790s steam power was beginning to be adopted locally as a motive source. The 'Soot Poke' in Stalybridge is reported to have had a steam engine installed between 1790 and 1793, while the first steam engine in an Ashton mill appears to have been ordered in 1799. In the first two decades of the nineteenth century, whilst water-power continued to be used in the old mills, it became common for new mills to be steam-powered from the outset. One of the earliest purpose built steam-powered mills was the large Castle Street Mills in Stalybridge (Fig. 3.4), which was established on the south bank of the River Tame in Stalybridge in 1805 by George Cheetham. The earliest mill on the site was a four-storey building which in 1807 was powered by a 20hp Boulton and Watt steam engine, and by 1811 contained 11,520 mule spindles. With the arrival of large steam-powered textile complexes the days of the farmer mill owner were over.

Hatting

The historical evidence suggests that hatting was a widespread activity throughout the eastern and southern zones of the area from the eighteenth century. Only two planking workshops from the early nineteenth century survive. These workshops were small buildings, owned by tenants, in which the felt was prepared and moulded into a rough hat. In the 1860s mechanisation of hatting was introduced into the area and one of the first sites, Joseph Howe & Sons, built in 1868 survives at Annan Street in Denton (see pp. 74–5). This factory looks on the outside like a row of terraced houses and so was ready to be converted to domestic use if the venture failed. At the end of the nineteenth century large hatting factories were being constructed, the largest becoming that started by Joseph Wilson which at its height employed 1,100 people (Burke & Nevell 1996). Immediately to the south around Stockport hatting played a small but significant role in the economy of the period with the rural hatters often also being farmers (Arrowsmith 1997, 156).

Enclosure

From the early medieval period a process of enclosing fields from the waste to form either new tenancies or freeholds had been taking place. By the seventeenth century much of the land that could be enclosed was already walled although even up to the middle of the nineteenth century some high upland intakes were developed (Nevell & Walker 1998).

Within the study area west of the high Pennine ridge there were a number of higher hills, often with moorland tops, that were not enclosed until relatively late. Werneth Moor was such a hill on which in the late eighteenth century the new lords of the manor, the Egerton family, enclosed the remnants of the local commons depriving the tenants not only of their right to dig for stone, with which to construct their houses, but also to graze their cattle and sheep. Initially the tenants of Werneth resisted but the Egertons prosecuted them for trespass. Archaeologically the removal of the tenants' rights are reflected in the drystone walls which enclose Werneth Moor and cut across many of the stone quarries there, and in the stone walls built to block some of the drovers' roads that ran to and from the Moor. In the same period, the last third of the eighteenth century, there was an upsurge in domestic textile activity in the manor of Werneth, reflected in the wills and inventories of the period and in the construction of at least eight handloom weavers' cottages in the village of Gee Cross. It is possible to suggest that the two events were connected and that the tenants attempted to offset the loss of their common rights by increasing domestic textile production which was an area free from lordly interference.

4.5 The Tenant's Strategy

There were a host of factors during the period 1642 to 1870 which favoured the development of industry amongst the tenantry. These included the availability of spare land, the local trading system which was free from restrictions and the fact that the tenants lived in a society in which, to judge from the use of initialed datestones, the accumulation and display of wealth attracted admiration. In 1969 Eric Wolf (Wolf 1969, 501–23) suggested a two-fold division of peasant societies; those that were conservative corporate societies; and those that were open innovative societies (Table 4.1).

Corporate Communties	*Open Communities*
Subsistence agriculture	Market production and subsistence
Strong control over access to free land	Weak control
Religion used to weld together the community	Religion not centralising
Antagonistic to wealth display	Allows display of wealth
Uniform culture	Diverse culture

Table 4.1 Two Types of Peasant Society

He argued that corporate societies mainly pursued subsistence farming and ensured their survival by creating a strongly centralised and controlled social structure. Open societies, in contrast, produced at least some products for the market as well as undertaking subsistence farming and were a diverse group lacking centralised control. As producing for the market required capital or credit this placed particular emphasis on acquiring the correct social links and status. These two concepts are useful in trying to assess the actions of the tenants during the industrialisation process. Wolf associated the open peasant societies in South America with a readiness to embrace changes in economy and agriculture. The Tameside tenants certainly showed such a similar readiness but tended, to judge from the archaeological sites that are most closely associated with them, to largely confine themselves to the area of least lordly control and, after agriculture, the area in which they had strong traditional interests, textile production.

The value of the archaeological approach taken in the last three chapters has been to show that, not only were the three social groupings linked to particular archaeological sites, but that the archaeology of the area corresponds with at least one major strand of historical and economic thought about the rise to industrial prominence of the most successful tenant families. In recent years it has been argued that throughout Europe early industry flourished in such open and innovative communities, all of which tended to be found in marginal areas such as Tameside (Pollard 1997). In England this view has its origins in the work of A. P. Wadsworth and J. De Lacy Mann in the mid-twentieth century (Wadsworth & Mann, 1931, 278–9) who argued that at each stage in the development of the Industrial Revolution new leaders arose from the ranks of the hillside weaver-farmers. In the early period of industrialisation, from the sixteenth to mid-eighteenth centuries, as industry developed on the farm and in the village there came from the, often Puritan, tenantry new leading families who developed small 'shops' and links to the middlemen and merchants of the local towns. In the late eighteenth and nineteenth centuries, with the advent of high capitalism, the hills produced a fresh generation of families ready to seize the opportunities of new technology and new foreign markets. Consequently, these entrepreneurial tenant families became, as they grew rich in the nineteenth century, the new landed elite, increasingly divorced from their industrial past.

CHAPTER 5

Conclusion

The trade of Manchester may be divided into four periods. The first is that, when the manufacturers worked hard merely for a livelihood, without having any accumulated capital. The second is that, when they had begun to acquire little fortunes, but worked as hard, and lived in a plain manner as before, increasing their fortunes as well by economy as by moderate gains. The third is that, when luxury began to appear, and when trade was pushed by sending out riders for every market town in the kingdom. The fourth is the period in which expense and luxury had made great progress, and was supported by a trade extended by means of riders and factors through every part of Europe ... towards the latter end of the last century traders ... began to build modern brick houses, in place of those of wood and plaster.

John Aikin 1795, 181–2

5.1 Introduction

When William Harrison (Withington 1876) wrote his description of England in 1577 he saw a country of growing changes and increasing wealth. In 1795, at the height of the industrial revolution when John Aikin wrote his description of the area around Manchester he too saw a landscape and society that was changing and growing richer (Fig. 5.1). This sense of growth and change noted by two observers separated by over two hundred years continues to appear in a range of local commentaries up to the present time.

It is difficult to explain that constant process of change in a way that sheds some light on life today but the first step towards it is to try to describe and chart the differences that have occurred over the last five hundred years. In building up such a description some disciplines such as history have a wealth of resources and extensive collections of documents about the minutiae of everyday life. A discipline like archaeology is made of coarser stuff, merely the physical remains of our ancestors and their activities.

If history has such rich resources then one might fairly ask what is the point of archaeology being bothered with the period? Archaeologists might answer, quite truthfully, that they have discovered remains that are not recorded in the historical documents, but is this the whole answer? Many archaeologists believe that by studying the physical remains of the past they can extract meaning not only about historic societies but the human condition throughout time. It is the belief that the 'mute stones can speak' which ultimately lies behind calls for 'archaeology to contribute to important debates and controversies (such as industrialisation) which have largely been the province of economic historians' (English Heritage 1997,45).

This book and its companion volume, *Lands and Lordships* (Nevell & Walker 1998), tries to explore, through the intensive study of two landholdings, whether or not archaeology is capable of aspiring to such heights. It is a partial exploration using particular techniques and therefore before we can offer an answer we need to look deeply at both what was done and what has been discovered.

5.2 Charting the Local Archaeology

The local archaeology has been charted in two ways, firstly by research leading to a series of particular volumes, secondly, by various fieldwork campaigns. The fieldwork in the last 19 years, when the authors started

Figure 5.1 A 1794 view of Ashton town looking west, showing the settlement on the northern bank of the River Tame. The parish church dominates the skyline, with the medieval Ashton Hall to its right. Prior to the Industrial revolution the lordships of Ashton and Longdendale had only three urban centres, of which Ashton town was the largest. During the period 1642–1870 the town's population expanded from around 550 to 31,984, with the fastest growth occurring in the period 1780–1820. Left of the church are many new buildings belonging to the Georgian town laid out by the Earls of Stamford in the period 1787–1803, and which from the 1790s increasingly included cotton spinning mills, one of which (a three-storey building with 12 bays) can be seen on the extreme left.

digging in the area, has consisted of surveys, excavations (Fig. 5.2), watching briefs and even a campaign of dendrochronological dating.

To order the resulting mass of data we have relied upon the Thesaurus of Monument Types which has resulted in the identification of 100 new types of archaeological site that were developed in the area between 1600 and 1900 (Fig. 1.4). As we saw in the first chapter because these sites survived in use for considerable periods we can draw a cumulative graph of their introduction over time. The resulting plot shows an s-shaped (sigmoidal) pattern of growth of a type found throughout Industrial England. The growth in miles of turnpikes shows such an s-shaped development between the 1690s and 1830s, canals between 1750 and 1845 and railways between the 1820s and 1925 (Pawson 1979). If these growth curves for increases in the transport network are added together they combine to produce a uniform s-shaped curve of growth. The same effect appears in Tameside where for each manor and for each type of site we have different growth patterns but in aggregate a clear pattern of sigmoidal growth occurs.

In compiling this graph we have classified as 'new' the archaeological remains classified as sites in the Thesaurus because of their distinct nature and form. There is the possibility that many types of sites defined in the Thesaurus should not really been seen as distinct sites but merely as elaborations of older forms. Whilst, for instance, the Haughton Green Glasshouse was a totally new type of site introduced by immigrants how should one view the emergence of the terraced house?

Figure 5.2 Excavations at the Bulls Head. The Bulls Head in Mottram is an example of an eighteenth-century tenant farm where the subsidiary income of inn keeping came to dominate in the nineteenth century, leading to the rebuilding of the farmhouse. This view shows the central room of the inn, with the fireplace closest to the camera, during excavation work. The fireplace produced a large hoard of clay pipes and creamware pottery from the late nineteenth and early twentieth centuries and may indicate that this was the room with the bar.

From one viewpoint it is the end of a chain that begins with the labourer's room in the farm being superseded by individual worker's cottage which, in turn, led on to the development of the terrace. This process of elaboration is shown particularly well in the clothing industries, schools and the church.

There were hatting industry sites such as Woolfendens' in Denton that in the 1870s consisted of a factory, workers' housing and three villas for the owner and his two sons. Today we might classify these remains as separate interrelated sites each arising out of a particular tradition. In fact they all originate from the phased growth of what originally consisted of a single farmhouse. In that dual economy structure we would have found, around 1830, rooms for the owner, rooms for the labourers and a central room (often called 'the house' in local wills) for industrial activity. With the growth in prosperity there is a gradual pattern of expansion in the working area by adding a workshop in 1860 and building a factory in 1873, and the creation of separate cottages for the workers and new homes for the family (Holding 1986).

With the schools we also have a process of increasing elaboration with increasing wealth; the first references are to masters without separate buildings, a phase which is followed by the construction of small buildings and eventually by large scale structures.

Contrary to some widespread opinions the introduction of pews in churches marks not some new social order but the elaboration of the old. The order of seating on the benches of the pewless Ashton church was, in 1422, already strictly controlled before the introduction of the pews. The 'new' pews were, initially at least, merely a more elaborate and expensive expression of an earlier system.

To try and resolve this problem of whether or not a site is really 'new' is extremely difficult. Recourse to the historical documents does not necessarily help simply because they are selective about what they record; factories, for instance, receiving a great deal more attention than stone quarries. At this stage we simply have to note the problem and rely upon the validity of the Thesaurus.

5.3 Classifying the local archaeology

Having charted and mapped the growth in archaeological sites the next issue is to try to search for some underlying order or structure in their occurrence. In *Lands and Lordships* (Nevell & Walker 1998) covering the period from 1348 to 1642 the more restricted number and range of archaeological sites made this task comparatively easy. After trying to link the pattern of archaeological sites from that period to various major influences such as climate it was found that the simplest and most all encompassing viewpoint was to see the sites as products of three main groups defined, ultimately, by land holding rights. We discovered that we could predict from the style, size and number of bays in a house the social status of its owner. More surprising was the discovery that we could explain strange patterns in the distribution of minor sites by such an approach. It was a shock to realise that the pattern of coal or stone pits was confined to either wayside verges, common land or land privately worked by the local lord or freeholder. The reasons for this distribution were clearly social. Wayside verges had uncertain ownership and control and were exploited by poor tenants. On the other hand mineral rights belonged to the owner of the freehold and were exploited on all his land except where digging pits would infringe the tenant's right. Here then was the social structure framing and shaping the nature of the archaeology.

To extend this simple approach into the more complex eighteenth and nineteenth centuries seemed likely to fail. Here was a new society with new ideas and new approaches. As we have seen, however, much of this newness may, to an archaeologist, be illusory. The preceding chapters of this volume have been about exploring the links between the new types of site built between 1642 and 1870 and their relationship to the major social groups identified in the earlier work (Fig. 5.3).

Chapter 2 seems to show that the lords, and their later local government replacement, tended to shape the same broad classes of sites in 1870 as they did in 1348. Civil buildings, public buildings, defensive structures, institutions, transport sites, towns and mines continued to be controlled and shaped by lordly interests. The prediction in the *Lands and Lordships* volume that the Lords had defined and limited rights that they would seek to maintain and exploit seems, on this basis, to be largely correct.

Ward and Wilson (Ward & Wilson 1971) did much to dispel the earlier historical concept of the aristocracy and greater landowners being highly conservative and resistant to change. In their view many of the great landowners 'were promoters of turnpikes, river navigation, canals, ports and harbours, banks and urban growth' (Ward & Wilson 1971, 10). This was a new understanding which this study only confirms although, in this volume, it is argued that the areas of industry in which the local lords were interested were precisely those which fell within their traditional sphere of control and interest.

In the earlier volume we predicted that the freeholders, to maintain their status, would tend to concentrate upon agricultural exploitation and would therefore be disadvantaged as industry grew in importance. Whilst we can see from Chapter 3 that the classic early agricultural freeholds decline the picture is more complex. Whilst both early and late freeholders are active in developing public buildings, educational facilities and religious sites the later freehold families, that arise from the tenantry, seem to replace the earlier agrarian freeholders bringing with them a strong interest in industry. Some historians dispute the importance of freeholds but in this area it gave distinct rights and social aspirations denied even to the most secure tenant. Harrison's definition of 1577 quoted in *Lands and Lordships* (Nevell & Walker, 1998, 48) that freeholders were yeomen and in this volume Aikin's statement from 1795 (Chapter 3) both infer that within the study area their status was lost if they took up trade. Aikin seems to report with some pleasure that as the traditional freeholders declined their replacements, those who had grown rich on manufacturing, were buying freeholds.

In *Lands and Lordships* we also suggested that the tenants would tend to exploit the opportunities presented by industrial growth as this was the area under least lordly control, a view which is the subject of Chapter 4. The relationship between lords and tenants appears to have been complex. There is clear local evidence to show that the lords converted labour service to cash payments and were quite keen to raise rent

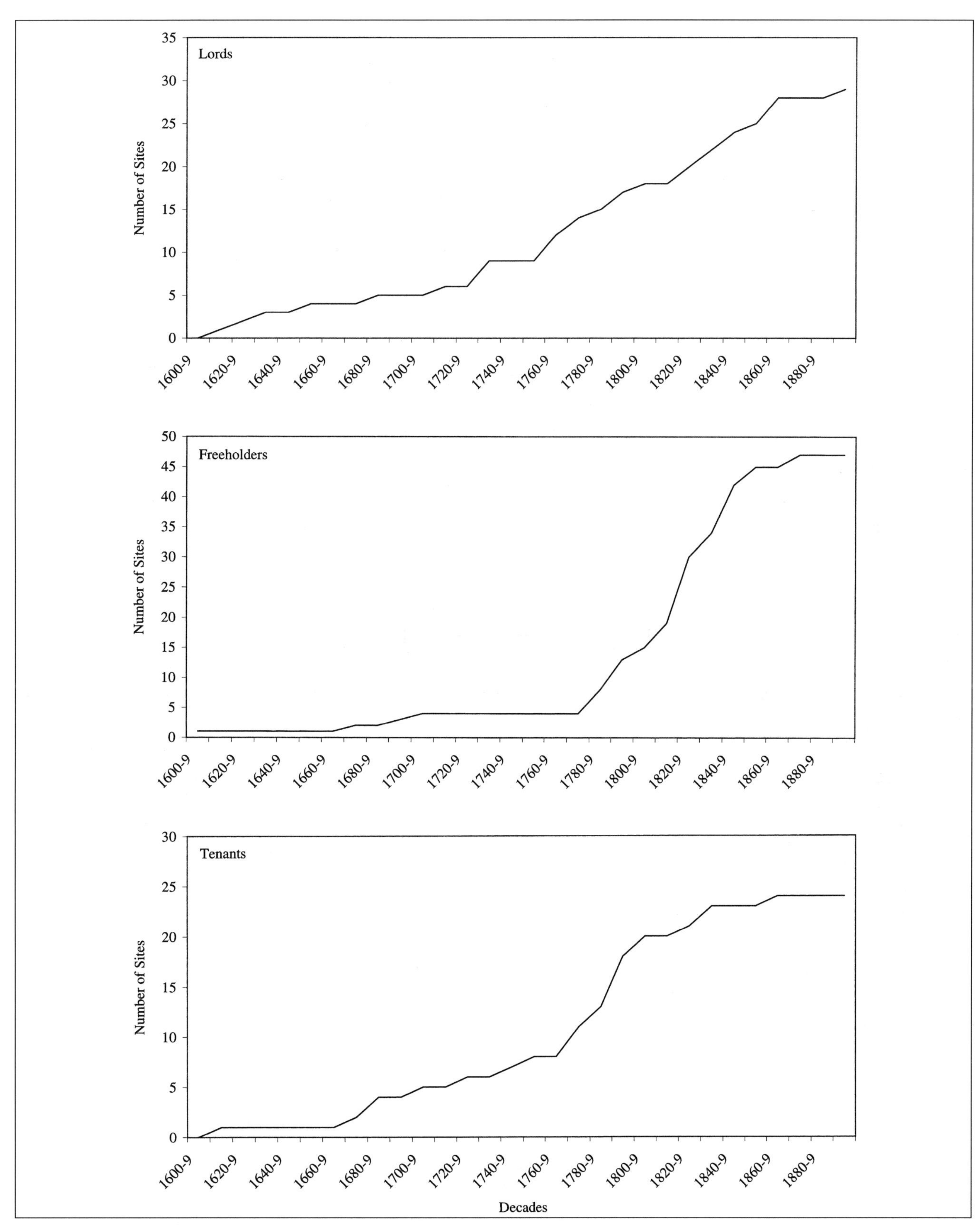

Figure 5.3 Lords (*top*), freeholders (*centre*) and tenants (*bottom*) graphs. These cumulative graphs of new archaeological monuments established by the three social groups we have identified do not show the same growth patterns. While those for the freeholders and tenants show an s-shaped growth pattern, that for the lords shows almost a straight-line growth, suggesting constant investment on their part. The reason for this may lie in the fact that the lords always had large financial resources to draw on throughout the period 1642–1870, whereas the freeholders and tenants did not.

which suggests they had little other than a commercial interest in their tenants. Ward and Wilson (Ward & Wilson 1971, 9) reported cases of lords who would forego immediate financial advantage to ensure they had loyal tenants. Perhaps the manorial lords needed both sound finances and loyal tenants to maintain their position. What is clear is that despite their close control over much of the tenants' activities the lords did not interfere with the industrial production that was taking place within their tenancies. The exception to this was the extraction of minerals or whatever else lay within the ground. Locally the view was always taken that minerals, stone and iron were part of the character of freeholds. It was a view that was bolstered at a national level both by the case of Regina versus Northumberland in 1568 and by national statute in 1688–89. Presumably as these minerals were part of the character of a freehold, their exploitation did not involve the possibility of loss of social status associated with working in trade or manufacturing.

Beneath the tenants were the poor who first surface in the archaeological record in the form of workers' cottages. It has long proved difficult for archaeologists to find the poor of the seventeenth and eighteenth centuries. They scarcely appear in the historical documents and in this area there are not the nucleated villages and their peasants' cots found farther south. Three facts may explain their apparent absence. Firstly, in this mainly pastoral area there was no great need for casual labour before the growth of industry. Secondly, some local eighteenth-century surveys suggest that many were housed in disused farmhouses or halls divided internally into smaller cottages. Lastly, there was the local tradition of housing labourers within the farmhouse. The fact that the tenants built the first worker's cottages may be no accident.

The theoretical basis

The cornerstone of this study is that the archaeological remains can be classified and explained by linking them to particular social groups. By linking groups to certain sites over which they had particular rights some clear patterns emerge:

A pattern of gradual development of elaboration in site complexity amongst tenants who had limited access to capital and resources;

A pattern of large scale change amongst sites that fall within the control of the lord who had access to greater capital and resources;

A decline in purely agricultural freeholds.

Taken individually all these patterns and the others described in the earlier chapters might be seen to be the result of individual factors. Grouped together they can be explained as aspects of one phenomenon; growth being shaped by social structure and social factors in accordance with the general schema offered by Closure Theory.

Rigby (1995) has produced a detailed analysis of Closure Theory related to real historical data from the later Middle Ages. In this volume we will simply highlight some aspects of the theory and its effect upon archaeological interpretation. A father of modern sociology developed Closure Theory, Max Weber (1864–1920). In recent years Weber's work has been elaborated and examined by historians (Nevell and Walker 1998, 95). In many ways Weber's approach was similar to that developed by Karl Marx but to Weber the causal factor in social change was not always the economy. To Weber identifying the causes of change depended upon an analysis of each case and in each case the cause could be different. To Weber social groupings would establish or justify their power by appealing to or using one of the following factors:

Legal or traditional factors;

Ideology, morals or charismatic factors;

Rational or economic factors.

Certainly we find all three factors used within our study area in cases of conflict between groups. Both tenants and lords appealed to different traditions and legal interpretations in Court Leet cases. Those parties involved in industry tried to present rational or economic arguments as to why they should be excluded from various national legislation. Various charismatic figures or ideological beliefs often welded the religious sects of the area together.

Where we are unable to follow Weber, because of the scale of work needed to prove it at a local level, are in his definitions of capitalism, its importance and the crucial role played by new, mainly Protestant, ethics (Weber 1927, 275–8, 352–69).

Closure Theory does not assume, that individuals

Figure 5.4 Excavations at Buckton Castle. This was the first site to be specifically targeted by the current research project. As the only castle within the lordship of Longdendale, it is likely that this was the centre of the lordship prior to its abandonment by 1359. However, the excavations shown here revealed archaeological deposits within the earthworks buried beneath over half a metre of rubble that dated to before the Norman Conquest of 1066, suggesting that the Lordship may have been older than was first thought.

may only belong to one group. The tenants of Dukinfield were just tenants but some at least were members of the select and secretive sect associated with Robert Dukinfield their lord. It should not be assumed that Closure Theory reduces the human being to an automaton; it merely assumes that interests or desires are often best served by membership of groups. Closure Theory predicts that social groups will attempt to close-off or enforce their rights by blocking access to resources, financial or social, to less powerful groups within the social order. Ultimately the dispossessed might be faced only with the option of attempting to usurp power, possibly through conflict.

Many of the local conflicts that took place between 1348 and 1870 seem to the archaeologist to have been very minor for from the decline of Buckton Castle before the fourteenth century (Fig. 5.4) to the construction of Ashton barracks in 1841 neither lordship contained substantive defensive installations. Ashton Old Hall contained gatehouses and gates but excavation of the towers coupled with a review of the documentary evidence suggests that these tall structures had very thin and easily toppled walls.

In 1548 and 1549 there were fights between minor lords that involved both gentlemen and husbandmen but up until the Civil War little open conflict although the area continued to provide troops to meet national demands. The Civil War resulted in both local lords trying to rally their tenants to their cause and, as we have seen, some tenants devising their own responses. Later in 1667 the lords of Ashton compiled a list of tenants ready to serve with either musket, halberd or bow. Many tenants offered a contribution to the town armoury whilst of the rest 23 would bring halberds, 12 a musket and six bows and arrows. In 1689 Lord Delamere called on his Ashton tenants to assist in driving James II from the throne promising in return that if they died their leases would pass to their children; some 50 men followed him. Whatever the experiences gained from the Civil War and the results of growth the local lords apparently had no qualms about the tenantry being armed.

During the 1715 rebellion the Lees family at Alt Edge organised some secret gatherings of Stuart loyalists but to little effect. During the 1745 rebellion highland troops inspected and scavenged the area both during their advance south and retreat north but failed to raise any support. Amongst the advancing loyalist forces was Thomas Heap who deserted his regiment as it marched north through the Ashton area to Culloden. Heap was never captured and was protected by his family.

In the 1750s the first signs of serious inter-group conflict emerged as the weavers and workmen began to form combinations to raise wages and protect themselves from changes in methods of textile production. By 1831 local houses were being searched for weapons by government troops. In 1841 Ashton barracks, which replaced a smaller temporary facility, was under construction in order to provide a ready supply of soldiers 'to quell the frequent risings of civilian employees in local industry' (Bowman 1960, 277). The construction of the barracks marked a period where serious local inter-group conflict was to assume a political and economic importance.

Before the eighteenth century local agricultural production dictated population size; sometime around 1750 as trade made good any local agricultural shortfall the dominant constraint became economic prosperity (see pp. 8–9). This history of local conflict coupled to the archaeological evidence suggests that between the Civil War and the nineteenth century serious inter-group conflict was probably minimised by the general growth in overall wealth in the various sectors of the economy under the control of the different social groups.

In recent years some sociologists and historians have brought the study of complex social networks to a level beyond that presented here (Griffin & Van Der Linden 1998). Wetherell (Wetherell 1998) has, for instance, felt able to justify the view that in the past:

all people were interdependent;

that links or relations between people channelled resources;

that the structure of these relations both eased and constrained actions;

that the pattern of that structure defined economic, political and social structure.

It is a view that this study tends to confirm. We might suggest that the proto-industrial culture of the North West was different and made up of a small range of distinct groups with their own interests. These small groups cannot only be detected in the archaeological record but actually shaped that record to a considerable extent by the pursuit of their own distinct strategies designed to seize the opportunities presented by growth.

5.5 Testing the Theory

In the companion volume (Nevell & Walker 1998) we defined a series of tests for theoretical viewpoints, following the work of Renfrew and Bahn (Renfrew and Bahn 1996, 441–74) and decided that before a theory could be acceptable it had to correspond with the data, be consistent with other statements about the period and provide predictions that could be 'tested'.

An approach underpinned by the Closure Theory concepts seems to pass that test not only for the period from 1348 to 1642 but also from then up to 1870. Before completely accepting that Closure Theory can provide the way forward in understanding and characterising the archaeology, and so our understanding of the period, there are some particular problems that must be addressed.

The aim of the project and its two volumes was to answer the call for archaeology to make a contribution in its own right to a study of the period as a whole. Many have tried to provide such an archaeological insight into the whole period but it has proved a difficult target to reach. Sometimes this has been due to the problems created by the huge wealth of available data and, sometimes, to difficulties in keeping pace with the latest insights of historians, economists and the scholars of other disciplines.

Even when these difficulties can be overcome or avoided we are left to confront the issue of what is meant by an archaeological viewpoint? Whilst most archaeologists agree that archaeology is the study of material remains few agree about how this might or should be done. Archaeological theory is currently uncertain and the subject of an intense debate. Most of the debate about theory lies beyond the scope of this volume but because we are presenting a particular interpretation the reader should be aware of some critical issues.

To some archaeologists many of the conclusions presented in this volume would be seen as fatally flawed. One reasoned criticism being that we have presented just one interpretation, derived as much from our own unavoidable prejudices as from the facts, of a past that is ultimately unknowable. Another criticism could be that if we wish to adopt an approach based upon social groups, it could be argued that it would have been better to present a multifaceted analysis in which equal weight was placed upon other groups such as the poor, women or the religious sects. All those groups appear in the local archaeological record and such a criticism has some merit. In a partial defence it should be noted that however important those groups were they did not dominate or shape as much of the archaeological record as the three major groups of manorial lord, freeholder and tenant.

It could also be argued that we should have placed greater emphasis upon the impact of new ideas such as the enlightenment and shown how the creation of totally new sites, such as canals, was only possible through the widespread adoption of the new belief that the application of reason could solve contemporary problems? It might even be argued that the real shaping force behind the patterns of the archaeological remains was not economic growth coupled to social structure but the underlying psychology of the human race.

As the past is probably unknowable and interpreted through our current perceptions all these criticisms have some validity. By producing eight volumes which range from traditional archaeological texts to local hagiography and onto to local mythology we hope we have provided information for those who wish to develop other interpretations.

The real problem is that if we accept the challenge of trying to provide an insight into the period from an archaeological viewpoint we must accept that archaeology has a viewpoint. The absence of a consensus among archaeological theoreticians has meant that we chose a sociological theory, Closure Theory, rather than an archaeological one.

5.6 A Useful Contribution to Wider Debate?

Given that the aim of this volume is to present a useful contribution from an archaeological perspective we might ask how our interpretation relates to wider and more important historical insights?

Pat Hudson (Hudson 1992) provided an analysis of all the major trends in historians' thinking about the Industrial Revolution. By simplifying, or perhaps over simplifying, the historical models described by Hudson we can divide these trends into three main classes:

Hypotheses about the nature or form of the Revolution;

Hypotheses about the way the Revolution worked;

Hypotheses about the causes of the Revolution.

In terms of its nature the Industrial Revolution has variously been seen as short and dramatic, long and evolutionary, cyclical, patchy, widespread or part of a worldwide imperial phenomenon. The workings of the Revolution have been seen as taking place in clear progressive stages or as the result of a series of positive feedback loops working in a less predictable fashion. The causes of the Revolution have been variously seen as technological growth, trade growth, capital growth, imperial growth or even (now somewhat discredited) heroic entrepreneurs.

In recent years, as we mentioned in the introductory chapter, attention has also turned to the view that the Industrial Revolution mainly took place in marginal areas and that to an extent in Britain the Revolution was unreal. The latter point seems to find favour among many modern social commentators who see British industrialists as never really being interested in industry but seeing it merely as a mechanism to obtain sufficient wealth to become part of the landed or cultural elite.

It was the detailed work of the economic historians particularly in the late 1980s that allowed the Industrial Revolution to be seen not as a revolution brought about by technology but as a broad process of growth throughout the economy as a whole (Crafts 1989, 25–43; Davis 1989, 44–68).

Paul Courtney (Courtney 1997, 9–24), who is both historian and archaeologist, has recently emphasised that new studies suggest both that the Industrial Revolution was an intensely regional affair and a period of steady long term growth.

The growing perception that the Industrial Revolution was in fact a broad process of growth in which regional variations played an important part opened up the possibility that broad holistic local archaeological studies of the type undertaken here might have some value. This research project took up this challenge of trying to present an archaeological understanding of the impact of a broad growth in wealth in a local context. The concept of a broad revolution not necessarily driven only by technological invention allowed us to approach the subject in the same way as traditional archaeologists might study the impact of the Roman Empire by exploring, charting and grouping a wide variety of sites and merely using historical sources to illustrate archaeological perceptions.

This approach has allowed us to draw up a historical narrative, based upon a series of archaeological conclusions articulated by Closure Theory, about the nature of the Industrial Revolution, in two lordships on the edge of the Pennines, as follows:

In the sixteenth century the two lordships were marginal in both a political and an economic sense. The backwater nature of the area meant there was a lack of direct central control and absent lords. The patchy quality of the landscape and the absent lords meant that there developed a short and dispersed social hierarchy based upon land and social rights. These social groups of lords, freeholders and tenants each gave birth to the distinct range of sites that characterised the area, halls, freeholds and tenant farms surrounded by commons.

This community evolved into a remarkably open society with a keen interest in new opportunities to gain additional resources. There was, probably because of the marginal nature of the land, a dual economy with active links to external markets. Religion did not play a strong centralising role and new types of religious sites were commonplace. The interest in religion and trade may have given additional impetus to the early and extensive interest in constructing schools.

Access to resources was strongly influenced by existing social and economic rules. The lords could generate additional income by exploiting the resources they, by tradition, controlled and which were appropriate to their status; stone and minerals, agriculture tenancies and, because they had some money, innovative capital projects. For the traditional freeholders their more limited rights coupled with a desire to maintain social status meant that in general additional income would have to come from agriculture. For the tenants weak control meant that industry was a source of largely untaxed income and any innovations were not controlled by strong local guilds or effective national legislation.

Other factors may also have made the area particularly suitable for industrial development; large areas of free land in the river valleys, a tradition of families working as one economic unit, a cheap and effective transport system, a society used to operating on credit and trust and a tradition of puritanism.

The causes quickening the pace of change from 1642 to 1870 remain unclear although the increase in the range and number of sites is obvious. Surprisingly the pattern of development in sites follows that laid down by the earlier social structure. These social groups are even reflected in the evolving folklore and myths of the area which tended to portray different groups as having different attributes.

At the forefront of the development of new industrial sites are the tenants. The tenants' sites show not a revolution but a gradual elaboration and evolution as material prosperity increases as a whole. Whilst agriculture increased in efficiency ultimately the traditional freeholders and free-holdings, based on farming, declined. They are replaced by a new form of freeholder interested not only in agriculture but also in industry. The lords on the other hand are responsible for, or closely involved with, all the major new capital and strikingly innovative projects which involved administrative, legal and social control or infrastructure.

The separate development of the groups possibly allied to high levels of social mobility against a background of economic growth meant that whilst the groups attempted to strengthen their own positions for long periods there was little serious local conflict. When either the ultimate path of these separate developments crossed or because growth declined conflict became more serious. Ultimately the social power of the lords was usurped by a political movement and their function was assumed by local government.

The Industrial Revolution in this area conforms to the pattern of many growing systems showing an s-shaped growth curve in new types of sites (Fig 5.3). To anyone living within the central portion of that curve, 1770 to 1820, the experience would be one of rapid and revolutionary change even though the pattern of growth was much longer and more complex. Individual industries also show their own distinct patterns of growth which if studied in isolation or in small groups would foster the impression of cyclical growth. The overall pattern of growth in archaeological sites makes it possible to speak of both a short and long revolution depending upon one's position on that graph. Both Harrison in 1577 and Aikin in 1795 were right; they lived in times of change and growth but in both cases the relative pace of change was different.

Although the driving force behind this change remains unclear there was a series of positive feedback loops and common interests. Both Lords and tenants had an interest in improving certain transport, administrative and legal systems. The pattern can best be described by adopting the precepts of Closure Theory to give an overall picture of contending social groups that largely acted as inadvertent co-conspirators and so became better placed than many other areas to seize the opportunities presented by major growth.

This local narrative derived from local archaeology clearly contains insights that might be useful to historians but the difficulty is to what extent does it represent an accurate portrayal of events? It satisfies the tests that we have chosen to adopt but difficulties still remain. In using the archaeology to develop a historical narrative we would be following in the path of previous writers such as Weber, Geertz and many historians (Tilley 1990, 123–9). At the same time we would be dismissing much modern thinking which sees each society in the past as essentially alien and in which the relationships of power were more complex than the simple model proposed here.

A narrative derived from archaeology of the type used in this volume has inherent limitations. The blunt and somewhat impersonal nature of the discipline means that the history of people and groups is rarely revealed. In this volume we have used individual histories only where necessary to explore the archaeological argument. An approach that compares poorly with the benefits of a truly historical approach demonstrated in such classic works as Bythell's study of the local weavers (Bythell 1969).

Clearly, there are various criticisms that could be offered of this narrative derived from archaeology coupled to sociology by the use of a selective approach to historical sources. Perhaps the criticism that does carries most weight is that Closure Theory, and this volume, might be taken to imply that social groups must close membership to those trying to enter them. How is it possible for Tameside tenants, such as Baron Ashton of Hyde, to become freeholders and ultimately lords if the driving force behind each group is to close off access to those from below, to keep what they hold? We might explain the Ashton case by saying that by this time control had already passed to the industrialists but this ignores the still potent social power of lords today. We could emphasise that there must have been occasions when it was easier to include new members into a group rather than promote conflict. A more satisfying view is to recognise that whilst we have explained much of the pattern of the archaeological remains by reference to social groups there are exceptions. In the end Closure Theory and the approach we have adopted are useful as a way of describing the changes that took place but their role in explaining the cause of those changes remains unclear but could be sought amongst such exceptions.

Beyond the surviving physical remains of the period many echoes of the past still continue within the area today. The Trustees of what remains of the Stamford estate in Ashton have a local agent and the estate continues to play an important role in urban development. The oldest firm in the area, Kenyons, continues the industrialist freeholder traditions with Sir George Kenyon providing pictures for the Tameside Central Art Gallery and his son, Christopher Kenyon, acting as Chairman of the University of Manchester Council. There is still a Lord of Longdendale, the local Member of Parliament, Tom Pendry. Tameside Borough Council continues the old lordship tradition of careful civic administration coupled to the pursuit of new opportunities. The people of Tameside continue to show a flexibility and an independence of mind that was the hallmark of the area from at least the fourteenth century. The area remains what it has been for many centuries, uniquely placed, by virtue of its culture, to make the best of change.

Acknowledgements

In the face of rapid change in social and economic affairs, perspectives created by our knowledge and understanding of the past can introduce balance and stability. The recent reorganisation of local administrative groupings in Greater Manchester reflects and continues a process of organic change which has taken place over the centuries. The possibility of translating these theoretical historic values into practical benefits for the community arose in the course of a meeting between the leader of the Council, Councillor Roy Oldham, then Director of the Greater Manchester Archaeological Unit, Phil Mayes, then Director of Planning, Mike Eveson, and Local Studies Librarian Alice Lock. Councillor Oldham pursued his belief in the value of the work and a publication programme was designed to cover the History and Archaeology of Tameside. The responsibility for monitoring the progress of the commission for Tameside fell to Barry Delve, Assistant Director of Leisure Services (Libraries and Heritage). His support and that of the staff of the Local Studies Library at Stalybridge are gratefully acknowledged.

Many individuals assisted in the research, writing, and production of this volume. Thanks are due to all the owners and occupiers of properties and buildings excavated or surveyed for this work; their co-operation and overall enthusiasm were both vital for the purposes of the volume and refreshing for the authors. Mr and Mrs Williams allowed access to The Fold which lies on their Stalybridge estate. Joyce Powell once more allowed free range of her archives as did Ron Braddock. Tanya McBurney assisted with the location of building plans and elevations held by Tameside MBC. Thanks are also due to Alice Lock, Tameside Local Studies Librarian, and the staff of the Cheshire, Greater Manchester and Lancashire Record Offices for their help and assistance.

Excavation work in Mottram and at Glasshouse Fold in Haughton was undertaken by John Roberts with the assistance of Stuart Holden and Graham Mottershead. Field survey and excavation work on Werneth Low was conducted by Philip Wilson and Peter Connelly. The building surveys were undertaken by Ivan Hradil and Peter Connelly. Thanks also to all the contributors to the cartouches: Tom Burke, Ivan Hradil and John Roberts.

Finally, thanks to all the staff at GMAU, especially Robina McNeil the County Archaeologist, UMAU, and the Department of Art History and Archaeology, University of Manchester, without whose help and support this book would not have been possible; especially those involved in the production of the book; Ivan Hradil who did most of the line drawings, Catherine Mackey, who proof read the volume and John Roberts who undertook drawing and research work. Thanks are also due to VUMAN Ltd for their administrative and technical support. If we have missed any persons from this list, our apologies. A work such as this necessarily rests on the goodwill of many individuals.

Michael Nevell and John Walker
University of Manchester Archaeological Unit
Field Archaeology Centre, University of Manchester

APPENDIX

Listing the first appearance of new monument types, 1600–1900

This list has been compiled from the work conducted on the previous seven volumes of the History and Archaeology of Tameside series. Listed are the earliest known dates for new monument types, as defined in the *Thesaurus of Monument Types* published by English Heritage and the Royal Commission on the Historical Monuments of England, introduced into the area between 1600 and 1900. The initials GMSMR refer to the *Greater Manchester Sites and Monuments Record* held at the University of Manchester. The numerals following GMSMR are the unique identifier for the individual site records which can be consulted on request to the Greater Manchester Archaeological Unit, University of Manchester. L = Lords, F = Freeholders, T = Tenants.

Agriculture and subsistence

F 1690s threshing barn, brick, Audenshaw Lodge GMSMR 806
T 1700 cow house, stone, Meadowcroft Fold GMSMR 832
T 1837 laithe house, Widowscroft Farm GMSMR 937
L 1840s model farm, Hyde Hall, Hyde GMSMR 762

Civil

L 1636 court house GMSMR 8201
L 1718 stocks, Gee Cross GMSMR 621
L 1823 public square, Henry Square, Ashton GMSMR 3256
L 1831 town hall, Stalybridge GMSMR 5895

Commemorative

L 1655 commemorative stone (Holland monument at St Lawrences) GMSMR 973
T 1680 external gravestone, Mottram Church GMSMR 812

Commercial

F 1787–1803 shop (fixed retail shop), 120 Stamford Street, Ashton GMSMR 6165
F 1820 savings bank, Warrington Street, Ashton GMSMR 745
F 1825 grain warehouse, Stalybridge cornmill GMSMR 3588
F 1828 wholesale warehouse, Peak forest canal, Hyde GMSMR 639
L 1830 market hall, Ashton GMSMR 752
F 1847 shopping arcade, Market Avenue, Ashton GMSMR 5853

Defence

L 1841 barracks, Ashton GMSMR 2195

Domestic

F 1604 date stone (building inscription) GMSMR785
F 1672 farmhouse, brick, Red Hall GMSMR 8159
T 1676 labourer's cottages, Hodgefold GMSMR 950
T 1682 hamlet, Gee Cross GMSMR 622
T 1742 rainwater head, Old Street, Ashton GMSMR 823
T 1755 double (depth) house, Oakdene GMSMR 1008
L 1762–87 workers cottages, brick, Dukinfield Circus GMSMR 3531
L 1770 country house, Dukinfield Lodge GMSMR 756
T 1772 handloom weavers cottages, stone, Wednesough Green GMSMR 3448
F 1784–95 workers village, Red Pump Street, Hyde GMSMR 3513
F 1787–1803 town house, no 121 & 135 Stamford Street, Ashton GMSMR 977
L 1780s circus, Stamford Street, Ashton GMSMR 6165
F 1790 terraced workers housing, Summerbottom GMSMR 939
F 1794 split level (cellar) house, Hollingworth GMSMR 3448
F 1800s ice house, Broadbottom Hall GMSMR 759
F 1812 detached house, Croft House, Ashton GMSMR 965
F 1817 through to light terrace houses, Old Street, Broadbottom GMSMR 3508
F 1820s gate lodge, Mottram Old Hall GMSMR 826
F 1820s courtyard terrace houses, Stalybridge GMSMR 3583
F 1820s steeped terrace houses, Well Row, Broadbottom GMSMR 3508
F 1830s backyard, Gair Street, Hyde GMSMR 3513
F 1840s back-to-back houses, Ashton GMSMR 3526
F 1840s semi-detached house, Hyde GMSMR 3513
F 1850s tunnel back terraces, Croft Street, Hyde GMSMR 3513

F 1850s, managers house, Dean Terrace, Park Bridge GMSMR 749
F 1877 villa house, The Hollies, Ashton GMSMR 6165

Education

L 1623 church school, Mottram Grammar GMSMR 819
F 1793 Sunday School, Moravian settlement GMSMR 628
F 1841 day school, St Paul's, Stalybridge GMSMR 1062
F 1856 mechanic's institute building, Ashton GMSMR 3526
L 1891 public library, Ashton GMSMR 803

Gardens, Parks & Urban Spaces

L 1865 public park, Stamford Park GMSMR 9175

Health & Welfare

L 1850 hospital, Ashton GMSMR 9175
L 1868 Turkish baths, Stalybridge GMSMR 3583

Industrial

T 1614 coal pit, Mottram Moor GMSMR 3369
L 1615 glass works, Haughton GMSMR 3319
T 1722 mine shaft, Crickety Lane, Ashton GMSMR 3526
L 1735 horse engine, Denton GMSMR 6290
L 1771 atmospheric engine house (Newcomen), Hague Colliery GMSMR 6284
T 1777 printing works, Shepley GMSMR 8139
T 1779 water-powered textile spinning mill (cotton), Throstle Nest, Ashton GMSMR 6351
T 1784 ironworks, Park Bridge GMSMR 6078
T 1790/3 steam-powered textile spinning mill (cotton), Old Soot Poke GMSMR 3583
T 1792 brick & tile making site works, Dukinfield GMSMR 6269
T 1796–97 hand-powered textile spinning mill, Dry Mill GMSMR 6301
T 1805 bleach works, Hodge Mill, Broadbottom GMSMR 6348
T 1808 Copperas Works, Bardsley GMSMR 183
F 1810 iron forge, Park Bridge GMSMR 6078
F 1812 gas works, Carrfield Mill, Hyde GMSMR 3431
F 1822 gas storage tank, Ashton Gas Works GMSMR 2272
F 1827 fire-proof textile mill, Copley mills GMSMR 3379
F 1820s weaving shed, Bayley Field Mill, Hyde GMSMR 3430
T 1823 pottery kiln, Pot House Farm, Matley GMSMR 5803
T 1839 hatters workshop, Joel Lane, Gee Cross GMSMR 6326
T 1868 hat factory, Howe & Sons, Denton GMSMR 481

Institutional

L 1730 workhouse, Ashton GMSMR 9175

Recreational

F 1870s theatre, Ashton GMSMR 6165

Religious, Ritual & Funerary

F 1707 nonconformist chapel, Dukinfield Old Chapel GMSMR 624
F 1784 Moravian settlement, Dukinfield GMSMR 628
F 1791 Methodist Chapel, Mottram GMSMR 815
L 1821 commissioners church, St Peter's, Ashton GMSMR 5899
F 1838–39 Catholic church, St Peter's, Stalybridge GMSMR 5899
L 1865 cemetery chapel, Dukinfield GMSMR 9157

Transport

L 1683 road bridge, stone, Broadbottom GMSMR 3508
L 1732 toll road, Manchester to Saltersbrook GMSMR 823
T pre 1781 coaching inn, Gunn Inn GMSMR 934
L 1792–97 canal, Ashton to Manchester GMSMR 6361
L 1794–99 canal roving bridge, Peak Forest Canal GMSMR 975
T 1790s tramway, Parkbridge GMSMR 629
T 1790s tramway tunnel, Parkbridge GMSMR 2253
F 1790s lock-keepers cottage, Droylsden GMSMR 646
L 1800 aqueduct, Stakes Aqueduct GMSMR 975
F 1820s toll house, Woodend Toll Bar Cottage GMSMR 634
F 1833 canal boat house, Droylsden GMSMR 646
F 1837–45 railway, Ashton & Woodhead GMSMR 949
F 1842 railway station building, Broadbottom GMSMR 6169
F 1842 station master's houses, Broadbottom GMSMR 6169
F 1843 railway goods shed, Broadbottom GMSMR 6169
F 1845 railway viaduct (brick), Ashton GMSMR 740

Water Supply & Drainage

L 1761 weir, Woolley Mill GMSMR 8175
L 1762–87 water tank, Dukinfield Circus GMSMR 3531
F 1808 water pipe, Flowery Field, Hyde GMSMR 9160
F 1825 reservoir, Tombottom Reservoir, Ashton GMSMR 5877

Sources

Primary Sources

Cheshire Record Office, Chester (CRO)

D 73/1 Deeds for Duckenfield property in Mobberley, 1662.
D 73/2 Will of Sir William Duckenfield Daniel, 8/12/1756.
D 3553/19–25 Mottram leases, 1780–99.
DAR/I/16 Werneth manor court book, 1588–1658.
DDX 16/1–5 Leases of Hyde and Duckenfield property in Brinnington, Romiley and Hyde, 1605–57.
DDX 67/5 Ashton of Hyde collection.
DDX 67/23 Deeds, Werneth township.
DDX 87/1/a The particulars of the demesne of Hollingworth.
DTW 2343/A/2/4 Mottram estate survey and valuation for 1785.
DTW 2343/F/16 Mottram estate, steward's accounts for 1826.
DTW 2406/12 Rental of Mottram in 1618.
DTW 2477/A/1 Tintwistle estate Accounts.
DTW 2477/B/9 A Survey of the land and tenements of Thomas Wilbraham Esq (Longdendale Survey) 1600.
DTW 2477/B/10 Mottram estate survey and valuation, 1799.
DTW 2477/B/12 Mottram estate survey and valuation 1813.
DTW 2477/B/13 Mottram estate survey and valuation, 1826.
DTW 2477/F/12 Mottram estate, steward's accounts and deeds for 1771–99.
DTW 2477/H Counterpart leases of premises in Longdendale, by Sir Thomas Wilbraham of Woodhey. All taken on 29th Sept. 1684, for 21 years.
DTW 2477/I Counterpart leases of premises in Longdendale, by Sir Thomas Wilbraham of Woodhey. All taken on 29th Sept. 1684, for 21 years.
DTW 2477/J Counterpart leases for premises in Mottram, by the Wilbrahams, 1623/4 to 1684.
EDP 198/10 Mottram parish records.
EDT 281 Tithe map and apportionment for Mottram, 1845.
EDT 366/1 Tithe map and apportionment for Staley, 1840.
QDV2/148 Dukinfield Land Tax Returns 1780–1831.
QDV2/217 Hollingworth Land Tax returns 1780–1831.
QDV2/231 Hyde Land Tax Returns 1780–1831.
QDV2/299 Mottram Land Tax Returns 1780–1831.
QDV2/313 Newton Land Tax Returns 1781–1831.
QDV2/393 Staley Land Tax Returns 1780–1831.
WS Wills and Inventories.

Lancashire Record Office, Preston (LRO)

DDX 350 Bowman collection.

Powell Collection (Private collections of Mrs Joyce Powell)

Sale catalogue for the Tollemache estate in Mottram 1841.
Sale catalogue for the Tatton estate in Werneth, 1857.

Tameside Local Studies Library, Stalybridge (TLSL)

DD 1/1/1–84 Day books of the Hyde Clarke family 1819–1902.
DD 161/2 Papers relating to George Clarke and family. Draft brief for the prosecution in the case of Clarke versus Bretland regarding the manors of Hyde and Haughton in Cheshire and Lancashire, to be heard on 5th August 1754.
DD 229/1 Dukinfield estate map, 1692.

Secondary Sources

Aikin J., 1795, *A Description of the Country Thirty to Forty Miles round Manchester.* London.
Allaby M., 1996 *Basics of Environmental Science.* Routledge
Arrowsmith P., 1997, *Stockport, A History.* University of Manchester Archaeological Unit and Stockport Metropolitan Borough Council.
Ashmore O., 1969, *The Industrial Archaeology of Lancashire.* London, David & Charles.
Ashmore O., 1982, *The Industrial Archaeology of North-West England.* Manchester University Press.
Aspin C., (ed.), 1972, *Manchester and the Textile Districts*

in 1849 by Angus Bethune Reach. Helmshore Local History Society.

Bann J. E., 1976, *The Changing Distribution of the Cotton Industry in Hyde. Unpublished BA dissertation, Newcastle-upon-Tyne University.* Copy in Tameside Local Studies Library.

Booker Rev. J., 1855, 'A History of the Ancient Chapel of Denton in Manchester Parish', in W. Langton (ed.), *Chetham Miscellanies.* Chetham Society, vol. 37.

Bowman W. M., 1960, *England in Ashton-under-Lyne.* Ashton-under-Lyne Corporation.

Britnell R.H ., 1996, *The Commercialisation of English Society, 1000–1500.* Second Edition. Manchester University Press.

Burke T. and Nevell M. D., 1996. *A History and Archaeology of Tameside. Volume 5: Buildings of Tameside.* Tameside Metropolitan Borough Council with the University of Manchester Archaeological Unit and the Greater Manchester Archaeological Unit.

Butterworth J., 1823, *History and Description of the town and parish of Ashton-under-Lyne, Mottram-long-den-dale and Glossop.* Oldham.

Butterworth J., 1827, *History and description of the towns and parishes of Stockport, Ashton-under-Lyne, Mottram-long-den-dale and Glossop.* Oldham.

Butterworth E., 1842, *An Historical Account of the Town and Parish of Ashton-under-Lyne in the county of Lancaster and the village of Dukinfield in the county of Chester.* Ashton-under-Lyne.

Bythell D., 1969, *The Handloom Weavers.* Cambridge University Press.

Caffyn L., 1986, *Workers' Housing in West Yorkshire: 1750–1920.* Royal Commission on the Historical Monuments of England, HMSO.

Calladine A. and Fricker J., 1993, *East Cheshire Textile Mills.* Royal Commission on the Historical Monuments of England.

Clark K., 1999, 'The workshop of the world: the industrial revolution', in Hunter J. and Ralston I. (eds), 1999, *The Archaeology of Britain. An Introduction from the Upper Palaeolithic to the Industrial Revolution.* Routledge, London.

Colinvaux P., 1993, *Ecology 2.* John Wiley and Sons.

Cootes R. J., 1982, *Britain since 1700,* 2nd edition. London. Longman.

Cordingley E. J., 1986, *The Effect of the Industrial Revolution upon Ashton-under-Lyne, in the Deramore Family's Lancashire Estates, and the Management of the Estate.* Unpublished BSc dissertation, Newcastle-upon-Tyne Polytechnic.

Cotton N., 1977, *Popular Movements in Ashton-under-Lyne and Stalybridge before 1832.* Unpublished Mlitt thesis, University of Birmingham Faculty of Arts. Copy in Tameside Local Studies Library.

Crafts N. F. R., 1976, 'English economic growth in the eighteenth century: a re-examination of Deane and Cole's estimates', *Economic History Review 29* (1976), 226–35.

Crafts N. F. R., 1989, 'The New Economic History and the Industrial Revolution', in Mathias P. and Davis J. A. (eds), 1989, *The First Industrial Revolutions.* Blackwell Ltd, Cambridge, 25–43.

Cronin P. and Yearsley C., 1985, 'Coal Mining in Denton and Haughton', in Lock A. (ed.), *Looking Back at Denton.* The Libraries and Arts Committee, Tameside Metropolitan Borough, 58–69.

Crossley D., 1990, *Post-Medieval Archaeology in Britain.* Leicester University Press.

Courtney P., 1997, 'The tyranny of contructs', in Gaimster & Stamper, 9–24.

Cunliffe-Shaw R., 1958, 'Two Fifteenth-century Kinsmen: John Shaw of Dukinfield, Mercer, and William Shaw of Heath Charnock, Surgeon', *Transactions of the Lancashire & Cheshire Antiquarian Society* 110, 15–30.

Davies J. A., 1989, 'Industrialization in Britain and Europe before 1850: New Perspectives and Old Problems', in Mathias P. and Davis J. A. (eds), 1989, *The First Industrial Revolutions.* Blackwell Ltd, Cambridge, 44–68.

Davies S., 1960, *The Agricultural History of Cheshire 1750–1850.* Chetham Society, 3rd series, vol. 10.

Dickinson J., 1855, 'Statistics of the Collieries of Lancashire, Cheshire and North Wales', *Memoirs of the Literary and Philosophical Society of Manchester,* 2nd Series 12, 71–107.

Dore R. N., 1966, *The Civil Wars in Cheshire.* A History of Cheshire, vol. 8. Cheshire Community Council.

Driver J. T. (ed.), 1954, 'A Subsidy Roll for the Hundred of Macclesfield, A. D. 1610', *Transactions of the Lancashire and Cheshire Antiquarian Society* 62 (for 1950–51), 54–67.

Earwaker J. P., 1878, *East Cheshire Past and Present,* vol. 1. London.

Earwaker J. P., 1880, *East Cheshire Past and Present,* vol. 2. London.

Eckersley T. P., 1991, *The Growth of the Cotton Industry in Mossley with Special Reference to the Mayalls.* Unpublished MA thesis, Manchester Polytechnic Dept of Economics and Economic History. Copy in Tameside Local Studies Library.

English Heritage, 1997, *English Heritage Research Agenda.* English Heritage.

Farrer W. and Brownbill J. (eds), 1911, *The Victoria History of the County of Lancaster,* vol. 4. London, Constable & Co.

Farrer W. and Brownbill, J. (eds), 1908, *The Victoria History of the County of Lancaster,* vol. 1, London, Constable & Co.

Feinstein C. H., 1978, 'Capital formation in Great Britain', in Mathias P. and Postan M. M. (eds), *Cambridge Economic History of Europe* (Cambridge 1978), vol. 7, part 1, 28–96.

Fitton R. S. (ed.), 1965, *The Family Economy of the*

Working Classes in the Cotton Industry 1784–1833, by Frances Collier. Chetham Society, 3rd Series, vol. 12.

Fleischmann R. K., 1973, 'Conditions of life amongst the Cotton Workers of south eastern Lancashire during the Industrial Revolution'. Unpublished PhD thesis, State University of New York at Buffalo. Copy in Tameside Local Studies Library.

Flinn M. W. with Stoker D., 1984, *The History of the British Coal Industry. Volume 2, 1700–1830: The Industrial Revolution.* Oxford University Press.

Gaimster D. and Stamper P. (eds), 1997, *The Age of Transition. The Archaeology of English Culture 1400–1600.* The Society for Medieval Archaeology Monograph 15 and Oxbow Monograph 98.

Garnett W. J., 1849, 'Farming in Lancashire', *Journal of the Royal Agricultural Society of England* 10, 1–51.

Griffin L. J. and Van Der Linden M. (eds), 1998, *New Methods for Social History.* International Review of Social History 43, 1998 Supplement.

Hamner J. and Winterbottom D., 1991, *The Book of Glossop.* Buckingham, Barracuda Books Ltd.

Harley C. K., 1982, 'British industrialisation before 1841: evidence of slower growth during the industrial revolution', *Journal of Economic History 42* (1982), 267–89.

Harris B. E. (ed.), 1980, *The Victoria County History of Cheshire,* Volume III. University of London Institute of Historical Research.

Harris B. E. (ed.), 1987, *The Victoria County History of Cheshire,* Volume I. University of London Institute of Historical Research.

Haynes I., 1987, *Cotton in Ashton.* The Libraries and Arts Committee, Tameside Metropolitan Borough Council.

Haynes I., 1990, *Stalybridge Cotton Mills.* Radcliffe, Neil Richardson.

Haynes I., 1993, *Dukinfield Cotton Mills.* Radcliffe, Neil Richardson.

Hill S., 1907, *Bygone Stalybridge: Traditional, Historical, Biographical.* (Republished 1987; Leeds, MTD Rigg Publications).

Hodson J. H., 1978, *Cheshire 1660–1780: Restoration to Industrial Revolution.* A History of Cheshire vol. 9. Cheshire Community Council.

Holding T., 1986, *An Archaeological Survey of the Hatting Industry in Denton.* Unpublished ms. Copy in Tameside Local Studies Library.

Hudson P., 1992, *The Industrial Revolution.* London.

Johnson M., 1996, *The Archaeology of Capitalism.* Oxford, Blackwell.

Jones J. V. and C., 1982, 'Financial Improvidence and political Independence in the Early Eighteenth Century: George Booth, 2nd earl of Warrington', *Bulletin of the John Rylands Library of Manchester,* vol. 65, No 1, Autumn 1982.

Kenworthy F., 1929, *The Industrial development of Ashton-under-Lyne. 1780–1850.* Unpublished MA thesis, University of Manchester Dept of History. Copy in Tameside Local studies Library.

King D., 1987, *A Study of the Probate Records for the Parishioners of Ashton-under-Lyne 1660–1680.* Unpublished Local History Certificate dissertation, University of Manchester Dept of Extra Mural Studies.

Littler J., 1993, *The Protector of Dunham Massey. Dunham Massey estate in the 18th Century. A study of the management carried out by George Booth, 2nd Earl of Warrington.* Altrincham, Joyce Littler Publications.

Manley G., 1974, 'Central England Temperatures: Monthly Means from 1659 to 1973', *Quarterly Journal of the Royal Metrological Society,* 100, 389–405.

Mathias P., 1989, 'The Industrial Revolution: Concept and Reality', in Mathias P. and Davis J. A. (eds), 1989, *The First Industrial Revolutions.* Blackwell Ltd, Cambridge, 1–24.

McNeil R. and Stevenson M. (eds), 1996, *Heritage Atlas 2. Textile Legacy.* The Field Archaeology Centre, University of Manchester.

McNeil R. and George A. D. (eds), 1997, *Heritage Atlas 3. Warehouse Album.* The Field Archaeology Centre and the University of Manchester.

Mendels F. F., 1972, 'Proto-industrialisation: the first phase of the industrialization process', *Journal of Economic History 32* (1072), 241–61.

Middleton T., 1907, *Legends of Longdendale. Being a Series of Tales Founded upon the Folk-lore of Longdendale Valley and its Neighbourhood.* Hyde.

Middleton T., 1932, *The History of Hyde and its Neighbourhood.* Hyde.

Middleton T., 1936, *The History and Denton and Haughton.* Hyde.

Mingay G. E. (ed.), 1989, *The Agrarian History of England and Wales. Volume VI. 1750–1850.* Cambridge University Press.

Morril J. S. and Dore R. N., 1967, 'The Allegiance of the Cheshire Gentry in the Great Civil War', *Transactions of the Lancashire and Cheshire Antiquarian Society* 77, 47–76.

Nevell M. D., 1991, *A History and Archaeology of Tameside. Volume 2: Tameside 1066–1700.* Tameside Metropolitan Borough Council with the Greater Manchester Archaeological Unit.

Nevell M. D., 1992, *A History and Archaeology of Tameside. Volume 1: Tameside Before 1066.* Tameside Metropolitan Borough Council with the Greater Manchester Archaeological Unit.

Nevell M. D., 1993, *A History and Archaeology of Tameside. Volume 3: Tameside 1700–1930.* Tameside Metropolitan Borough Council with the Greater Manchester Archaeological Unit.

Nevell M. D., 1994, *A History and Archaeology of Tameside. Volume 4: The People Who Made Tameside.* Tameside Metropolitan Borough Council with Greater Manchester Archaeological Contracts.

Nevell M. D., 1997, *The Archaeology of Trafford. A Study of the Origins of Community in North West England Before 1900*. Trafford Metropolitan Borough Council with the University of Manchester Archaeological Unit and the Greater Manchester Archaeological Unit.

Nevell M. D. and Walker J. S. F., 1998, *A History and Archaeology of Tameside. Volume 6. Lands and Lordships in Tameside: Tameside in Transition 1348–1642*. Tameside Metropolitan Borough Council with the University of Manchester Archaeological Unit. s

Nevell M. D. and Walker J. S. F., 1999, 'Introduction: Models, Methodology and Marginality in Roman Archaeology', in Nevell M, (ed), *Living on the Edge of Empire: Models, Methodology and Marginality. Late Prehistoric and Romano-British Rural Settlement in North-West England.* Council for British Archaeology North West, the Field Archaeology Centre, University of Manchester and Chester Archaeology.

Ormerod G., 1882, *The History of the County Palatine and City of Chester* (revised and enlarged by T. Helsby), 3 volumes. London.

Orser, 1999, 'Negotiating Our 'Familiar' Past', in Tarlow S. and West S., 1999, *The Familiar Past?* Routledge, London and New York, 273–285.

Palmer M. and Neaverson P., 1998, *Industrial Archaeology, Principles and Practice.* Routledge, London & New York.

Pawson E., 1979, *The Early Industrial Revolution.* Batsford.

Phillips C. B. and Smith J. H., 1994, *A Regional History of England: Lancashire and Cheshire from AD 1540*. Longman, London and New York.

Platt C., 1994, *The Great Rebuildings of Tudor and Stuart England: Revolutions in Architectural Taste.* London, UCL Press Ltd.

Pollard S., 1997, *Marginal Europe. The Contribution of Marginal Lands Since the Middle Ages.* Clarendon Press, Oxford.

Powell J., 1976, *The Parish of Mottram-in-Longdendale, 1570–1680*. Unspublished Local History Certificate dissertation, University of Manchester Dept of Extra Mural Studies.

PP 1874, *Return of Owners of Land 1873 Part I.* Parliamentary Papers 1874, volume lxxii.

Preece G., 1981, *Coalmining. A Handbook to the History of Coalmining Gallery,* Salford Mining Museum. City of Salford Cultural Services.

Preece G., 1989, 'The Art Collection of the Cheetham Family and the Encouragement of Cultural Provision in Stalybridge', in Lock A. (ed.), *Looking back at Stalybridge.* The Libraries and Arts Committee, Tameside Metropolitan Borough, 104–19.

RCHME, 1996, *Thesaurus of Monument Types.* Royal Commission on the Historical Monuments of England, London.

RCHME, 1998, *English Farmsteads 1750–1914*. Royal Commission on the Historical Monuments of Engalnd, HMSO.

Renfrew C. and Bahn P., 1996, *Archaeology. Theories, Methods and Practice.* Second Edition, Thames and Hudson, London.

Richardson J., 1986, *The Local Historian's Encyclopedia,* 2nd edition. Hertford, Historical Publications.

Rigby S. H., 1995, *English Society in the Later Middle Ages. Class, Status and Gender.* Macmillan, London.

Rostow W. W., 1960, *The Stages of Economic Growth. A Non-communist Manifesto.* Cambridge.

Scard G., 1981, *Squire and Tenant: Rural Life in Cheshire 1760–1900*. A History of Cheshire, vol. 10. Cheshire Community Council.

Sheppard M., (n.d., *c.* 1984), B*ankwood Mills, Stalybridge. The Story of a Victorian Cotton Family. Manchester,* H. M. Frecketon & Co. Ltd.

Smith R. E. and Smith R. M., 1998, *Elements of Ecology.* Fourth Edition, Benjamin Cummings and Co.

Smith W. J., 'The Architecture of the Domestic System in South-East Lancashire and the Adjoining Pennines', in Stanley D. Chapman (ed.), *The History of Working Class Housing. A Symposium.* David & Charles, Newton Abbot, 249–75.

Speake R. and Witty F. R., 1953, *A History of Droylsden.* Stockport, Cloister Press Ltd.

Stewart-Brown R. (ed.), 1934, *Cheshire Inquisitions Post Mortem, Stuart Period, 1603–60. Volume I, A-D.* Record Society of Lancashire and Cheshire, vol. 84.

Stewart-Brown R. (ed.), 1935, *Cheshire Inquisitions Post Mortem, Stuart Period, 1603–60. Volume II, E-O.* Record Society of Lancashire and Cheshire, vol. 86.

Swain J. T., 1986, *Industry Before the Industrial Revolution. North-east Lancashire c. 1500–1640*. Chetham Society 3rd series Volume 32, Manchester University Press.

Tarlow S. and West S., 1999, *The Familiar Past? Archaeologies of Later Historical Britain* Routledge, London and New York.

Thirsk J. (ed.), 1967, *The Agrarian History of England and Wales, Volume IV. 1500–1640*. Cambridge at the University Press.

Tilley C. (ed.), 1990, *Reading Material Culture.* Blackwell, London.

Wadsworth A. P. and Mann J. de L. (eds), 1931, *The Cotton Trade and Industrial Lancashire 1600–1780*. Manchester University Press.

Walker J. S. F. and Nevell M. D., 1998, *The Folklore of Tameside. Myths and Legends. The Ashton and Longdendale Lordships.* Tameside Metropolitam Borough with the University of Manchester Archaeological Unit.

Walton J. K., 1987, *Lancashire: A Social History 1558–1939*. Manchester University Press.

Ward J., 1973, *Chapel into Church. How Denton Chapel became St Lawrence's Church.* Ashton-under-Lyne, Drew & Co Ltd.

Ward J. T. and Wilson R. G. (eds), 1971, *Land and Industry: the Landed Estate and the Industrial Reolution.* David & Charles, London.

Weber M., 1927, *General Economic History.* Greenberg.

Wetherell C., 1998, 'Historical Social Network Analysis', in Griffin L. J. and Van Der Linden M. (eds), *New Methods for Social History.* International Review of Social History 43, 1998 Supplement, 125–144.

Wilkins-Jones C., 1978, *Tameside. An outline history of those parts of Lancashire and Cheshire now in Tameside Metropolitam Borough.* Tameside Metropolitan Borough Libraries & Arts.

Williams M. with Farnie D. A., 1992, *Cotton Mills in Greater Manchester.* Preston, Carnegie Publishing Ltd.

Withington L. (ed.), 1876, *Elizabethan England by William Harrison.* London.

Wolf E., 1969, 'South American Peasant Societies', in Dalton G. (ed.), *Tribal and Peasant Economies: Readings in Economic Anthropology.* Natural History Press for the American Museum of Natural History.

Wrigley E. A. and Schofield R. S., 1981, *The Population History of England 1541–1871: A Reconstruction.* London.

Young J., 1982, *Some aspects of the history of Denton and Haughton, Lancashire, prior to the eighteenth century.* Unpublished Local History Certificate dissertation, University of Manchester Dept of Extra Mural Studies.

Index

Entries in bold indicate pages on which figures or plates and their captions occur.